T0312126

Regionalism in Latin America

This interdisciplinary edited volume explores the political economy of regionalism in Latin America. It identifies convergent forces which have existed in the region since its very conception and analyses these dynamics in their different historical, geographic and structural contexts. Particular attention is paid to key countries such as Argentina, Brazil and Mexico, as well as sub-regions like the Southern Cone and Central America.

To understand the resilience of regionalism in Latin America, this book proposes to highlight four main issues. Firstly, that resilience is linked to mechanisms of self-enforcement that are part of the accumulation of experiences, institution building and common cultural features described in this book as regionalist acquis. Secondly, the elements and driving forces behind the promotion and expression of the regionalist acquis are influenced and shaped by nested systems in which social processes are inserted. Thirdly, when looking at systems, there is a particular influence by national and global ones, which condition the form and endurance of regional projects. Finally, beyond systems, the book highlights the relevance of agents as crucial players in the shaping of the resilience of regionalism in Latin America.

This insightful collection will appeal to advanced students and researchers in international economics, international relations, international political economy, economic history and Latin American studies.

José Briceño-Ruiz is Professor at the Center of Latin American and Caribbean Studies, National Autonomous University of Mexico.

Andrés Rivarola Puntigliano is Associate Professor in Economic History and Director of the Nordic Institute of Latin American Studies at Stockholm University, Sweden.

Routledge Studies in the Modern World Economy

For more information about this series, please visit: www.routledge.com/
Routledge-Studies-in-the-Modern-World-Economy/book-series/SE0432

Regionalism in Latin America

Agents, Systems and Resilience

**Edited by José Briceño-Ruiz
and Andrés Rivarola Puntigliano**

 Routledge
Taylor & Francis Group

LONDON AND NEW YORK

First published 2021
by Routledge
2 Park Square, Milton Park, Abingdon, Oxon OX14 4RN

and by Routledge
52 Vanderbilt Avenue, New York, NY 10017

Routledge is an imprint of the Taylor & Francis Group, an informa business

British Library Cataloguing-in-Publication Data
A catalogue record for this book is available from the British Library

Library of Congress Cataloging-in-Publication Data
A catalog record for this book has been requested

ISBN: 978-0-367-37680-2 (hbk)
ISBN: 978-0-429-35558-5 (ebk)

Typeset in Bembo
by Apex CoVantage, LLC

Contents

Tables

Contributors

José Briceño-Ruiz holds a PhD in political science (Institute of Political Studies of Aix-en-Provence – IEP Aix, France). He holds a master's degree in international relations (Durham University (England) and a DEA in comparative political science (Institute of Political Studies of Aix-en-Provence – IEP Aix, France). He is a professor-researcher at the Research Center about Latin American Studies Latina and Caribbean (CIALC) of the National Autonomous University of Mexico (UNAM). He was a professor at the Universidad de los Andes in Venezuela and the Cooperative University of Colombia, and he has been a visiting professor at the University of Buenos Aires, the University of San Pablo, Pontificia Universidad Católica de Minas Gerais, Aoyama Gakuin University in Tokyo and the University of Sonora in Mexico. He is currently a member of the National System of Researchers (SNI), (level II) in México. He is a regional editor of *Latin American Policy*. His papers have been published in several journals in Latin America, Europe and Asia. His most recent book is *The Political Economy of the New Regionalisms on the Pacific Rim* (Abingdon, Routledge, 2019) with Philippe de Lombaerde.

Enrique Catalán Salgado is Professor-Researcher of the Autonomous Metropolitan University in the Department of Politics and Culture in Mexico City. He holds a BA in international relations from the FCPyS UNAM, MA in international relations and PhD in social sciences from the UAM-Xochimilco. He has published in several national and international journals and has various specialised publications. His main research areas are regionalism in Latin America, foreign policy of the United States, globalisation, regional integration and rights of Indigenous peoples.

María Antonia Correa Serrano holds a PhD in international relations from the Faculty of Political and Social Sciences of the UNAM. She is professor and researcher of the Department of Economic Production of the UAM-Xochimilco, in the degree of economy, the master of international relations and in the PhD program in social sciences. Member of the National System of Researchers of México, Level 1. She is specialist in foreign direct investment, globalisation and regional integration, sustainable development and environment, trade and international finance. She has given conferences in national and international universities, among which stand out: University of Stockholm, University of Warsaw, University of Utrecht, Institute of Higher Studies of Latin America in Paris, University of Externado (Colombia) and National University of Colombia. She has published 80 chapters of books and articles in national and international journals.

Rita Giacalone is PhD and MA in history (University of Indiana, United States); historian graduated from the Faculty of Philosophy and Letters (National University of Buenos Aires). She is a researcher at the Center for Agri-Food Research (Universidad de Los Andes, Venezuela); Visiting Professor of the Latin American Integration Institute (University of La Plata, Argentina) and Associate Researcher of the Latin American Research Center (University of Calgary, Canada). She was Professor of economic history (Faculty of Economic and Social Sciences), director of the School of Political Science of the University of Los Andes, Venezuela and Project Coordinator of the ALFA Program (European Community). Among her recent publications are "A Cooperative Scenario for Latin American Regionalism and International Insertion" in the Jean Monnet/Robert Schuman Paper Series 18 (2) 2018; "Asymmetric regionalism as the axis of the South American resistance to Brazil (2000–2013)" in *Journal of International Relations, Security and Defense* 13 (1) (January–June 2018) and *Geopolitics and geo-economy of the globalization process* (Bogotá: Editorial UCC, 2016).

Giovanni Molano Cruz is a sociologist of the Universidad Nacional de Colombia. He holds a master's degree in development studies from the Graduate Institute Geneva and a master's degree in international relations from l'Université Paris I Panthéon Sorbonne, where he obtained the degree of doctor in political science. He is Professor at Instituto de Estudios Políticos y Relaciones Internacionales (Iepri), Universidad Nacional de Colombia. His teaching and research topics are: international political sociology, processes of regionalism, foreign policy of Latin America and the Caribbean, relations European Union–Latin America and the Caribbean. His more recent publications are: Global Drug Governance: Rules designed to protect some uses and eliminate others. *Análisis Político*, (95), 2019, pp. 144–162; The construction of a world of regions. *Revista de Estudios Sociales*, (61), 2017, pp. 14–27; A view from the South: The Global Creation of the War on Drugs. *Contexto Internacional*, 39 (3) 2017, pp. 633–653 and L'interégionalisme euro-latino-américain. Quel partenariat stratégique ? In: Santander, S. (Ed.) Concurrences Régionales dans un monde multipolaire émergent. Bruxelles: P.I.E. Peter Lang, 2016, pp. 329–344. His contribution to this book is part of one of his research projects at Iepri (Coc Hermes 46149).

Kevin Parthenay holds a PhD in political science at Sciences Po. He is currently associate scholar at the Centre d'Etudes et de Recherches Internationales

(CERI). Parthenay is member of the Observatoire Politique de l'Amérique latine et des Caraïbes (OPALC) as well as guest lecturer at the Institut diplomatique du Ministère des Relations extérieures de El Salvador (IEESFORD) and a master course in regional integration and development at Universidad Rafael Landivar. Parthenay has recent published articles at the *Journal of European Integration* and the *Revista Centroamericana de Ciencias Sociales* de l'Université du Costa Rica (UCR) comparing Central American and European civil societies.

José Ramiro Podetti holds a degree in humanities from the University of Montevideo and a PhD in history from the Universidad del Salvador (Argentina). He is director of the Institute of Latin American Studies 'Alberto Methol Ferré' of the University of Montevideo, academic coordinator of the Master in Latin American Studies and professor of "Communication and Culture", "Latin American Culture", "History of Latin American Thought" and "History of Ideas", in the same University. Since 2015, he is dean of the Faculty of Humanities and Education of the University of Montevideo. He has taught courses and conferences at universities in Mexico, Venezuela, Chile, Paraguay, Brazil and Argentina. He received in 2007 the Mariano Picón Salas International Essay Prize granted by the Rómulo Gallegos Foundation. He is a founding member of the Rodonian Society, the Alberto Methol Ferré Association and the Uruguayan Association of International Studies (AUEI). He is a member of the Latin American Association of Literature and Theology and the Historical and Geographical Institute of Uruguay. His areas of interest are history of ideas, history of culture, Latin American studies.

Andrés Rivarola Puntigliano has a PhD in economic history of the Stockholm University and is associate professor in economic history. Rivarola Puntigliano is director of the Nordic Institute of Latin American Studies at Stockholm University and lecturer of Latin American Studies at the same university. He has written and edited various publications, some of these are: The Geopolitics of the Catholic Church in Latin America (*Territory, Politics, Governance*), 'Geopolitics of Integration' and the Imagination of South America (*Geopolitics*), Prebisch and Myrdal: Development Economics in the Core and on the Periphery (*Journal of Global History*), 21st-century geopolitics: integration and development in the age of 'continental states' (*Territory, Politics, Governance*), State and Globalization, a Latin American Perspective (*Iberoamericana Nordic Journal of Latin American and Caribbean Studies*), Latin America: Left, Right or Beyond? (*Stockholm Review of Latin American Studies*), Global Shift: The U.N. System and the New Regionalism in Latin America (*Latin American Politics and Society*), Mirrors of change: Industrialists in Chile and Uruguay (*CEPAL Review*), Going Global: An Organizational Study of Brazilian Foreign Policy Organization (*Revista Brasileira de Política Internacional*, RBPI).

Carlos Eduardo Vidigal holds a PhD in international relations from the University of Brasília (UnB) (2007), a degree in history (1987), specialisation (1993) and a master's degree in history (2001) from the same university. He is professor of the history course of UnB, in the area of history of America. He has developed studies in the area of history of international relations and international politics, with emphasis on international relations of Latin America and Brazil–Argentina Relations, and has as master's dissertation: "Brazil–Argentina relations: the first essay (1958–1962)" and as doctoral thesis: "Brazil–Argentina relations: the construction of understanding (1962–1986)". He is currently developing research on (a) contemporary history of South America: power, conflict and geopolitics; (b) history of America: themes, approaches, perspectives; and (c) power and politics: history of Latin American thought.

Liliana Weinberg holds a PhD in Hispanic literature from El Colegio de México and a BSc in anthropology from the University of Buenos Aires. She is principal investigator at the Centre for Research in Studies of Latin American and the Caribbean (CIALC, UNAM) and Professor in Latin American studies at the National Autonomous University of Mexico (UNAM), where she leads the Essay in Dialogue Research Group. She was formerly the editorial assistant of *Cuadernos Americanos* and editor-in-chief of *Latinoamérica*. She is a fellow of the Mexican Academy of Sciences, as well as a member of the board of the Cátedra Alfonso Reyes. Among her recent publications are "José Martí: chronicler of the invisible" (CELEHIS), "El Aleph" y las estructuras elementales de la imaginación (México: Coordinación de Humanidades, UNAM, 2019), "El ensayo: un ejercicio de lucidez" (México: Dirección de Literatura, UNAM, 2019), "El ensayo como espacio de diálogo intelectual" (Fractal), "Hopscotch: a novel of translation" (Signos Literarios 15), "Alfonso Reyes and the Ateneo de la Juventud", (Iberoamericana).

Introduction

Resilience and regionalism: agents and structures

José Briceño-Ruiz and Andrés Rivarola Puntigliano

The aim of this book is to deepen the understanding about regional integration and cooperation processes in Latin America, in particular its resilience despite crises and setbacks. Most of the literature about Latin American regionalism is concentrated on specific periods of time and geographic areas. Concerning the first, the analysis of regionalism is generally boxed in by specific temporal contexts, generally with a beginning and end, which generally leads to the view that integration and cooperation (at least in Latin America) always ends in failure. In relation to geography, we hold that a separate geographic outlook narrows the complexity that exists in the intertwinement among different processes of integration across the continent. In this book, we choose a different vantage point. Instead of looking at single periods, we seek to identify long-term processes with the objective of understanding the resilience of regionalism; a resilience that can be observed across periods of time, sub-regions and countries.

The intention of this volume is to show how forces pushing for convergence have existed in the region since its very conception. We seek here to identify and analyse them in their particular historical, geographic and structural contexts. They will also be studied within a broader geographic, continental framework, as well as in a long-term time span that allows the identification of processes. Our goal is to find variables that explain their survival across time.

Regionalism is a relevant subject of analysis not only in Latin America but across the world. Regions are, in fact, being pointed out as the very basis that sustains the structuration of a new world order, referring to a 'global order of strong regions' (Buzan & Waever, 2003), 'regional orders' (Solingen, 1998) or to a 'world of regions' (Katzenstein, 2015). Along this track, scholars are increasingly acknowledging that the order established and proclaimed as universal by the Western countries stands at a turning point, where a new kind of multipolarity appears to be on the rise. The big puzzle concerns how this will be structured and by whom. It is here where the study of 'regions' becomes more relevant, as the geographical framework around which states pursue new forms of control and influence, locally, in the regions, and through them towards the international system. The era of 'superpowers' might be over, and a new multipolar order seems to be an alternative. In this new context, as we adress in this book, regions should be taken into account. However, it still remains to be seen if they will become central actors in world politics at the end of the Western era.

The presidential election of Donald Trump in the United States (2017–) has represented a change of direction in this process. The United States was actively involved in regionalism since the 1980s, examples of which were the participation in the Asia Pacific Economic Forum (APEC), the North American Free Trade Agreement (NAFTA), the failed Free Trade Area of the Americas (FTAA) and more recently the Transpacific Partnership (TPP) and Transatlantic Trade and Investment Partnership (TTIP). If one adds factors such as the crisis in the European Union (EU) after 2010, the rise of China as a global power, the creation of new international groups organised on a non-regional basis (like BRICS – Brazil, Russia, India, China and South Africa) and the Brexit, the scenario of a world of regions should be put in relative terms. This does not mean that the regional dimension has lost importance as a unit of analysis in international relations. In the case of America, NAFTA was replaced by the United States–Mexico–Canada Agreement (USMCA) in 2018. China, on its side, is increasingly involved in regional initiatives such as the Shanghai Cooperation Group or the Regional Comprehensive Economic Partnership. Besides Asia, regional initiatives in Africa and Latin America continue to maintain relevant spaces, as is the case with the Common Market of the South (MERCOSUR). In what refers to Europe, the EU is gradually recovering from its economic crisis and reshaping its role after Brexit.

Therefore, despite its setbacks, a closer scrutiny of the formative and development stories of regions is still a relevant topic of research in the study of international relations and international political economy (IPE). One of the hurdles has been a strong Eurocentric bias in the underlying assumption and understandings about the nature of regionalism (which most often stem from a particular reading of European integration). A way out of this is the analysis of the European process from new perspectives, as well as more in-depth research about regions and regionalism in other parts of the world. There is here an imperative to make comparisons by broadening the agenda, bringing in new cases and views to improve comparisons as well as to avoid simplistic and imprecise theoretical propositions.

This volume intends to fill a void that exists in the analysis of regionalism in Latin America. In the study of this region we take up questions raised by pundits concerning the formative dimension, analysing who determines the shape of regional integration and cooperation processes and their role as building blocks in the regional and international order. However, we also add one question, which is particularly related to Latin America: that is, what makes pro-regional forces survive across time and setbacks? Or, as is argued in this book, what makes regional integration and regionhood, become a 'resilient' social phenomena?

A point of departure of this study is the hypothesis that regionalism in Latin America is not a new issue but an ongoing process with roots back in the colonial formation and independence of states on the American continent. America, meaning the continent, may be seen as one of the geographic places where 'modern regionalism' was fostered.

If one analyses this from a long-term perspective, as we intend to do, the list of initiatives, successful or not, is long and impressive; the initiative of Simón Bolívar to create a Confederation of Hispanic-American States at the Congress of Panamá in 1826 – or the subsequent Hispanic American Conferences in 1846, 1856 and 1864 – are just some of the earlier examples of regional integration projects and processes that would be followed by more initiatives during the 20th century.

The analytical vectors: history, geography, economics and politics

Regional integration could be analyzed from the perspective of two analytical dimensions: temporal (history) and geographic. Starting with the temporal, following Ferdinand Braudel (1958), we take distance from a kind of 'history of events' that analyses different integration projects as isolated initiatives. There are studies that focus on early integration initiatives around the 19th century. Some scholars identify 'early' integration initiatives around the 1950s, while others highlight the relaunch of integration in the late 1980s. A common element among these is that periods are singled out without connection to prior processes. Moreover, there is also a tendency to narrow studies to certain spatial frameworks. For example, in specific analysis of integration initiatives in Central America, the Andean region, South America or the Southern Cone. To be sure, we do not *a priori* reject any of these studies. There is much of value to find there at what could be identified as the 'micro', national or sub-regional levels. However, in our study we choose to analyse these 'micro' and 'short-time' perspectives in a broader temporal and spatial framework. Concerning the our position is that history matters. Along with Braudel, we hold that 'today's time is the result of yesterday, the day before yesterday and many days before that'. We also share the view that 'structure' dominates the problems of long duration. For Braudel (1958), 'structures' are regarded as the relationship between certain realities and social masses, a reality that persists in long-lived structures that functions as stable elements for many generations. These 'structures' can be identified as geopolitical, economic, political and cultural vectors through which we will explain the resilience of regional integration. Geopolitics, is here regarded, as part of the spatial framework and implies the territorial dimension of state action, that is, the spatial framework in which the construction, fragmentation and (in general) policymaking of states take place. With its origin in the Latin word *terra*, the idea of a territory is related to a bounded space under the control of a group of people, with fixed boundaries and exclusive internal sovereignty (Elden, 2013, p. 18). In short, 'territory' becomes geopolitical when it is related to the control and managing of terrain.

A methodological guideline of our analytical framework is that the relation between history and geography (or territory) is of crucial importance, since it conditions the formation of states (Gottmann, 1973, p. 15). The history of states is also the tale of the construction of legal, cultural and mythical sources of legitimacy to connect 'nation(s)', 'territory' and 'state'. If successful, these foundations of the power of a state might survive the passing of time and even conquerors. There are, of course, examples in history in which nations have grown without states, but we dare to say that, in most cases, it has been the other way around. As we see it, the selection of geographic setting might influence the analysis of regional integration processes in the same way as the selection of periods of study. For example, if one selects a specific geographic setting, such as South America, and a particular period, such as the so-called post-hegemonic period (starting in the early 2000s), the result would be quite distinct in comparison to a scenario in which one would take into account a broader geographic setting and time span.

The economic vector relates to the way the international economic structures and Latin American states interact. The argument of the subordinated insertion of the countries of that region into the global economy, basically centred on the exports of raw materials or commodities and excluded from the technological revolution that took place since the 18th century, is widely known. As a result, the place of Latin America in world economic affairs has been secondary, and the region has been influenced by the vicissitudes of the global markets, sometimes in a positive way, as was the case of the recent boom of commodities from 2003–2013, but sometimes in a negative way. The place of Latin America in the international economy was explained by Raúl Prebisch (1962) in his famous centre–periphery dichotomy, and by the 'dependency school' that was strongly influenced by neo-Marxist ideas highlighting the role of external influences on the economic development of Latin America (see Frank, 1966; Cardoso & Faletto, 1979). There is, in our view, no doubt that the structure of the international economic system has influenced the development of regionalism in Latin America. This influence was clear during the period of import substitution industrialisation that led the so-called old regionalism. Prebisch's ideas on regionalism claimed that it was using it as a mechanism to further industrialisation. Regionalism was a core element in the strategy aimed at modifying Latin America's subordinated position in the global economy (see Prebisch, 1959; ECLAC, 1959). In the era of open regionalism, the proposals of economic integration in Latin America were perceived as a mechanism to achieve a better insertion into the global markets (ECLAC, 1994). Thus, the economic vector is crucial to understanding the resilience of regionalism in Latin America.

A third vector is politics. Mainstream literature defines the international system as anarchic, where material capabilities define the position of the diverse countries in the global hierarchy of power. According to this approach, the military and, more recently, economic power determine the place a country has in the international system. However, Latin American scholars such as Juan

Carlos Puig (1971, 1980) and Helio Jaguaribe (1979) have criticised this view of the international system. For them, hierarchy is a feature of that system, in which some countries are the main producers of norms and others just recipients. Thus, the system is not anarchic but hierarchic, and the position of a country in it does not depend only on its material capabilities. Certainly, they recognise that Latin American states have a subordinated position in the international hierarchy, but they think that the region could improve that position by fostering policy to achieve autonomy. Puig calls it a 'process of autonomization' in which Latin American countries promotes policies to improve their room for maneuvering in the international system. There is a misunderstanding when talking about autonomy because it is assimilated to autarky, and that is incorrect. Autonomy does not mean isolation in a globalised world but a joint strategy of Latin American countries to enhance their position in the international structure of power. Therefore, the political structure of the international system and its effects on Latin American countries are also variables to be analysed.

The cultural vector is often set aside, but we see it as crucial. Recent constructivist literature on regional integration and cooperation has highlighted the role of ideas, narratives and identities in the construction of international regions (see Checkel & Katzenstein, 2009; Checkel, 2014; Santa-Cruz, 2014). In the case of Latin America, regionalism has often been connected to the idea of a shared identity and the belief of considering the region as a 'broken nation' (see Herrera, 1967). This identity factor derives from centuries of shared Spanish and Portuguese colonial rule and similar experiences of political and economic development after independence. The connection here between history and culture is crucial to understanding the two regionalist trends that have existed in the Americas since the 19th century. One is Latin Americanism, which includes proposals of regional unity embracing all the Latin American countries based on political, economic but also cultural (identity) reasons. The other is Pan-Americanism, with the United States as a driving force.

Thus, to propose, as we do, a Braudelian long-term perspective for evaluating these four vectors implies viewing success and failure as part of social, economic and geopolitical processes. It also implies taking into account shifting hegemonic powers, broader geographic connections, transformation in the international economic structure and cultural variables. South America, in this sense, might be distinct but also connected to Latin America and the Caribbean (at least the Spanish-speaking Caribbean). In fact, as the contributions of this volume show, the recent 'post-hegemonic' South American processes are, in many ways, linked to other at Latin American, American and even Caribbean levels. However, as this book intends to show, the fate of Latin American integration is not just in the hands of structures of the international system. Local agency matters. In the case of Latin American regionalism we identify and analyze the role of state leaders, diplomats, businessmen, intellectuals, military and clergy.

A methodological clarification is needed at this point, especially considering the systemic-structural bias of previous paragraphs. We agree with Anthony Giddens in rejecting explanations where social life is regarded as the result of social structures that constrain individual action, or just the result of the aggregation of utility-maximising individuals. Both pure structuralism and individualism provide a limited explanation of social life. As a result, we subscribe to the belief that agency and structure are mutually constituted. Giddens developed the idea of structuration, according to which:

> The basic domain of study of the social sciences (. . .) is neither the experience of individual actors, nor the existence of any form of social totality, but social practices ordered across space and time. Human social activities like some self-reproducing in nature, are recursive.
>
> (Giddens, 1984, p. 2)

These ideas are critical to formulating our approach to understanding the resilience of regionalism in Latin American and the Caribbean. Certainly, the economic and political structure of the international system has influenced the way the regional initiatives were born and developed in Latin America. No doubt the Congress of Panama was a response to fears that the Holy Alliance could restore Spanish power in America, and the Congress of Lima in 1864–1865 was the result of the increasing European interventionism in México and South America. The same is true concerning Prebisch's proposals, that were part of a strategy to adapt the region to the post-war scenario, or the later case of open regionalism as a response to globalisation. The international system has established both constraints and opportunities for Latin American regional initiatives. This fact notwithstanding, we cannot explain the fate of regionalism as a mere result of structural and systemic factors.

The strategy followed by nation states and societies and their agents is crucial to understanding regionalism in the resilience of Latin American regionalism. Agents such as presidents and ministers of foreign affairs have played an important role in the promotion of regionalism. Simón Bolivar, Lucas Alamán, José Maria da Silva Paranhos Junior (known as the Barão do Rio Branco), Juan Domingo Perón, Raúl Alfonsín, Dante Caputo or Luis Inácio Lula da Silva are examples of heads men at the commanding hights of the state that fostered regional initiatives. There are also important intellectuals and politicians such as Francisco Bilbao, José Martí, Manuel Ugarte and Alberto Methol Ferré, whom analysed the events of their time in regional terms. Technocrats as Raúl Prebisch, Felipe Herrera, Enrique Iglesias and Victor Urquidi were also very important by fostering initiatives of regional integration. In the case of Prebisch and Herrera, they could be considered both intellectuals and technocrats at the same time. The actions of all these agents demonstrate the existence of recursive practices across the space and time centred on the ideas of: regional unity, cooperation and integration. These practices have, in our view, contributed in the construction of a Latin

American regional acquis and have to a great extent explained the resilience of Latin American regionalism.

Resilience and regionalism

The concept of resilience have been used in natural sciences to understand the capacity of ecosystems to persist in their original state in spite of perturbations. When applied in social sciences, scholars generally use it as synonymous with some kind of 'resistance' in time. That is correct, but there is more one could borrow from natural sciences, where resilience is also referred to as part of ecological memories in the form of information and legacies of evolutionary adaptations to disturbances (Johnstone et al., 2016, p. 2). 'Memory' is a key principle of resilience, and it depends on three main factors: (a) the diversity and quantity of surviving memory carriers, (b) the diversity of vectors that bring in new memory carriers and (c) the collective forming of complex mnemonic infrastructure.

Resilience is then, in our view, linked with a *longue durée* perspective, since it refers to the accumulated 'memory' sustaining continuity in new forms of integration initiatives. This 'memory' contains different kinds of experiences, successful or not, that are accumulated and developed by 'carriers' and 'vectors'. In our study, 'carriers' refers to actors, organisations and even individuals that play central roles in the processes; some examples are the state, social movements, business, the church, the military or intellectuals. The concept of 'vectors' is more concerned with the different dimensions presented above.

One more element concerning resilience is that it is not only concerned with 'continuities' but also with 'adaptation' and 'transformation'. The first reflects the capacity of a system to adjust its responses to change in external drivers and internal processes, although it does not necessarily need to alter any of the structures that surround it. Transformation, on the other hand, describes the change that might take place in processes of adaptation. This is also a reason for historical and cross-regional analysis, since regional processes differ in time and space.

In sum, our resilience approach to Latin American regional integration and cooperation sets the attention on certain hypotheses. To start with, that regionalism in Latin America cannot be understood in terms of a single process but as a complex web of different ones, sometimes converging and sometimes not, but generally influencing each other. Secondly, regionalism should be considered as part of a process. In this way, it cannot be understood by focusing on single periods of time but only with a long-term perspective, the roots of which are found in the pre-independence colonial states. Since colonisation, the creation of states in Latin America has been part of the global system in both political (territorial) and economic terms. In this way, all geopolitical and economic strategies, for or against integration and cooperation, have been linked to systemic limitations or driving forces, sometimes expressed in anti-systemic reactions and sometimes as forms of adaptation. Yet, local agency matters, and as a result, the recursive practices of political and social actors are critical to understanding the origins, features and development of regionalism in Latin America. We are aware that all the elements outlined here cannot be covered by this edited book. We see this, however, as a good start to a new interdisciplinary vantage point, focusing on different actors as well as disciplinary perspectives from areas such as history, political science, political economy, literature and international relations.

Structure of the book

The authors of the book were asked to analyse the different aspects described above, explaining the resilience of regionalism in Latin America. The *first section* of the book focus in the theoretical dimension in the sense that explore use of the idea of resilience in the study of regionalism. The *second section* is devoted to examining the resilience of the regional idea in some parts of the Latin American sub-continent. The *third section*, which constitutes the core of this book, include a series of chapters that evaluate how particular political and economic actors have furthered regional initiatives throughout the Latin American history. However, it is not just about describing concrete actions of diplomats, intellectuals, businessmen or militaries. As described in the previous sections of this introduction, the goal is to evaluate the extent to which structural factors linked to geography, history, politics and economy influence the behavior and initiatives of individual actors.

The first section includes the chapter written by José Briceño-Ruiz and Andrés Rivarola Puntigliano. These authors discuss two categories that are crucial in the historical analysis of Latin American regionalism: resilience and acquis. It is a theoretical inquiry, based on the overall hypothesis that regionalism in Latin America is not a new issue but an ongoing process with roots back in the colonial formation and independence of states in the American continent. An evidence of that process is the resilience that regionalism has showed in Latin America. Despite the patterns of fragmentation that have been part of the history of the region, despite failures, regionalism is never abandoned. New generations of Latin American leaders and social actors always return to regional projects, taking these to new levels and dimensions. To understand what we call the resilience of regionalism integration in Latin America, we propose to highlight four main issues. Firstly, that resilience is linked to mechanisms of self-enforcement that are part of the accumulation of experiences, institution building and common cultural features described in this chapter as regionalist acquis. Secondly, that the elements and driving forces behind the promotion and expression of the regionalist acquis are influenced and shaped by nested systems in which social processes are inserted. Thirdly, when looking at systems, there is a particular influence by national and (global) international ones, which condition the form and endurance of regional projects. Finally, it is not only a matter of systems but also of its agents, with crucial players in the shaping of the resilience of regionalism in Latin America.

The second section evaluates sub-regional experiences of resilience. Kevin Parthenay's chapter evaluates Central American regionalism through its long-lasting logic. According to him, although there has been much written about this issue, most scholars concentrate on specific actors, states, and specific periods, mainly the activation of the 1950s and the reactivation of the 1990s. It discards, however, a long-term process that takes its origins in the very initial formation of the 'region' at the time of the independences. The formation of this original 'mental map' has constituted a vector of the Central American project resilience. In this chapter, Parthenay sheds a new light on the Central American regionalism, exploring its intellectual roots since the 19th century and taking into consideration the agents that contributed to give birth to that project. To study this Central American experiment, international political economy is articulated to a classical framework of historical institutionalism in order to explain the resilience of this sub-regional case of Latin American regionalism.

Carlos Eduardo Vidigal argues, in the following chapter, that there is a Brazilian project for regional integration that, since the beginning of the 1960s, has been arousing sectors of the political, military, diplomatic and academic elites of that country. He studies diverse initiatives proposed in different political conjunctures that Brazil has gone through during this period: (a) the independent foreign policy of the Janio Quadros and João Goulart governments (1961–1964); (b) the military regime (1964–1985); (c) the first phase of the recent democratic period (1985–2000/2002); (d) the government of the Workers Party (2003–2016). The central argument presented by Vidigal is the existence of a long-term Brazilian project for South American integration. This argument is backed by the hypothesis that the Brazilian project of South American integration did not configure itself as an instrument of domination, although hegemonic aspirations have not been absent from it. In other words, in the pursuit of its project of regional integration, Brazil has sought to convince its neighbors of the importance and the format of the integration.

In the next chapter, José Briceño-Ruiz, María Antonia Correa and Enrique Catalán analyzes the role of the diplomats and technocrats in regional integration processes in Latin America. For them, one of the main forces behind the proposals of regional integration has been the ministers of foreign affairs. Lucas Alamán, Jose Gregorio Paz Soldan, José Maria da Silva Paranhos Junior (known as O Barão do Río Branco), Dante Caputo and Celso Amorim have been, in their respective periods of time, central figures in pushing regional initiatives such as the Family Pact in the 1830s, the Hispanic-America Congress of Lima in 1847–1848, the ABC Pact in the 1910s, the Bilateral rapprochement between Argentina and Brazil in the 1980s (that led to the creation of MERCOSUR) and the Union of South American Nations in the 2000s. Similarly, technocrats such as Raul Prebisch, Felipe Herrera, Victor Urquidi and Enrique Iglesias have also played a crucial role in the promotion of regional unity. This chapter analyses the role of these diplomats and technocrats in the promotion of regional initiatives in the Latin American sub-continent.

The role of the military in Latin American regionalism is the focus of Andrés Rivarola Puntigliano's chapter. The Latin American military have for a long time been considered a negative force. Their role in repression during the 20th century, and particularly during the regimes in the 1970s, have indeed contributed to this view. This is generally attributed to a subordinated position towards 'imperialism', repression of popular movements, neo-liberal policies and, fundamentally, an elitist and anti-democratic stance. There is also a relation between this position and a negative actions concerning regional integration and cooperation. However, Rivarola Puntigliano presents a broader perspective on Latin American military forces, which shows that during different periods of time the military also had both close links to popular forces and a pro-active position concerning regionalism. In fact, in some cases, the military where a pivotal group behind the promotion of regional integration and industrialisation.

In the following chapter, Liliana Weinberg analyses the cultural dimension of Latin American regionalism. With the suggestive title of 'Latin America and the Caribbean: from geopolitics to geopoetics', Weinberg's chapter argues that integration as a project can only be possible if it is done from a perspective of the future and attending to the specificity its cultural dimension. In consequence, literary and artistic practices and other cultural components should be considered, and integration cannot be reduced to the commercial endeavours. In this sense, the author gives particular attention to the role of essay in the formation of the idea of unity in Latin America. For her, the artistic creation is the cause of the resurgence, rebounding, resistance and resilience of the idea of unity in Latin America.

José Ramiro Podetti's chapter focuses on the role of the Catholic Church in the construction of regionalism in Latin America. Podetti argues that the 19th century was a turning point in the history of the Catholic Church in Latin America: born and developed for three centuries under the wing of the monarchy, as a result of the separation of church and state and the secularisation processes, it suffered a severe crisis. Additionally, since the new Hispanic American republics had drifted apart not only from Spain but also from each other, the episcopal polity and the clergy, both secular and regular, lost the mobility across dioceses, from Mexico to the Río de la Plata, that they had enjoyed for three centuries. Thus, churches became more local – 'national' – during the 19th century. During the 20th century, the Church in Latin America went through a 'reconstitution' process, especially at a presbyterial and episcopal level. A key feature of this process was the 'Latin Americanisation' of the Catholic Church in the region. This chapter explains this process, starting with the creation and development of the Latin American Episcopal Council, continued in the five Latin American Episcopal General Conferences between 1955 and 2007, with major reflections upon their connection to Latin Americanism and its importance to the resilience of regional integration.

Finally, Rita Giacalone and Giovanni Molano analyse the role of the economic actors in the integration agreements, whether they support them or reject them or (more infrequently) they feel indifferent. They argue that along more than three-quarters of a century, the private sector has been involved in the process of regional integration. The business sector has sometimes showed an ambiguous attitude and other times an outright support or rejection vis-à-vis regionalism. This chapter examines the history of business associations involvement in regional integration, emphasising as the main explanatory factor their relations with their national state apparatus. In the concluding chapter, Briceño-Ruiz and Rivarola Puntigliano present a final analysis concerning a theoretical framework for the study of the resilience of Latin American integration in the light of the empirical contributions in the chapters of this book.

The diverse chapters of this book give some insights about the reasons for the resilience of Latin American regionalism. From an interdisciplinary view, the diverse chapters show the political, economic and cultural reasons behind the initiatives of regional unity, the role of diverse actors such as the Catholic Church, the military, the business sector, the diplomats and technocrats, and the way in which systemic variables interact with those agents. This constitutes a contribution in the study of the resilience of Latin American regionalism.

References

Braudel, F. (1958). Histoire et sciences sociales: la longue durée. *Annales. Histoire, Sciences Sociales, 13*(4), 725–753.

Buzan, B., & Waever, O. (2003). *Regions and powers: The structure of international security*. Cambridge: Cambridge University Press.

Cardoso, F. H., & Faletto, E. (1979). *Dependency and development in Latin America*. Berkeley, CA: University of California Press.

Checkel, J. F. (2014, June). *Regional identities and communities* (Simons Papers in Security and Development, 36/2014). Vancouver: School for International Studies, Simon Fraser University.

Checkel, J. T., & Katzenstein, P. J. (Eds.). (2009). *European identity*. Cambridge: Cambridge University Press.

ECLAC. (1994). *Open regionalism in Latin America and the Caribbean: Economic integration as a contribution to changing production patterns with social equity*. Santiago, Chile: ECLAC.

Economic Commission for Latin America. (1959). *The Latin American common market*. New York: United Nations.

Elden, S. (2013). *The birth of territory*. Chicago, IL: University of Chicago Press.

Frank, A. G. (1966). *The development of underdevelopment*. Boston, MA: New England Free Press.

Giddens, A. (1984). *The constitution of society: Outline of the theory of structuration*. Berkeley, CA: University of California Press.

Gottmann, J. (1973). *The significance of territory*. Charlottesville, VA: The University of Virginia Press.

Herrera, F. (1967). *Nacionalismo Latinoamericano*. Santiago, Chile: Editorial Universitaria.

Jaguaribe, H. (1979). Autonomía periférica y hegemonía céntrica. *Estudios Internacionales, 12*(46), 91–130. https://doi.org/10.5354/0719-3769.2011.16458

Johnstone, J. F., Allen, C. D., Franklin, J. F., Frelich, L. E., Harvey, B. J., Higuera, P. E., . . . Turner, M. G. (2016). Changing disturbance regimes, ecological memory, and forest resilience. *Frontiers in Ecology and the Environment, 14*(7), 369–378. https://doi.org/10.1002/fee.1311

Katzenstein, P. J. (2015). *A world of regions: Asia and Europe in the American imperium.* New York: Cornell University Press.

Prebisch, R. (1959). El Mercado Común Latinoamericano. *Comercio Exterior, 9*(9), 509–513. Retrieved from http://revistas.bancomext.gob.mx/rce/magazines/477/4/RCE4.pdf

Prebisch, R. (1962). The economic development of Latin America and its principal problems. *Economic Bulletin for Latin America, 7*(1), 1–22.

Puig, J. C. (1971). La vocación autonomista en América Latina: heterodoxia y secesionismo. *Revista de Derecho Internacional y Ciencias Diplomáticas, 39/40,* 60–66.

Puig, J. C. (1980). *Doctrinas internacionales y Autonomía latinoamericana.* Caracas, Venezuela: Universidad Simón Bolívar, Instituto de Altos Estudios de América Latina.

Santa-Cruz, A. (2014). Liberalism, constructivism and Latin American politics since the 1990s. In J. I. Dominguez & A. Covarrubias (Eds.), *Routledge handbook of Latin America in the world* (pp. 109–123). Abingdon: Routledge.

Solingen, E. (1998). *Regional orders at century's dawn: Global and domestic influences on grand strategy.* Princeton, NJ: Princeton University Press.

1 Resilience and acquis in Latin American regionalism

José Briceño-Ruiz and Andrés Rivarola Puntigliano

Introduction

The point of departure for the theoretical inquiry proposed in this chapter is based on the overall hypothesis that regional integration in Latin America is not a new issue but an ongoing process with roots back in the colonial formation and independence of states on the American continent. Thus, as proposed by the French historian Fernand Braudel, we regard Latin American regionalism as a process of *longue durée*. A central question here is how to understand and analyse this process, its origins, driving forces and patterns of change. A clear-cut evidence of that process is the resilience shown by regionalism in Latin America. Despite the patterns of fragmentation that have been part of the history of the region – despite the failures and setbacks of initiatives of cooperation and integration, regionalism is never abandoned. New generations of Latin American leaders and social actors always return to integration projects, taking these to new levels and dimensions.

To understand what we call the resilience of regional integration in Latin America, we propose to highlight four main issues. Firstly, that resilience is linked to mechanisms of self-enforcement that are part of the accumulation of experiences, institution building and common cultural features described in this paper as *regionalist acquis*. Secondly, that the elements and driving forces behind the promotion and expression of the regionalist *acquis* are influenced and shaped by nested systems in which social processes are inserted. Thirdly, when looking at systems, there is a particular influence by national and (global) international ones, which condition the form and endurance of regional projects. Finally, it is not only a matter of systems but also of their agents, as crucial players in the shaping of the resilience of regionalism in Latin America.

The concept of resilience

Resilience has received different kinds of definitions ranging from distinct disciplinary areas. Thus, in the natural sciences, resilience refers to the quality of a material or an ecosystem. In this case, "a trestle of steel is more or less resilient depending on its capacity to recover from load bearing and return to its previous state unchanged. A natural environment that sustains an industrial disaster and recovers also demonstrates resilience" (Ungar, 2012, p. 13). Ungar explained that resilience is also used in the psychological sciences to describe "the ability of individuals to recover from exposure to chronic and acute stress." In cybernetics, the term refers to individuals who return to a state of homeostasis or experience change and growth (morphogenesis) following exposure to a toxic environment (p. 13). From an ecological point of view, resilience refers "to the ability of socio-ecological systems (SES) to absorb disturbance without flipping into another state or phase" (Cote & Nightingale, 2012, p. 1).

In all the different definitions described above, there is a common denominator: resilience entails the capacity of an individual or social system to deal with adverse situations and continue working on a regular basis. A deeper analysis of the category implies a review of how it has been understood in disciplines such as psychology and ecology, where the concept has been extensively developed for decades.

In psychology, resilience is usually understood as "the process of adapting well in the face of adversity, trauma, tragedy, threats or even significant sources of stress" (Southwick, Bonanno, Masten, Panter-Brick, & Yehuda, 2014a, p. 2). This concept was proposed by the American Psychological Association. Another definition describes resilience as "the capacity of people to recover from trauma, to cope with high levels of stress or to demonstrate competence and coping despite continuous or cumulative adversity" (Bottrell, 2009, p. 323). However, recent literature on the issue describes these concepts as useful but limited. There is a further need to explore what resilience really entails. This implies exploring whether resilience is a trait, a process, or an outcome (Southwick, Bonanno, Masten, Panter-Brick, & Yehuda, 2014b). If resilience is a *trait*, it could be understood as "the capacity of individuals to deal with adverse situations and is regarded as an 'individualized' feature" (p. 2). In this line of thought, resilience would be "the ability to draw on personal or social resources, the ability to detect contingencies and predictability in complex situations and the capacity to react flexibly" (Rauh, 1989, p. 165). Resilience can also be considered as a *process*. In this framework, resilience might be regarded as a stable trajectory after a highly adverse event or as a trajectory "characterized by a relatively brief period of disequilibrium, but otherwise continued health" (Southwick et al. 2014a, p. 2). If resilience is conceptualized as an *outcome* in the face of adversities or risk, the concept refers to "the fact of maintaining adaptive functioning in spite of serious risk hazard" (Kaplan, 2002, p. 20). These three ways of understanding resilience (as trait, as a process and as an outcome) are useful when applying this category to the study of regionalism.

A different view emerged in the 1970s from ecologic systems theory. Along this track, the concept 'resilience' was used to understand the capacity of socio-ecological systems (SES) in dealing with changes. This included recovery from unexpected shocks and avoiding undesirable 'tipping points' but also the capacity to adapt to ongoing change and fundamentally transform SES if needed (Biggs, Reinette, Schlüter, & Schoon, 2015, p. 21). Along this line, some of the elements pointed out in studies of SES concerning resilience are as follows: (a) capacity to self-organise, (b) forms of adapting and learning in response to internal or external changing conditions, (c) adaptation and change following non-linear dynamics and (d) assuming strong interdependence and different levels of interaction with systems, which are interconnected at multiple scales. Recent trends also describe resilience as contextually and culturally embedded. Thus, as Bottrell (2009) explained, "cultural practices, social processes, social change and the nature of individual-social relations are all significant aspects of the context for analysing resilience" (p. 322). These contextual factors are located in different system levels, from individual agency in microsystems to social structures at macrosystems (p. 125).

When applying the category of resilience to the study of regionalism, some of the ideas explained earlier should be considered. Pundits, such as Pia Riggirozzi, have argued that the idea of resilience developed by Rivarola Puntigliano and Briceño-Ruiz (2013) seems to be just "the persistence of the idea and the value of identity, autonomy, and development. In other words, resilience seems to be defined as merely the preservation of an 'idea'; that is, the perpetuated need to achieve greater autonomy and independence through regional integration" (Riggirozzi, 2014, p. 465). This criticism deserves to be considered. Resilience is not just the preservation of an idea. In our view, the *resilience* of regionalism in Latin America is a *trait* that can be seen in the initiatives of integration and cooperation. It should also be regarded as a *process*, related to the capacity of local social systems to resist disturbances and setbacks caused by international and domestic crises. Finally, resilience is an *outcome* of a process in which structural variables linked to the function of the international system are critical but in which the role of the agents is also crucial.

Thus, in respect to regional integration, resilience can be regarded as the capacity of the regional process of integration and cooperation to recover from crises and setbacks. A long-term historical analysis shows the capacity of Latin American regionalism to recover from crises. The Congress of Panamá of 1826 is often considered the first formal attempt to create a regional institutional framework to deal with common problems, but its results were limited because most of the agreements subscribed in the Congress were never ratified. Despite this, a new cycle of regionalism, which De La Reza (2012) described as the Confederative Cycle, began in the 1840s and concluded in the 1860s. Three regional Congresses to promote cooperation and integration were held: in Lima (1846), Santiago (1856) and Lima (1865). When this confederative cycle ended, regionalism seemed to stall, but new initiatives would emerge again. That was the case of the ABC treaty between Argentina, Brazil and Chile or economic proposals around a South American Custom Union, that were fostered in the early decades of the 20th century. After a period of slowdown, new attempts at regional cooperation emerged in the 1940s, the most important of them being the creation of the Economic Commission for Latin America (ECLA) in 1948 and the later creation of the Latin American Free Trade Association (LAFTA) in 1960, which led to the period known as 'old regionalism'. The period between late 1990s to early 2000s is called the era of open regionalism, followed by a new period from 2003 to 2015 dominated by what has been named 'post-hegemonic regionalism'. This brief historical review shows the capacity of regionalism to recover from crises and return in new forms and models. The question remains; if regionalism is just a sum of failures, as some scholars argue, why does the regional process not disappear from the political agenda? Our point is that this is because resilience has been a *trait* of Latin American regionalism.

In our view, resilience in Latin American regionalism should also be seen as a *process*, with ups and downs as well as changes and continuities. For example, if one looks at regional schemes from the mid-20th century, such as LAFTA, the Central American Common Market (CACM) or the Andean Pact, they had an initial period of successes (ups) that were followed by setbacks (downs), leading to their review as integration processes (changes). A similar process can be observed in the era of open regionalism. The Southern Common Market (MERCOSUR) was initially quite successful but entered into crisis in the late 1990s going through several transformations. Once again, these initiatives experienced ups, downs and changes, but they do not disappear. Regional context changed over the time, but the idea or regional unity did not because the factors that fostered resilience remained. These factors are, as our study intends to show, systemic and agential.

Resilience is also an *outcome* in the sense that it has the capacity to maintain the adaptive functioning of most regional processes. Despite their crises, regional processes function in many dimensions. For example, some claim that trade interdependence is quite low in most Latin American regional schemes such as MERCOSUR and the Andean Community. It is hard to reject such empirical data. This notwithstanding, it does not imply that other dimensions of integration are not working, for example in the domains of migration and freer movement of persons, areas in which both regional processes have achieved some success. The resilience of Latin American regionalism is evidenced in the capacity of regional schemes to adapt and reformulate themselves as response to shifting internal (local) and external conditions. Regionalist initiatives have always returned, in spite of civil wars, shifting political systems and economic crisis. They have also survived as part of alternatives and solutions that deal with shifting global processes such as the economic crisis or world wars of the early 20th century, the Cold War or debt crisis in the second part of the 20th century, the changes produced by the process of globalisation or the emergence of a new multipolar world order in the early 21st century. Hence, resilience has meant adaptation and change through regional blocs, at different systemic levels within the global system(s).

Resilience as contextualised process: the role of systems and agency

Since resilience is contextually and culturally embedded, the context matters when analysing the resilience of Latin American regionalism. This implies the analysis of cultural practices, social processes, social changes and individual – social relations that shape resilience. As explained, the analysis of those factors must be made at the micro and macro levels. In the study of the resilience of regionalism, this implies the analysis of the impact of both the international system and its agents in the regional schemes.

The nature of systems depends on their composition, where one might find an ample variety of forms and outcomes. The eco-system model, with its attachment to systems, forms of adaptation and change, is a source of inspiration for our approach to regional integration. There is, however, a trend in the studies of social systems to see these as disconnected to agents. We are here closer to the position of Alexander E. Wendt (1987) in the field of international relations concerning the importance of the interaction between system and agency in global affairs. According to Wendt:

> Despite their many differences . . . the 'agent-structure', 'parts-whole', 'actor-system', and 'micro-macro' problems all reflect the same meta-theoretical imperative – the need to adopt, for the purpose of explaining social behaviour, some conceptualisation of the ontological and explanatory relationship between social actors or agents (. . .) and social structures.
>
> (p. 338)

In respect to systems, including in the framework of international/global studies, we turn to scholars Barry Buzan and Richard Little (1993), who asserted that a system refers to a group of parts or units whose interactions are significant enough to justify seeing them in some sense as a coherent set. A group of states forms an international system when "the behaviour of each is a necessary factor in the calculations of the others" (Buzan & Little, 1993, p. 129).

Thus, a system comprises structure, units and interactions. For Buzan and Little, the term 'international system' has two senses. The first refers "to the system of states, and reflects the puzzling, but firmly established use of nation as a synonym for state" (Buzan & Little, 1993, p. 129), while the second refers "to the totality of human interaction on the planet, and incorporates a range of units varying from individuals, through firms, nations and a great variety of other nongovernmental organizations or entities, to states" (Buzan & Little, 1993, p. 129). It is valid to argue that regional institutions are also units of the international system, since these are also part of the great variety of 'sub-systems' that conforms the international system(s).

A first element of a system is the structure. This is certainly a controversial concept in the social sciences, where there is no unique view. As Giddens and

Sutton have pointed out, the history of sociological thought is evidence of this diversity. For Herbert Spencer and August Comte, social structures were groups, collectivities and aggregates of individuals, but Durkheim used the notion of social facts and society as an entity in its own right. Talcott Parsons devised a theory of action in which social structures were to be less 'thing-like' and become patterns of normative expectations and guidelines governing acceptable behavior (Giddens & Sutton, 2014, pp. 52–53).

Douglas V. Porpora (1989) describes at least four ways to understand structure: (1) as patterns of aggregate behavior that are stable over time; (2) as law-like regularities that govern the behavior of social facts; (3) as systems of human relationships among social positions; and (4) and as collective rules and resources that structure behavior. In all those meanings, structure implies interactions (p. 339). As Porpora argues, "social structures such as the class system, the family or the economy are built from social interactions, which endure and change over time" (Giddens & Sutton, 2014, p. 54). Giddens, for example, highlights the "social practices that are 'ordered across space and time', and it is through these that social structures are reproduced" (p. 56). For Archer (2017), "structure is the conditioning medium and elaborated outcome of interaction" (p. 50).

Two challenges emerge when discussing which units comprise the system. The first one is the identification of the ontological framework in which the 'original units' are placed. The second one is about the insertion of these units into a broader context that might explain their emergence and patterns of change. This challenge appears regardless of whether one focuses on 'institutions', ideas, discourse or different forms of materialist-based points of view. An additional problem, particular to the discipline of international relations, was identified by Alexander Wendt as the explanatory use given by two influential perspectives of international relations, 'realism' and 'world-system theory', to what he calls the 'primitive units'. The latter are those selected as the ontological basis for the agent-structure issue: 'the state' in the case of realism and the 'capitalist world system' in the case of world-system theory. According to Wendt, the common problem is that "both of them precludes an explanation of the essential properties of their respective primitive units" (p. 340). In the case of realism, systems are made up of states, but realists fail to provide an explicit theory of the state, its 'primitive unit'. In the case of world-system theory, the system is treated as operating independently of state action, where "the whole is seen as ontologically prior to its parts". The problem, in Wendt's view, is that this theory does not explain "why the system developed that particular structure, nor does it guarantee that that structure will endure" (pp. 347–348).

In sum, our point is that in order to explain and understand regionalism and its resilience in Latin America, systems and agents must be part of the analytical framework. Setting aside one of these two dimensions is a serious shortcoming in the understanding of regional integration and its resilience.

Regions, adaptation and change in systems: *longue durée,* acquis and resilience

A region is generally the meso-level of a broader system, be it defined in cultural, geographic or economic terms. At the broadest macro level, we have the international system, whose shifts and framework of action influence local levels, such as national and regional units (Millner, 2007, p. 2). Braudel (1979) argued that at the macro-level, there are (a) economic systems, characterised by an increasingly inter-connected global economy; (b) political systems containing several dimensions such as mega-regions and regions as well as national and sub-national units; and according to Meyer (1999) also macro world-cultural systems, where the spread of norms and cultural institutions also shape the creation of local level, regional or national organisations. At the meso-level, there are macro-regional units that might contain other regional and, of course, national, entities. Finally, at the micro level, there are nation-states that might also be key units (systems themselves) that are part of regional systems. Nation-states, particularly if they are large in size, also have sub-regional units, some of which might be stronger than other systems that are part of a particular region. There can also be other forms of micro-systems related to other social dimensions than those mentioned.

All these units are constantly changing in different ways their relation towards other units of the system(s). A study of forms, leverage and changes of system and their units is of great importance to understanding the framework in which regional units exist. There is a tendency in some schools of thought to overemphasise the role of macro/structural systems over single units or micro-systems. Indeed, we share the view that broader systems condition the units within them, yet agency at micro-levels also has the power to influence broader changes in macro-systems.

Another issue relevant to understanding a system's patterns of change and adaptation lies in the historical perspective. Systemic short-term impacts might imply changes at regional levels, yet generally, the deeper changes should be followed by an analysis of the longer trends in systemic change. This issue is clear in the case of economic cycles, which are, in turn, deeply connected to geopolitical changes (Arrighi, 2006). As pointed out in the introduction, the long-term (*longue durée*) perspective is particularly relevant for the analysis of the resilience of regional systems. Also, as argued earlier, the *longue durée* of these systems is relevant because it refers to the accumulated 'memory' that sustains continuity in new forms of integration initiatives. This 'memory' contains different kinds of experiences that, successful or not, are accumulated and developed by 'carriers' and 'vectors'. We turn to the issue of 'carriers' in what follows, but for now our aim is to point out the link between historical perspective, 'memory' and the accumulation of experience with regard to the resilience of regional systems.

In systems theory, this can be related to Niklas Luhmann's view of 'auto-referential systems' (De la Reza, 2015, p. 54). By an accumulation of experience, the units conforming the system develop a capacity to differentiate themselves from the external environment. In the case of Latin American regionalism, that is what we here refer to as the 'acquis' of regional integration. Its origin might very well be a form of 'culture of resistance', which has in time elaborated its own forms of identity, organisation or what Coriún Aharonián (2002) calls 'technology for resistance'. Beyond the logic of resistance, the acquis implies the creation of norms and patterns of behaviour that are particular to a regional system.

Acquis is a concept that emerged in the legal debates of European integration. The French expression *acquis communautaire* does not have an exact translation in English, but in the *Glossary the Reform of the European Union in 150 definitions*, it is just described as "the acquis communautaire or Community patrimony is the body of common rights and obligations which bind all the Member States together within the European Union" (European Commission, 1997, p. 11). For Goebel (1995):

> 'Acquis communautaire' essentially conveys the idea that the institutional structure, scope, policies and rules of the Community (now Union) are to be treated as 'given' ('acquis'), not to be called into question or substantially modified by new States at the time they enter.
>
> (p. 1095)

In addition, for Philippe Schmitter (1996), the acquis "refers to the sum total of obligations that have accumulated since the founding of the ECSC and are imbedded in innumerable treaties and protocols" (p. 162).

A Eurocentric view on the concept of acquis rejects the idea of a Latin American acquis. Thus, Mario Carranza denied the existence of an "acquis communautaire" in Latin America, because this concept has a "precise meaning". By quoting McCormick (1999), Carranza describes acquis as "all the principles, policies, laws, practices and goals agreed and developed within the EU" (Carranza, 2014, p. 164). Acquis is a legal concept that for Carranza "cannot be loosely applied – without changing its meaning to the 'build-up' of the 'idea' of regional integration in Latin America since the early nineteenth century" (Carranza, 2014, p. 164). This approach to the issue is clearly a Eurocentric approach. In this research the terms 'Latin American acquis', 'theoretical acquis' or 'historical acquis' are used but not the word 'communautaire', as with Carranza. The idea of communautaire comes from a time when the idea of acquis was beginning to be developed and the formal denomination of the integration process on the old continent was the European Community. For this reason, the adjective 'communautaire' is not part of our explicative framework. In our research, acquis has an historical and theoretical meaning, not a legal one. To think that acquis should just possess a legal meaning because it had that meaning in the European integration is a static and inflexible way to understand the constructions of concepts. Some concepts can have different meanings according to the area of analysis. For example, in a previous section of this chapter, we have demonstrated how a single concept, resilience, is understood differently in psychology and ecology.

Furthermore, a term is not a concept. Acquis is originally a French term that means 'given' in English. Acquis communautaire is a legal concept developed in the early years of the European Community. It is also valid to argue about the existence of a 'historical acquis' or 'theoretical acquis' as concepts of their own. From an epistemological point of view, Mario Bunge has described a concept as a unit of thought:

> Accordingly, the theory of concepts should be the philosophical equivalent of the atomic theory. Concepts, like material atoms, are not given in experience but must be sought by analysis. Analysis of what? Clearly, of the linguistic expressions of knowledge, since conceptual knowledge comes wrapped in signs: words, symbols, diagrams, etc.
>
> (Bunge, 1998, p. 51)

Thus, acquis as a concept must not be understood in a static way given by the European legal tradition but in a dynamic way that includes the analysis of the different linguistic meanings that acquis could have to explain realities beyond Europe.

In consequence, acquis in this chapter has a twofold meaning. On the one hand, it has a historical meaning and refers to the historical trajectory of Latin American regionalism and the lessons and experiences learned from that trajectory. This is the 'historical acquis' that, according to pundits as Carlos Closa, can be found in the nineteenth-century American integration projects, "from the Pan-American Conference to the Central United Provinces" (Closa, 2015, p. 6). On the other hand, acquis has a theoretical meaning and describes a long tradition of thought on regional unity that goes back to Francisco de Miranda or Simón Bolívar in the 19th century. In this theoretical acquis, regionalism is linked to the concepts of autonomy and development.

Understanding agency is here of key importance, both as a form of resistance towards systems and also as a driving force for the creation and shaping of norms and patterns of behaviour. Indeed, we are here in front of dialectical processes, a connection of systems from micro- to meso- and macro-levels. That is, systems that are nested into each other, sometimes in the form of conversion, as sources of opposition, and at other times carrying both forms. In this book, Latin America is the case of study, containing sub-regional meso-system(s), such as the Andean Region, Central America, the Caribbean, the Amazon or Rio de la Plata Basin, as well as local national and sub-national systems. To understand the interaction among systems, Samuel Cohan refers to 'geopolitical systems', where systems are seen as; (a) evolving in predictably structured ways, (b) open to outside forces, (c) with hierarchy, regulation and entropy as important characteristics, (d) and self-correcting. In this model, change and adaptation might be regarded through a progressional line where the earliest form is called *undifferentiated* or atomised – identical systems – followed by *differentiation*, when parts develop own characteristics but are still isolated. The next stage is specialisation, in which an exchange of complementary outputs of the system leads to an integration of the system. The parts of the system are hierarchically ordered, increasing its efficiency, as one level fulfils certain functions but leaves other functions to units belonging to different levels. What helps to bring balance to the system is the drive of less mature parts to rise to higher levels (Cohen, 2009, p. 57).

Systemic factors are critical to understanding the resilience of Latin American regionalism. Such factors can be found in structural constraints that existed since the early years of political independence, and remain to this day, making regional integration a recurrent policy option for Latin American governments. The first constraint is what the Argentinean scholar Juan Carlos Puig (1980) described as a "hierarchical international system". For him, the international order is a political regime in which a command structure exists. Some countries command and impose norms, while other ones are in an intermediate position or just recipients of those norms. The Latin American countries are included in the category of recipients, and their room to maneuver in international affairs is limited. This implies a problem of autonomy: those countries were formally independent but with a limited autonomy. The structure of the international political system created conditions for the endurance of that hierarchical order. From this perspective, regionalism could be seen as a mechanism to improve the autonomy of Latin American countries. This durability of this international structure of power is an incentive to promote regionalism and explains its resilience.

Regionalism in Latin America has been perceived as a mechanism to improve the 'autonomy' of Latin American countries. A long historical analysis of Latin American regionalism provides evidence that autonomy was behind many regional proposals in the immediate decades after independence in the 19th century (Briceño-Ruiz, 2015). By the same token, regional initiatives in the era of the so-called old regionalism of the 1960s and 1970s also aimed at autonomy in the context of the Cold War. For example, Puig (1986) thought that that autonomy could be achieved by promoting a model of regional integration based on solidarity and the sharing of common values. Thus, one can argue that regionalism is a mechanism to deal with a structural problem of the political insertion of Latin America into the world that has remained for centuries, where it has a subordinated role in global affairs. This structural factor might be an explanation of the resilience of Latin American regionalism.

The second factor is the unequal division of the international economic system between developed and underdeveloped countries. This was described by the Argentine economist Raúl Prebisch as a dichotomy centre–periphery. Certainly, the world has changed since the time Prebisch wrote his contributions to economic development. The world economy is currently globalised, and a new category of countries called 'emerging' has appeared. These facts notwithstanding, the unequal division of the international economic system is still a feature that has not changed substantially. Latin America is part of the developing world, and despite the efforts to diversify its economic structure, this remains closely linked to the production of raw materials. Since the ECLA's and Prebisch's proposals in the 1950s, economic regionalism in Latin America has been related to the goal of improving the Latin American position in the international economic system and the achievement of economic development. Once again, a structural feature of the international system (the division between developed and developing countries) is a factor that influences the emergence of regional blocs in Latin America. This might also explain the resilience of regionalism.

Agents of integration and resilience

In his classical book *Man, State and War*, Kenneth Walz considered the state and human beings as units, even if the state was what Wendt called the 'primitive units', while war was the international system. David Singer proposed two levels: the international system and national sub-systems. More recently, Barry Buzan and Ole Waever introduce the regional level. Up to this point most positions concern definitions of systems, their interconnectedness, nested systems, adaptation and change and how this could shape resilience. The meso level represented by the regions has also been considered. However, units are crucial in the working of a system. The units are the agents that deploy activities in the system. They have a function of agency in a system. However, there has been a debate on what the units of the system are. As explained, the state is the unit for the realist and capitalist regime of world system theories, but what about the individuals or non-state actors such as the business associations, social movements or the Roman Catholic Church? Arguably, some of these agents influence not only the behaviour of nation states but also the international system itself. Arguably, they play a role in the resilience of regionalism. In the case of human beings, Herbert Kelman (1970) pointed out that:

> We sometimes tend to forget that is individual human beings who make the decisions and carry out the actions that constitute international relations. It is individuals who threaten or fell threatened, who perceive o misperceive, who give and withhold support, who compete or cooperate, who kill and die. In formulating policies, the ultimate guide must be their implications for the needs and interests, the welfare and dignity, of individual human beings, rather than for the alleged sanctity of symbols and institutions – important and real though these may be. Such policies are more likely to emerge when the analysis of international relations gives some considerations to the role of individual actors – among decision-makers as well as publics, in national as well as international systems.
>
> (p. 1)

An area in which individuals play an important role is foreign policy. Thus, political leaders, diplomats or foreign policy makers have been crucial in certain countries and historical periods. The Barão of Rio Branco in the early decades of republican life in Brazil or Henry Kissinger in the 1960s and early 1970s in the United States, are examples of individual men of state that shaped significant foreign policy decisions. Hermann, Preston, Korany, and Shaw (2001) have written about the effect of powerful leaders in foreign policy. According to them, "when a single individual has the power to make the choice concerning how a state is going to respond to a foreign policy problem, he or she becomes the decision unit and acts as a predominant leader" (p. 84). However, the actions of these leaders are contextualised (Rathbun, Kertzer, Reifler, Goren, and Scotto, 2016). Both personal values matter and structural factors play a crucial role since, as Valerie Hudson (2005) argues:

> The mind of a foreign policy maker is not a tabula rasa: it contains complex and intricately related information and patterns, such as beliefs, attitudes, values, experiences, emotions, traits, style, memory, national, and self-conceptions. Each decision-maker's mind is a microcosm of the variety possible in a given society. Culture, history, geography, economics, political institutions, ideology, demographics, and innumerable other factors shape the societal context in which the decision-maker operates.
>
> (p. 11)

Non-state actors are also units in the international system. They could be defined as "organizations largely or entirely autonomous from central governments funding and control: emanating from civil society, or from the market economy, or from political impulses beyond the state control and direction" (Josseli & Wallace, 2001, p. 3). Fred Halliday has outlined some aspects that define what a non-state actor is in contemporary international relations. Firstly, the term encompasses not only Non-governmental organisations (NGOs) but also business, religious movements, social movements and even criminal organisations. Secondly, it must be highlighted that non-state actors have played a role in world politics for centuries. It is not just a phenomenon associated with the contemporary erosion of the state power. As Halliday (2001) holds:

> A rethinking of the 'non-state' can, it may be argued, take us back to the very origins of the modern system: arguably, Christopher Columbus was a non-state actor, as were Vasco de Gama and Martin Luther, and as were the East Indian Company, the Hudson Bay Company, the French revolutionaries, the nationalist movements of the nineteenth and twentieth centuries and much else besides.
>
> (p. 21–22)

Thirdly, non-state actors may impact policies and affect the state itself. Thus, states and non-state actors are units of the international system. They have played a role in the resilience of regionalism. Individual human beings have been important. Political leaders such as Simón Bolívar, José Martí, Juan Domingo Perón and Raúl Alfonsín fostered regional initiatives. Diplomats such as Lucas Alamán, the Barão of Rio Branco, Dante Caputo and Celso Amorim also played an important role in furthering regionalism. A similar role was also played by intellectuals and thinkers such as Francisco Bilbao, Manuel Ugarte, Francisco García Calderon, Raúl Prebisch, Leopoldo Zea, Juan Carlos Puig and Hélio Jaguaribe. These were 'carriers' of regionalism and 'agents of regional integration'. Their role is critical to understanding the creation, transfer and survival of the acquis. As is adressed in this book, non-state actors such as the Roman Catholic Church and networks of intellectuals have been part in the construction of the idea of Latin America. The same is true for entrepreneurs, business associations and social movements, that have encouraged economic integration in certain periods of time. Accordingly, the activities of all these actors are key to explaining the resilience of Latin American regionalism.

System, units and resilience

As explained beforehand, both systemic and agential factors are behind the resilience of Latin American regionalism. This seems to be contradictory in terms of the explanation of social life. As Buzan and Little (1993) point out, structural explanations often consider human agents as lifeless puppets whose behaviour is regulated by impersonal social forces. Explanations couched in terms of agency conversely presuppose that it is human beings who control events in a social system. However, the 'structuration theory' proposed by Anthony Giddens in the 1980s challenged this alleged duality agent-structure. For Giddens, there is a dialectical relationship between structure and agency. Very far from being cultural dopes, pushed around by impersonal social structures, Giddens depicts social agents as knowledgeable and reflexive, having not only a sophisticated view of the world and how it is structured but also the ability to monitor their actions in the light of this knowledge. As a consequence, social agents are con-stantly performing actions, often intentionally but sometimes unintentionally, which ensure that social structures are reproduced (Giddens, 1984).

Alexander Wendt adopts that view in the discipline of international relations by highlighting the need to "take into account human intentionality and moti-vation" as well as systemic and structural factors. According to Wendt (1987), this is a "dialectical synthesis" (p. 356). That overcomes the subordination of macro to micro and vice versa. That is the approach adopted in this chapter. Both structures and agents are crucial to explaining and understanding the resilience of Latin American regionalism. Under the premise that a system is constituted by agents and structures and that these two latter mutually con-stitute, it is argued that the recursive practice of agents also plays a role in the resilience of regionalism in Latin America. The units of analysis in our research are states and societies and the agents acting on their behalf.

Conclusions

The concept of 'resilience' to explain international regionalism is inspired by its use in other disciplines and areas of research, in particular the study of eco-systems and psychology. This allows us to go beyond the general use of the concept as synonymous with 'resistance'. There is of course also much 'resistance', but in ecosystem theory 'resilience' is also linked to a broader analysis of systems. One can here go beyond single units or particular 'events' in a certain period of time, searching for cultural, social, geopolitical and economic systems. These are created and act within a particular territorial setting, which is the framework of existence and interaction. As an example, a cultural system might be composed by units belonging to a national territory, or 'space', but this might be connected and sometimes takes its own form within a regional space. The same happens with other dimensions of society, economy or geopolitics. Regional systems are generally connected to and often originated in national or sub-national systems; they might sometimes also be connected to broader international and global ones. These connections might sometimes be in the form of 'integration' or 'cooperation', but there are also many conflicts.

Since colonisation, Latin America has been part of the formation of a global system. This has an important economic side, but there are also cultural, security and geopolitical dimensions. Sometimes acting as separated systems, other times as interwoven parts, a web of systems are identified with different names. A more recent one could be 'globalisation'. Yet there is no, and there has never been, a one-dimensional 'global' or even 'hegemonic' system that confronts local ones such as those from Latin America. As everything in life, there is a constant change in dominating features of the 'global' framework, pushing for changes at local levels. Often, the global systemic changes are also caused by the emergence of new local systems, pushing for processes of transformation. Systems react to external shifts or challenges – by broader systems of other units – through rejection, adaptation or transformation. In all cases, resilience is a strong component.

Resilience implies 'adaptation'. This reflects the capacity of a system to adjust its responses to change in external drivers and internal processes, although it does not necessarily need to alter any of the structures that surround it. This might take the form of an 'isomorphism'. In the case of transformation, resilience involves changes that might take place through processes of adaptation that might differ in time and space. That is, some parts of the regional system might, during some periods or places, act as drivers of continuities (perhaps even drawbacks), while in others they become a bearer of transformations.

This shows the need of transcending time and space to grasp the complexity of this process. A central element to understanding systems and resilience is history. As for the case of Latin America, many of these systems, or units, have existed for a long time or might be composed of units with long history. Thus, the systems and/or their units contain memories of past exposures to disturbances that transform them into 'memory carriers'. Hence, resilience is, in our view, linked with a *longue durée* perspective in which systems accumulated 'memory', sustaining continuity in new forms of integration initiatives. This 'memory' contains different kinds of experiences, successful or not, that are accumulated and developed by 'carriers' and 'vectors'. Actors play a central role in our study. Actors are not just objects in a relationship of power (Dahl, 1957, p. 203). They are also agents through which we can understand local reaction to structural (systemic) changes.

In our view, the interaction between system and units is critical to understanding resilience. The systemic influences on Latin American regionalism exists since the early years of political independence. Thus, the Congress of Panamá in 1826 was the outcome of Simon Bolivar's fears of an attempt by the Holy Alliance to reconquest the former Spanish territories. Later on, the Hispanic Americanism led by José Enrique Rodó and Manuel Ugarte was a respons to the increasing US hegemony in the continent. In these two cases, a systemic factor – an uneven distribution of power in the international system – led Latin American countries to promote regionalism as a mechanism to strengthen their relative power in that system. With Raúl Prebisch and ECLA promoted a Latin American Common Market in the 1950s, the idea was to use economic regionalism to modify the pattern of insertion of the region in an international economic system, shaped on the centre–periphery dichotomy. Latin America was part of the periphery, and economic regionalism was conceived as an instrument to advance regional industrialisation and a mechanism to overcome that 'peripheral' status. Along this line, we see regionalism as a response to a systemic constrain: the asymmetric configuration of the international economic system.

These systemic variables are crucial in countries' decisions to promote regionalism. For example, where systemic factors such as the Cold War and the US hegemony in the Americas led to promote closer relation with the other countries of the region. That was the case of Brazilian national-developmentalism, aimed to improve the Brazilian position in the world economic system through the creation of a regional market in which the industrial production could find preferential treatment.

However, as argued previously, the action of the units is fundamental to understanding the resilience of Latin American regionalism. For example, in the case of Latin American armed forces, that are at the inner core of national state systems. The military also have been part of the creation of regional systems, contributing with their own 'memories' and views of society and the future. The idea of 'autonomy' or the concept of 'development' are two elements through which the military found regional synergies with other militaries across the region, as well as also with other groups. In this way, they several times joined forces to create regional platforms related to security, economy and even culture.

One of the organizations that was part of these synergies was the Catholic Church. Like the military, the Catholic Church has deep roots in Latin American history, dating back to colonial times, from where a 'continental' identity took form. The Catholic Church has been a leading actor in the emergence of 'Latin America' as concept and institution, through entities such as the Latin American Episcopal Council. During the 20th century, the Church has recreated itself and its role in the region in a process of 'Latin Americanisation' of its organization in the region.

Diplomats have also played an important role in the promotion of regional initiatives. The diplomats have been bearers of institutional 'memories'. These contain early initiatives, related to security or economic issues, to integrate Latin American countries in order to confront external challenges, as those promoted by Lucas Alamán in the 1830s (the so called Family Pact) or by the Barão of Rio Branco in the early 1900s (the ABC Treaty). Thus, when the region, again, confronted external (systemic or not) challenges, the diplomats have played a key role in fostering and leading the creation of regional systems. This long tradition has been continued in the 20th century by figures, such as Dante Caputo, in the rapprochement between Argentina and Brazil during the 1980s, and Celso Amorim, in the formation of UNASUR during the 2000s.

Technocrats, in particular, those working in international institutions such as the ECLA and the Inter-American Economic Bank also fostered regionalism in Latin America. Without doubt, Raúl Prebisch was the leading figure, but other international public servants such as Felipe Herrera, Felix Peña, Juan Mario Vacchino, Enrique Iglesias and Gert Rosenthal also were committed in furthering regionalism in Latin America. They were important drivers whose actions helped in the construction of the resilience of regionalism in that part of the world.

Finally the private sector, economic agents, have been relevant actors of regional integration. It is important to note that this group, like the others mentioned, has had components that at sometimes have rejected or simply been indifferent to regionalism. Yet, at moments they have also been highly relevant in regional integration processes.

Altogether, the different actors studied display their political action in a web of regional systems that compose Latin American integration and cooperation platforms and initiatives. It is in their history, interests and identities that we find the driving forces of regional integration processes and their resilience. There is still much more to analyse and research on this issue. Our hope is that this is a step forward in the understanding of the complex issue around the persistent resilience of Latin American regionalism.

References

Aharonián, C. (2002). Technology for the resistance: A Latin American case. *Latin American Music Review*, *23*(2), 195–205.

Archer, M. (2017). Morphogenesis realism's explanatory framework. In T. Brock, M. Carrigan, & G. Scambler (Eds.), *Structure, culture and agency selected papers of Margaret Archer* (pp. 1–35). Abingdon: Routledge.

Arrighi, G. (2006) [1994]. *The Long Twentieth Century*. London: Verso.

Biggs, R., Schlüter, M., & Schoon, M. L. (Eds.). (2015). *Principles for building resilience*. Cambridge: Cambridge University Press.

Bottrell, D. (2009). Understanding "marginal" perspectives. Towards a social theory of resilience. *Qualitative Social Work*, *8*(3), 321–339.

Braudel, F. (1979). *The perspectives of the world: Civilization & capitalism, 15th-18th century* (Vol. 3). New York: Harper & Row Publishers.

Briceño-Ruiz, J. (2015). Saber y teoría: reconstruyendo la tradición autonómica en los estudios de integración en América Latina. In J. Briceño-Ruiz & A. Simonoff (Eds.), *Integración y cooperación regional en América Latina. Una relectura a partir de la teoría de la autonomía* (pp. 29–70). Buenos Aires, Argentina: Biblos.

Bunge, M. (1998). *Philosophy of science: Volume 1, from problem to theory*. New Brunswick and London: Transaction Publishers.

Buzan, B., & Little, R. (1993). *The logic of anarchy*. New York: Columbia University Press.

Carranza, M. E. (2014). Resilient or declining? Latin American regional economic blocs in the postneoliberal era. *Latin American Politics and Society*, *56*(3), 163–172.

Closa, C. (2015). *Mainstreaming regionalism* (Research Paper No. RSCAS, 12). Florence: Robert Schuman Centre for Advanced Studies. https://doi.org/10.2139/ssrn.2559777

Cohen, S. B. (2009). *Geopolitics: The geography of international relations* (2nd ed.). New York: Rowan & Littlefield Publishers.

Cote, M., & Nightingale, A. J. (2012). Resilience thinking meets social theory: Situating social change in Socio-Ecological Systems (SES) research. *Progress in Human Geography*, *36*(4).

Dahl, R. (1957). The concept of power. *Behavioral Science*, *2*(3), 201–216.

De La Reza, G. (2012). *El ciclo confederativo: historia de la integración latinoamericana en el siglo XIX*. Lima, Peru: Universidad Nacional Mayor de San Marcos, Fondo Editorial.

De la Reza, G. (2015). *Creación Interdisciplinaria. Orígenes, fundamentos y aplicaciones de la teoría de sistemas*. Lima, Peru: Universidad Nacional Mayor de San Marcos, Fondo Editorial.

Economic Commission for Latin America. (1950). *The economic development of Latin America and its principal problems*. New York: United Nations.

European Commission. (1997). *Glossary the reform of the European Union in 150 definitions*. Luxembourg: Office for Official Publications of the European Communities.

Giddens, A. (1984). *The constitution of society: Outline of the theory of structuration*. Cambridge: Polity Press.

Giddens, A., & Sutton, W. (2014). *Essential concepts in sociology*. Cambridge: Polity Press.

Goebel, R. (1995). The European Union grows. The constitutional impact of the accession of Austria, Finland and Sweden. *Fordham International Law Journal*, *18*(4).

Halliday, F. (2001). The romance of non-state actors. In D. Josselin & W. Wallace (Eds.), *Non-state actors in world politics* (pp. 21–37). Basingstoke: Palgrave Macmillan.

Hermann, M., Preston, T., Korany, B., & Shaw, T. (2001). Leaders, groups, and coalitions: Understanding the people and processes in foreign policymaking. *International Studies Review*, *3*(2).

Hudson, V. M. (2005). Foreign policy analysis: Actor-specific theory and the ground of international relations. *Foreign Policy Analysis*, *1*(1), 1–30. https://doi.org/10.1111/j.1743-8594.2005.00001.x

Josseli, D., & Wallace, W. (2001). Non-states actors in world politics: A framework. In D. Josselin & W. Wallace (Eds.), *Non-state actors in world politics* (pp. 1–20). Basingstoke: Palgrave.

Kaplan, H. B. (2002). Towards an understanding of resilience. A critical review of definitions and models. In D. Glantz, J. Meyer, & L. Jeannete (Eds.), *Resilience and development. Positive life adaptations* (pp. 17–83). New York: Kluwers Academic Publications.

Kelman, H. (1970). The role of the individual in international relations: Some conceptual and methodological considerations. *Journal of International Affairs, 24*(1).

McCormick, J. (1999). *Understanding the European Union: A concise introduction.* New York: St. Martin's Press.

Meyer, J. (1999). *Constructing world culture: International nongovernmental organizations since 1875.* Stanford: Stanford University Press.

Millner, B. (2007). *States, nations, and the great powers: The sources of regional war and peace.* Cambridge: Cambridge University Press.

Porpora, D. (1989). Four concepts of social structure. *Journal for the Theory of Social Behaviour, 19*(2).

Puig, J. C. (1980). *Doctrinas internacionales y autonomía latinoamericana.* Caracas, Venezuela: Universidad Simón Bolívar.

Puig, J. C. (1986). Integración y autonomía en América Latina en las postrimerías del siglo XX. *Integración Latinoamericana, 109,* 40–62.

Rathbun, B. C., Kertzer, J. D., Reifler, J., Goren, P., & Scotto, T. J. (2016). Taking foreign policy personally: Personal values and foreign policy attitudes. *International Studies Quarterly, 60,* 124–137.

Rauh, H. (1989). The meaning of risk and protective factors in infancy. *European Journal of Psychology of Education, 4*(2), 161–173.

Riggirozzi, P. (2014). Resilience of regionalism in Latin America and the Caribbean: Development and autonomy. *Canadian Journal of Latin American and Caribbean Studies/Revue canadienne des études latino-américaines et caraïbes, 39*(3).

Rivarola Puntigliano, A., & Briceño-Ruiz, J. (Eds.). (2013). *The resilience of regionalism in Latin America and the Caribbean: Autonomy and development.* Basingstoke: Palgrave.

Schmitter, P. (1996). Imagining the future of the Euro-Polity with the help of new concepts. In G. Marks, F. W. Scharpf, P. C. Schmitter, & W. Streeck (Eds.), *Governance in the European Union* (pp. 121–150). London: SAGE Publications Ltd. http://doi.org/10.4135/9781446279328.n6

Southwick, S. M., Bonanno, G. A., Masten, A. S., Panter-Brick, C., & Yehuda, R. (2014a). Resilience definitions, theory, and challenges. *Interdisciplinary Perspectives, 8*(3).

Southwick, S. M., Bonanno, G. A., Masten, A. S., Panter-Brick, C., & Yehuda, R. (2014b). Resilience definitions, theory, and challenges: Interdisciplinary perspectives. *European Journal of Psychotraumatology, 5*(1), 25338. https://doi.org/10.3402/ejpt.v5.25338nk

Ungar, M. (2012). Social ecologies and their contribution to resilience. In M. Ungar (Ed.), *The social ecology of resilience: A handbook of theory and practice* (pp. 13–31). New York: Springer. https://doi.org/10.1007/978-1-4614-0586-3_2

Wendt, E. A. (1987). The agent-structure problem in international relations theory. *International Organization, 41*(3), 335–370.

2 Why Central American regionalism never ends dying: a historical exploration of regional resilience

Kevin Parthenay

Introduction

The aim of this chapter is to deepen the understanding of regional integration process in Central America. Since its reactivation in 1990s and the creation of the Central American Integration System (SICA, with Spanish acronym), most monographs concentrate on a specific actor, states and their presidents, and focus on how Central American regional project are mainly characterized by dysfunctionality and shaped by external actors. Indeed, SICA has faced, since the early 1990s, low level of institutional performance. How could it be assessed? Among major characteristics, it is worth observing the high reiteration of presidential mandates, the problems of compliance and the lack of political will towards strengthening political integration (Parthenay, 2013). In addition, the public knowledge about regional institutions remains low, and SICA has frequently been the target of many social critics. It is even more problematic when those critics emerge from the presidents themselves, who are central authorities of the regional system. Among the constant criticisms addressed by the presidents, the lack of 'regional institutions' performance is regularly targeted. The Costa Rican Minister of foreign affairs, Bruno Stagno (2006–2010), declared in 2009, while leaving a presidential summit, that the Costa Rican President Oscar Arias (1986–1990 and 2006–2010) had decided not to attend, and that President Arias believes that many summits are being held, with few results. We wish more informal meetings that serve to advance the negotiations so that, when appropriate, the presidents participate. This argument explains the low participation of President Arias (Elnuevodiario. com, 28 May 2019).[1]

Even if SICA has initially benefited from a high legitimacy thanks to its central role in the pacification and democratization of the region, it has suffered a series of political crises that regularly jeopardized its *raison d'être*. In the recent period, we can record the Guatemalan institutional crisis (2015), the Salvadorian one (2011), Nicaragua's surge of authoritarianism (since April 2018), the Honduran coup d'état in July 2009 and several "exit crises" by Honduras (2004), and more recently by Costa Rica (2018) when the country faced the Cuban migrants' crisis. Moreover, regional asymmetries (in economic and administrative terms) also currently affect the pace of regional cooperation

(Sanchez, 2009). The depiction of such a dark panorama on SICA's performance and legitimacy among its constituencies and in the national societies paradoxically echoes its high resilience. A regional bureaucrat stresses the fact that SICA's tale surrounds "a death that never happens". Indeed, despite all the difficulties mentioned, SICA is still alive and even has an extended regional bureaucracy with about 143 regional entities. It has also developed its external relations with a wide spectrum of actors across the globe. In 2019, SICA counts 33 observers, gathering 31 states and two international organizations (European Union, Ibero-American Youth Organization).

How to account for the resilience of Central American regionalism? In this chapter, we argue that a long-term approximation of the regional political and institutional logic is required in order to understand why despite so many weaknesses and difficulties Central American regionalism never ends dying. The main issue is not to know whether history matters or not, but how "history matters". How do historical processes help to consider failures and setbacks not as part of a normative discourse on regional organizations weakness or lack of performance but as part of a resilient process? To follow this thread, the chapter is organized as follows: in a second section, we review the literature that brings elements to explain the reasons why Central American regionalism is still a living experiment despite many failures and setbacks. In a third section, we present the research design and the principal concepts that will help to shed a new light on a long-run explanation of regional process. The concept of "mental map" is particularly at the core of our analysis. In the fourth section, we proceed to the empirical exploration of Central American regional history, going back to the colonial era. In the fifth section, we interpret the results of the empirical examination and draw some lessons from this long-term historical process in order to explain the resilience paradox. We finally offer some concluding remarks.

The Central American resilience: from state bargaining to an outward-oriented model of regionalism

In the vast literature on Central American regionalism published since the early 1960s, mainly by North American neofunctionalists, few have focused on the paradox of its resilience. To date, we identified three analyses that have provided comprehensive elements in order to understand why Central American regionalism never ends dying. In this section, we review how those three perspectives have contributed to answer this paradox.

Following an intergovernmental approach, Rafael A. Sanchez, in *The Politics of Central American Integration* (2009), pointed out that Central American resilience comes from a specific combination of compromise culture and structural economic factors. His approach focuses on the idea that:

> Integration arises primarily as a result of the convergence of preferences in the larger states of a region. To achieve integration, governments

co-operate and get involved in asymmetrical bargaining where the larger states will attempt to shape outcomes in line with their preferences; this analysis focuses on the interests and preferences of the larger states in Central America.

(Sánchez, 2009, p. 5)

Interstate bargaining has given rise to compromises under lowest-common denominators which have limited the pace and scope of integration but also major conflicts. According to him, "when conflict disrupt[s] integration, some analysts see it as a consequence of institutional failure to conduct integration, class conflicts and imperialist designs rather than politics or clashes of government preferences" (Sanchez, 2009, p. 5). In that perspective, he considers that the resilience of Central American regional institutions lies on the "slow pace of the process itself, the impact of distributive conflict and (. . .) the strategic interactions of the states at both regional and global level" (p. 5). He evokes a variation of institutional pace according to states' preferences that are fluid and changing. The regional project is then closely related to political fluctuations. However, if Sanchez explains well why the member states are led to assume some domestic stances, he does not explain why the regional project has regularly reborn and above all, how and under what design. In addition, it is difficult to sustain a debate around the concept of resilience with an intergovernmental approach, as the centrality of state preferences and interests prioritize the questions of institutional performances and cyclical political commitments towards regionalism.

With distinct lenses, Olivier Dabène explored the question of regional "resilience despite frequent crises" in Latin America. He explains this paradox by the fact that "most Latin American integration processes have been highly politicized during their foundational sequence, which created institutions that proved to be very sticky in the long run" (Dabène, 2012, p. 45). According to the French political scientist, a strongly politicized initial phase puts an integration process on a path that is not easy to deviate from. What does he mean by "politicization"? Adjusting the neofunctionalist definition, he stresses that "politicization implies that the actors consider economic integration as an instrument to reach political goals. As corollary, politicization also implies a commitment of key political actors sharing a conception of common interests. Finally, it implies institutional arrangements and a regional public space where the agendas and outcomes are discussed" (Dabène, 2012, p. 42). From that point on, he explains that two factors determine the resilience of Central American regionalism: collective presidentialism and differentiated integration. For the first variable, Dabène (2010) explains that politicization went through founding presidential summits that entailed the sharing of common interests and constituted a regional public space. Moreover, the light definition of regional institutions enabled to reinforce informal institutions that favour adaptation or adjustment to crises or periods of instability. Regarding variable geometry, Dabène (2012) explains that the practice of variable geometry has characterized the Central American regional patterns since its reactivation in the early 1990s. Here, economic integration, even differentiated, serves political common goals such as fostering interdependence and promoting international insertion. He asserts that "states pick the piece of communitarian legislation that favored their interest" (Dabène, 2012, p. 19). Assuming different levels of regional commitments offers opting-out strategies in case of disagreement or prioritizes ad hoc flexibility to confront political turmoil. Dabène's explanation of Central American resilience, based on historical institutionalism and the concept of politicization, discards however a large amount of the regional institutional thickness as it focuses mainly on the modern period (since the 1950s). It then discards the heritage of the initial regional Central American experiment as foundational steps of the regional institutions' pattern. As Dabène points out that Central American institutions are sticky, the observation would benefit by taking into account the whole process. In fact, the "regional integration" sequence of the 1950s does not emerge from the ground. Many attempts have previously vivified the Central American project.

More recently, Kevin Parthenay presented another perspective to observe the resilience paradox, arguing that Central American regionalism has become an outward-oriented model of regionalism (Parthenay, 2013). Despite repeated crises, Parthenay explained that SICA's institutionalization had been promoted by unanticipated factors that contributed to create an outward-oriented model of regionalism. This model refers to regional institutions that are characterized by the active participation of external actors (state and non-state), which finance their regional budgets and shape their institutional designs. Regional policy making is also shaped by external actors, which influence member states in the formulation of common policies/strategies in specific sectors. Despite the weak political will of member states, regional institutions have been fuelled by external resources (finance and technical support) and help explain how, without political inputs, regional institutions have always maintained a minimal level of activities. To illustrate this, we observe that the Central American Health body (COMISCA), gets the bulk of its funding from external actors. To COMISCA, member states are expected to pay an annual quota of US$ 13.000, yet many have been delaying payments or even missed them altogether, making the COMISCA's Executive Secretary (Secretaría Ejecutiva del COMISCA, SE-COMISCA) @ heavily dependent on extra-regional funds. In 2016, a budget assessment showed that 90.74% of SE-COMISCA's budget was funded by external state and non-state actors, such as Spain, Taiwan, and US cooperation agencies (SE-COMISCA, 2016). This pattern, shared by almost all Central American regional institutions, lies on two main explanation: regional bureaucratic autonomy (or leadership) and the presence of external actors. In a way, external funds have helped keep SICA's head above water. However, the limit of Parthenay's analysis (2013) comes from its focus on the recent sequence of regionalism in Central America, that is to say from the 1990s to date. Indeed, if regional bureaucratic autonomy may be rooted in current institutional patterns, the presence of external actors refers to a historical pathway dating back to the spread of liberalism across the region (Mahoney, 2001).

All those explanations shed different light on a same reality: Central American resilience. However, they all converge on the same limitation. If they offer periodic patterns of explanation, they failed in identifying long-standing explanatory factors to the resilience of the regional project in Central America. The Central American regional legacy is, however, much older but has never been integrated in the debate on the resilience of Central American regionalism. To understand it beyond the four standard variables we identified in the state of art: state preferences, politicization, bureaucratic autonomy and external actors. In that respect, the historical approximation of the process has been limited and deserves to be stressed in order to understand the Central American regional project on a much longer perspective.

Analysis and research design

The main characteristics of Central American regionalism is the constant re-emergence of regional-oriented initiatives, many times in superior forms that previous ones. This constitutes a mystery that deserves to be dealt with through a historical approach to regionalism. Indeed, if previous monographs have explained contemporary factors that explain why Central American regionalism still is operating despite crises and weak institutional performances, they do not offer explanation of the regional resilience in the long run. In fact, the Central American regional projects date back to the nineteenth century, to the foundational Central American Federation (1823–1839), that has its own roots in the anterior colonial period. In our case, history matters, as many historical institutionalists have already demonstrated (Pierson, 2004; Thelen & Mahoney, 2010; Mahoney, 2001), not as an isolated intellectual fancy but above all to explain contemporary processes. In that perspective, resilience can be understood as the result of a regional longstanding pathway that has been built by the action of political, economic and social actors and intellectuals.

Arising from that pattern, the concept of "mental maps" gains strength in order to explain and understand the resilience of regional projects. In this chapter, an importance will be conferred to history through this central concept in order to explain how regionalism has become a common and constant standardized diplomatic strategy for Central American states. The concept of "mental map" comes originally from the field of perception studies. In that regard, the idea of a mental map is defined as "a model of the environment which is built up over time in the individual's brain". It has been later applied to other fields of social sciences, in particular geography. As an "image in the head" of a larger environment, the mental map "provides for the orientation, comfort and movement of man within his environment" (Pocock, 1972, p. 115). Like choosing a specific road to get from one point to another, the mental map can act in a wider sense, as a general representation of what to do, how and under what limits. More recently, and thanks to the theoretical contribution of constructivists, it has fed the debate on regionalism studies. Defined as "cognitive and ideational projects associated with the invention of regions and construction of identities and delineation of mental maps" (Bach, 2016, p. 6), it has renewed the approximation of space within the study of why and how regionalism is built up. Daniel Bach has recently pointed out that "colonial policies and politics, in Africa, as earlier on in Latin America, have contributed to shape the landscapes, topographies and mental maps associated with region building" (p. 30).

This opens a renewed perspective on how space, time and ideas are intertwined. As Franck Mattheis (2014) underlined, more often the "notion of regional space corresponds to an agglomeration of nation states as basic units" (p. 36). In that sense, regionalism "has become a synonym for visible institutionalization and less for ideas and projects" (2014, p. 36). To fill this gap, he applies the spatial turn initiated by Henri Lefebvre (1974) to regions and regionalisms. Lefebvre's contribution implies taking into account three dimensions of space: space as social practices; space as imagination; space as social mode. The second dimension is the one that has the most implications for our purpose. Indeed, "the space conceived from the imagination of regionalist elites (. . .) is represented and expressed in their ideas and discourses that impose regionalising mode" (Mattheis, 2014, p. 76). The constant reshaping of material conditions, social patterns and political and institutional experiments produces space as a mental map that becomes in return influential and somehow constraining.

From that point on, the challenge is to open an exploration of how the regional space has been built and explore it through the *longue durée* (Braudel, 1949). What is *longue durée* to regionalisms? In 2004, Louise Fawcett published a fundamental contribution to the field, stating that the study of regionalism lacked historical roots. She argued "that regionalism should be understood as an evolutionary and cumulative process" and that, "broadly speaking, regionalism has always been with us. Regions as empires, spheres of influence, or just powerful states and their allies have dominated in different international systems" (Fawcett, 2004, p. 436). Furthermore, she underlined, contrary to common thinking that locates the creation of regional groupings after World War II, that the international system of the League of Nations gave some place to regional groups even during the 1920s. In this perspective, up until recently (Söderbaum, 2016, pp. 16–30), many have called for a reconsideration of the historical roots of regionalism (Parthenay (2019). Fawcett pointed out that "more interesting is a longer view which maps the development of regionalism over time" (Fawcett, 2004, p. 430). Considering that "history of regionalism shows how regions have been defined and redefined in such selective terms" (p. 432), she called for a "historical turn" in regionalism studies. However, the "longer view" has been limited to World War I. In that perspective, I propose to take into consider a wider time perspective, getting back to the colonial period in order to understand how the regional space has been initially shaped and how it has come to influence practices.

This chapter goes back to the old foundations of the Royal Audience of Guatemala (or General Captaincy of Guatemala) under the Spanish Empire.

Table 2.1 Regional sequences under comparison

Sequence	Institutions	Period
Colonial era	General Captaincy of Guatemala	1542–1821
Post-colonial era	Multiple "reunification" attempts	1821–1950
Contemporary era	Organization of Central American State (ODECA)	1951–1973
	Central American Integration System (SICA)	1991–present

Source: Author's elaboration.

Actually, some contemporary political trends echo some economic, social and political ones inherited from the colonial period. To develop this exploration, a special focus is made on the cumulative construction of "Central America" as a regional space and on the numerous – and various – attempts at regional "unification" through time. On that empirical basis, a sequential comparison is used as a revelation of the existing threads that gave substance to the so-called colonial legacy and to understand the inner logic and pace of Central American regionalism. For that purpose, three sequences are compared (see Table 2.1): the emergence of a regional space under the colonial era (1542–1821), the regional space under the post-colonial era (1821–1951) and the contemporary era (1951–1973 and 1991 to present).

Through a narrative approach and using thick description (Geertz, 1973), we explore why and how elites resorted systematically to the regional option and how this strategy has been shaped by a specific representation of the Central American territory, constitutive of a regional mental map.

The historical roots of Central American resilience

The emergence of a regional space under the colonial era (1542–1821)

Under the Spanish crown's domination, Latin America was organized according to a precise administrative structure. Various territorial entities were identified (from the largest to the smallest): *Virreinato, Reinos, Real Audiencia, Capitanía General and Intendencias (since 1785)*. The General Captaincy of Guatemala corresponded to a territorial entity that covered since its creation in 1542 the current understanding of the Central American space, Guatemala, Belize, El Salvador, Honduras, Nicaragua and Costa Rica, plus the additional Provinces of Chiapas (a current Mexican territory), Chiriquí and Bocas del Toro (current Panamanian territories). The rest of what is currently known as the Republic of Panama was included in the Vice-Royalty of Peru as the Audience of Panama. The General Captaincy of Guatemala was created by Charles I of Spain. With the New Laws of the Empire promulgated in 1542, the Captaincy became *Real Audiencia de los Confines de Guatemala and Nicaragua* and *Reino* de Guatemala. Under the Colonial Rules, the *Capitania General* referred to military government, the *Real Audiencia* to justice administration and the *Reino* to the political administration (even if there is no king). Notwithstanding this, the term "General Captaincy of Guatemala" has been kept to refer to the territorial entity as a whole. In terms of administrative competences, it held a singularity, as it was given the military, government and justice administration. Indeed, the Representative of the *Real Audiencia* was at the same time General Captain and Delegate to the *Real Hacienda*. Moreover, since 1570, the captaincy did not depend on any viceroyalty but on the *Consejo de Indias*.

Since the origins, the General Captaincy of Guatemala (GCG) endorsed a singularity that raises the question of why this foundational shaping of the Central American territory. One convincing explanation is linked to the lack of administrative control and difficulties for ores' circulation. In Quesada Saldaña's book, *Estructuración y desarrollo de la administración política territorial de Guatemala. En la colonia y la época independiente* (2005), it is stressed that:

> Until the time when the New Laws[2] were enacted, there existed in the Central American territory, Governations and territorial demarcations that were disconnected from the power of the Audiences created to date due to distances. Thus, for example the Province of Honduras was outside the power, both of the Audience of Mexico, and of the Panama, since it belonged to the Audience of Santo Domingo. On the other hand, the Audience of Panama comprised from what is now Nicaragua, up to the Strait of Magellan.
>
> (p. 45)

The logic of creation of the American audiences and the new dynamics dictated by the Spanish crown during the sixteenth century allowed the Spanish crown to incorporate communication routes drawn from the links between the different regions of the continent. Since the origins, the Central American space was considered an intermediate territory located between two mighty Audiences, the ones of Mexico and Panama, the latter being the strategic point for gold exportation to Spain. It is even more interesting to observe that one major constitutive element for the shaping of this regional territory came from how conquest expeditions were held and how initial authority has been conceded.[3] From an uncontrolled territory, the Spanish colonial order has progressively built the outlines of the Central American space. In 1570, the Real Audience of Guatemala gained its definitive shape and was divided among five governorates: Guatemala, Comayagua in Honduras, Nicaragua, Costa Rica and Soconusco (current Mexican territory). This design has an economic explanation, granting a differentiated importance to the territories according to their capacity to export towards Spain, mainly the ores. The objective is then to establish a homogeneous territorial framework, to harmonize and organize in order to impose a new economic form of social relation with a reasoned exploitation of the native labour force and an appropriation of the lands.

Until the Bourbons' reforms, few changes disrupted this Central American territory. Nation-states were not yet in formation and the future territorial states of Guatemala, El Salvador and Honduras remained fragmented between a vast number of "corregimientos" and "alcaldias".[4] Nicaragua and, above all, Costa Rica benefited from more stability in their territorial construction. Costa Rica was then sparsely populated and economically poor. As a consequence, the Bourbons' reforms, which came into force on 22 of April 1787 for the "Kingdom of Guatemala" (see Note n°4), establishes intendancies (San Salvador, Chiapas, Honduras, Nicaragua) did not change the status of Costa Rica, which remains a "*Gobernación*". It is worth noting that a "*Gobernación*" was at the time under the direct command of the king on official appointments (but depending on the audience for justice matters). Like Panama, which benefited from its own audience, Costa Rica remained remote to the legal and institutional hazards of the declining Spanish Empire.

The Bourbons' reforms, which intended to centralize power to better exploit the territory economically, had the opposite effect of reinforcing the vibrancy of local particularities. At this stage of pre-national constructions, the Central American territory had been built around Guatemala as a centre (at least under the Spanish rule), with a close competing periphery (El Salvador, Honduras) and a remote periphery (Nicaragua and Costa Rica). At the end of the eighteenth century, El Salvador was regularly criticizing the "tyranny of Guatemala" (Del Carmen Muñoz, 2006, p. 74) that was attempting to concentrate the regional trade and become a regional economic power. By the same token, Costa Rica and Nicaragua asked the Spanish crown to be separated from Guatemala. In 1814, Costa Rica and Nicaragua were both integrated in their own captaincy. Meanwhile, Costa Rica was already trying to separate from Nicaragua, as they considered it a restraint to their own development.

This colonial sequence illuminates the regional reflection around several realities. The first one is the gradual formation of a Central American "mental map", with a territorial anchorage. It progressively excluded the Mexican provinces in the north, and the Panamanian lands in the south always remained apart of the regional dynamic. The second is the emergence of a "regional centre" built around Guatemala with a competing rival, El Salvador. The third is the remoteness of Costa Rica and Nicaragua opposed to a greater convergence in the northern territories (Honduras, El Salvador, Guatemala) gathered in the contemporary category of "Northern Triangle".

The regional space under the post-colonial era (1821–1951)

Once forged this regional "imagined space" through a historical common legacy, the new emerging Central American states and their political elites decided to extend the regional experiment. The fear of independence mainly explains what will become a true regional quest. Due to the fragile regional economies and the weak legal and administrative regulation capacities, autonomy represented a danger that explained the initial choice to be integrated within the Mexican Empire of Augustín Iturbide. As Héctor Perez-Brignoli pointed out, the Central American political elites were hoping that the annexation would offer a solution to the endless administrative conflicts and hope in face of extended economic dependency (Perez-Brignoli, 1985). After a short episode of annexation, the newborn Provinces of Central America decided to meet at Guatemala Ciudad on 1 of July 1823 and declared the absolute independence of Central America. They convened a Constituent General Assembly. During this congress, the deputies proclaimed the "United Provinces of Central of America" as a free nation, sovereign and independent from the Spanish crown, Mexico and any other power. On 22 November 1824, the members of the Congress elaborated a Constitution that gave shape to a federal system. The New Republic was then called the Central American Federation and was officially composed by five states: Guatemala, El Salvador, Honduras, Nicaragua and Costa Rica.

The fate of this initial step of regional cooperation in Central America fell short. The Federation lived a hectic and troubled life, weakened by a fierce ideological cleavage between liberalism (*federalistas*) and conservatism (*anti-federalistas*). The Federation's dislocation, resulting from the successive desertions by emerging unitary states, ended the first federal experiment in Central America. Notwithstanding this and considering the harsh political rivalries between liberals and conservatives, the political elites constantly tried to revive the regional dynamics until the middle of the twentieth century. Up to the surge of the contemporary Central American regionalism and the creation of the Organization of Central American States (ODECA), Spanish acronym. Table 2.2 shows 16 attempts to revive the regional experiment, from mere cooperation to unification.

During the whole eighteenth century, Central American political elites constantly attempted to revive the regional unification. The reflex of the Central American elites to seek unceasingly unification and cooperation between states comes mainly from a quest for common protection vis-à-vis external threats. In that respect, the Pacto Permanente de la Confederación Centroamericana (1842) stipulates that the Central American states "commit themselves if the Central American territory is threatened, invaded or weakened by a foreign power, to work in perfect agreement to denounce the offense, to repair it if possible and to promote the respective rights of all Central America" (García Laguardia, 1988, p. 24). In the same token, the declaration of the Representación Nacional de Centroamérica stressed:

> The need to form a united front that, representing them all abroad, also provides them with effective means to strengthen internal order, stability and peace and that, threatened as they are by a foreign power, they could not defend themselves, be divided or put themselves in communication with the other nations, whose friendship, relationships and alliance form the moral and political force that makes everyone respect each other's rights at the same time.
>
> (p. 25)

The defence against external aggressions of threats has been a constant vector of reunification attempts, mainly by the one from Great Britain and the United

Table 2.2 Historical attempts of Central American regional unification

Name	Date	Member states	Main objectives
1 Convención de Chinandega	17 March 1842	El Salvador, Honduras, Nicaragua	Defense against external aggressions and internal search for peace
2 Pacto Permanente de la Confederación Centroamericana	27 July 1842 (7 October 1842)	El Salvador, Honduras, Nicaragua (Guatemala)	Protection of the Central American territory
3 Proyecto de Reunión de Sonsonate	15 June 1846	El Salvador, Honduras, Nicaragua, Guatemala, Costa Rica	Ensure internal and external peace and achieve uniform representation of foreign relations (from the United Kingdom)
4 Pacto de Nacamoe	7 October 1847	El Salvador, Honduras, Nicaragua	Providing reciprocal assistance for the preservation of their independence and sovereignty (UK)
5 Representación Nacional de Centroamérica	November 1849	El Salvador, Honduras, Nicaragua	Foreign threat (from the United States of America)
6 República de Centroamérica	13 October 1855	El Salvador, Honduras, Nicaragua	Foreign threat (from the United States of America)
7 Pacto de la Unión	17 February 1872	El Salvador, Honduras, Guatemala, Costa Rica	Territorial integrity, defense of liberal institutions, economic cooperation, peaceful settlement of conflicts.
8 Pacto de la Unión	15 September 1875	Guatemala, Honduras, El Salvador	Foreign threat
9 Decreto de Unión Centroamericana	28 February 1885	Guatemala (unilateral)	
10 Tratado (tentativo) de Unión	12 September 1885	Guatemala, Honduras, El Salvador	
11 Pacto de Unión Provisional de los Estados de Centroamérica	15 October 1889	El Salvador, Honduras, Nicaragua, Guatemala, Costa Rica	Unify the external representation and unify the administrative interests of Central America
12 Pacto de Amalapa (República Mayor de Centroamérica)	20 June 1895	Honduras, Nicaragua, El Salvador (and in 1897 Costa Rica, Guatemala)	Foreign threat
13 Tratado de Paz y Amistad	July 1906	El Salvador, Honduras, Nicaragua, Guatemala, Costa Rica, USA	Collaborate against aggression, not recognition of military coups, control of belligerent emigrants.
14 Pacto de Unión	January 1921	El Salvador, Honduras, Guatemala, Costa Rica	
15 Plan de Confraternidad Centroamericana	15 March 1934	Honduras, Nicaragua, Guatemala	Approach measures in legal aspects, transit, communication, education and economic union.
16 Pacto de Santa Anna (Pacto de Unión Confederada de los Estados de Centroamericana)	September 1946	Guatemala, El Salvador	Approach of the Central American peoples for political union.

Source: Author's own elaboration, based on Parlamento Centroamericano, Libro Azul del Parlacen 1991–2006, recopilación histórico–documental del Parlamento Centroamericano, Centroamérica, August 2006

States of America (for instance the expedition of William Walker). An important characteristic in the unification project is then to promote the territorial integrity of the Central American nations, to guarantee their sovereignty and peace within the region. Salvadorian president Gerardo Barrios (1859–1963) stresses after Walker's invasion – and its failure – that it underscores the liberal argument that underpins all attempts at the end of the century to unite: "I know how Republics are today. Central Americans go wrong, because they do not have the means for a safe and dignified existence. They are parodies of nations, and their governments are parodies" (in García Laguardia, 1988, p. 28). In this regard, he repeatedly promoted reunification of the region.

In this historical record of regional attempts, we observe that the states that have been most engaged in the search for regional cooperation are El Salvador and Honduras, respectively present in 14 and 15 unification revival initiatives. Guatemala and Nicaragua participate respectively in 11 and 10 of these initiatives. Conversely, we find Costa Rica still in a remote position vis-à-vis the unifying projects, participating in only 6 of 16 regional attempts. It appears as the legacy of the previous period and the stronger assertion of the local particularisms nourished by a more important and anticipated consolidation of its territorial integrity, initiated under the colonial period.

Despite such a regional reiteration, why have all those attempts finally failed? It is worth observing that during the whole century, Guatemala and Costa Rica have promoted a singular stand towards unification. As pointed out by García Laguardia (1988), Costa Rica has advocated a position qualified as an "extraordinary distance" and Guatemala as a "magnificent separatist remoteness" (p. 28). As far as Guatemala is concerned, the paradox of participation (11 attempts over 16) despite separatism comes from sound political divergences with the conservatives in power (in particular under the Presidency of Rafael Carrera, self-proclaimed president for life, embodying the trend of conservative separatism). The Guatemalan conservatives reacted positively towards regional construction while facing threats of external aggressions but systematically formulated reservations on political unification. Moreover, many national rivalries, doubts and suspicions have jeopardized and weakened all those reunification projects. Finally, many of those regional unification attempts have failed due to coups d'état or violent regime destabilization, mainly in Honduras and El Salvador.

The contemporary Central American regionalism (1951 to present)

What we call "contemporary regionalism in Central America" can be traced back to the following years of the Second World War, at a time when the United Nations system built up and with it, perspectives of regional arrangements indicated under Chapter VIII of the United Nations Charter. In that post-war period, a new era emerged for regionalisms across the world (Fawcett, 2004). The contemporary Central American regional experiment revived in the pathways of the Santa Anna pact, signed between Guatemala and El

Salvador's presidents, Juan José Arevalo (1945–1951) and Salvador Castañeda Castro (1945–1948), on 12 September 1946. Indeed, those two countries have historically tried to endorse regional leadership, Guatemala benefiting from the colonial legacy of administrative regional centralism and El Salvador by challenging Guatemala as regional power. The Santa Anna pact was a constructive attempt to revive regional cooperation. In January 1947, it led to the *Pacto de Unión Confederada de los Estados de Centroamérica* that would give birth a few years later to the Central American State Organizations (ODECA). The Salvadorian president and foreign minister, Oscar Osorio (1950–1956), and Roberto Canessa (1954–1955) were the promoters of this renewed idea of regionalism in the isthmus. In the same line as the United Nations System, the ODECA aimed at defending legal equality of the states, mutual respect and no intervention. The ODECA experience gets back to the many previous attempts of regional unification and tries to take profit of the modern system of international law. Indeed, in the preamble of the San Salvador Charter, it is written that although previous attempts to integrate the Central American republics have failed, "modern international law offers adequate formulas for this purpose, through the making of the regional organizations". Notwithstanding this, the ambitious regional structure quickly faced functional weaknesses and suffered political crises.

Those difficulties were increased by different visions for Central American regionalism endorsed by the member states. As Rafael Sanchez stressed, Costa Rica and El Salvador "have supported integration since the signing of ODECA and the Central American Common Market (CACM) in 1951 and 1960 respectively. However, while El Salvador has placed the emphasis on community building and the completion of the common market, Costa Rica has favoured intergovernmentalism and the building of a free trade area" (Sanchez, 2009, p. 32). This various stand dates back to the colonial and post-colonial logics presented earlier. Sanchez accounts that "in colonial times, Costa Rica was the poorest part of the isthmus both in economic resources and populations. However, by the turn of the nineteenth century it has gained the reputation of being the 'most highly civilized, the most politically mature and the most advanced and prosperous nation in the region" (Robinson, 1977, quoted in Sanchez, 2009, p. 33). The allegiance to a territory that had a long-standing stability and homogeneity since the colonial era explains the cautious behaviour of Costa Rica towards regionalism. In an opposite perspective, El Salvador views the regional project as "vital" to its economic life (Sanchez, 2009, p. 35). This is reason why this country has endorsed a leadership in the making of the CACM, accompanied by Guatemala.

The ODECA did not survive the US intervention in Guatemala in 1954 to force leftist President Jacobo Árbenz (1951–1954) out of power. Central America was still not keen to build political integration out of diversity. However, it proved much easier to create a common market. In 1951, the Mexican office of the UN Economic Commission for Latin America (ECLA) sponsored the creation of a Central American Committee for Economic Cooperation (CCE) and organized its first meeting in August 1952, in Tegucigalpa. While the newly created ODECA had an Economic Council, composed of the regional ministers of economy and in charge of making recommendations to "promote development and Central American economic integration", the CCE, composed of the same Ministers, clearly duplicated its functions. However, while the ODECA was paralyzed right from its beginning, the CCE took advantage of the ECLA's technical and political support and met immediate success, creating a Central American School of Public Administration (ESAPAC) in 1954 and a Central American Institute of Research and Industrial Technology (ICAITI) in 1955. In June 1958, a multilateral treaty on free trade and Central American economic integration was signed and, during the CCE 7th ordinary meeting on 13 December 1960, the Central Americans signed in Managua a General Treaty of Central American Economic Integration and several other important agreements (one of them creating the Central American Economic Integration Bank) that put the integration process on a promising path (Dabène & Parthenay, 2017).

However, domestic Central American politics were once again responsible for the regional process stopping as the region got diverted from integration issues, as Guatemala, Nicaragua and El Salvador were ravaged by civil wars at the end of the 1970s (Rouquié, 1992). It was not until the beginning of the 1990s that Central America convalesced from a two-decade period of violence and instability. A pacified and politically more homogeneous region could reboot its integration process. The crisis resolution efforts in Central America put the integration process on a new path. Central America entered the 1990s with a very rich agenda of collective action, concerned with building a lasting peace in the region.

In December 1991, the Central American states signed the Tegucigalpa Protocol and gave birth to the Central America System of Integration (SICA), the current and living pattern of regional cooperation in the isthmus. Since its creation, the SICA has faced an intense institutionalization sequence to 1997, date of a first general but uncompleted reform. In particular, this reform tried to solve an old division between economic integration promoted by the Economic Integration Secretariat (SIECA) located in Guatemala (Ciudad) and political integration promoted by the General Secretariat (SGSICA) located in El Salvador (San Salvador). In addition, since its reactivation in the early 1990s, SICA has suffered a lack of political will and variable geometry. While Guatemala and El Salvador try to promote regional cooperation with Honduras, as a follower, in the frame of the "Northern Triangle", Costa Rica remains apart from most of political integration initiatives. Regularly disrupted by political, economic or environmental crises, regional cooperation is marked by a strong instability and a relative (financial) commitment of the states, compensated by an unprecedented binomial composed of regional bureaucrats and actors of the international cooperation (non-governmental organizations, international organizations, and national cooperation agencies etc.) (Parthenay, 2013).

A sound evolution in the contemporary period is the progressive adjustment of the "regional territory" and the "Central American mental map". In 1991, Panama, for the very first time, fully participated in the foundation of SICA. The country adhered tardily to the Central American economic system, in 2013, in the strategic perspective of the bi-regional Agreement with the European Union. On 27 December 2000, the Belize (ex-British Honduras), English-speaking country and member of the Commonwealth, integrated the regional system as well as the Dominican Republic in 2013 (after being an Associate State since September 2004). This double enlargement entails a silent redefinition of the Central American mental map, more open to the Caribbean. In practical terms, the existing variable geometry that precedes SICA's operation facilitated the integration of those two Caribbean-oriented countries. This enlargement has political motivation, as stated by the Santo Domingo Declaration (6 November 1997) which underlined "the creation of an integration space in the Caribbean Sea area".[5]

While previous regional initiatives were based on a rather stable and homogenous approximation of the regional territory – even with variable geometry – the current regional cooperation focuses on a distinct representation of "Central America" as a historical construction. The presence of Panama, Belize and the Dominican Republic initiated a new sequence for the regional experiment. In that perspective, SICA opened a new approximation of the Central American space. Moreover, while the previous attempts focused mainly on the defence and protection of territorial integrity and sovereignty in the postcolonial era and on economic development in the early stage of the contemporary sequence, the current regionalism targets in priority the economic and political global insertion. Weak states' capacities remain the main standards that still justify why Central American authorities still bet on regional cooperation.

Interpreting the results

Many explanations of Central American regionalism's resilience have focused on the tools that enabled such a resilience without entering into its explanatory deep factors. In such a perspective, the study of long-term historical threads is useful to understand contemporary regional processes and diplomatic practices. This is the major lesson learnt through the empirical presentation.

From the empirical exploration, we observe that Central American unification, integration and cooperation have always served a specific purpose to compensate one fundamental and transversal characteristics of the region: weak states' capacities. In our perspective, the Central American weak states' capacities refer to a mix between an economic dimension and a regulation consideration. Indeed, economists and historians have frequently assessed those state capacities through tax incomes, or the ability to raise revenues, and declared weak those states that were not endowed by this virtue and able to foster economic development (Besley & Persson, 2010, p. 1). From a political science perspective, it has rather been considered through an institutional and a regulatory dimension, for instance the capacity to "penetrate (the) territories and logistically implement decisions" (Mann, 1993, p. 59). Since the colonial period, we observed that the Central American states have always needed the support of regional cooperation in order to compensate for their weaknesses and defend their territorial integrity and the full exercise of their sovereignty.

In that respect, the regional initiatives have served a variety of purposes: the protection against external aggressions (or threats of external aggressions) and protection of territorial integrity and sovereignty (in the colonial era); the economic development (in the post-colonial era); the economic and political global insertion (in the contemporary era). This long-term segmentation of the regional process in Central America offers insights to understand its resilience.

We observe long-lasting dynamics that have slowly been adapted to a trans-formative context. Moreover, it turns out to be also explanatory of many dip-lomatic practices. The struggle to defend territorial integrity and sovereignty explains why Costa Rica has remained remote from the regional project since its genesis. Indeed, its national territory has benefited, even under the colonial era, from a long stability. Its later economic development also explains why it stays apart in a sequence that seeks to foster the industrialization of the region under ECLA's hegemony (Cohen Orantes, 1972). In the last sequence, it is interesting to see the progressive extension of the regional mental map, as the main targets of the regionalism is oriented towards a global insertion. In that perspective, it is worth mentioning the inclusion of Panama, a regional eco-nomic power, and the opening to the Caribbean space (with Belize and the Dominican Republic).

When the New Laws were enacted in 1542, the Central American territory was considered as an intermediate space between two mighty blocs (Panama[6] and Mexico Audiences), with less wealth and already characterized by a sin-gular administrative regulation from the Spanish crown. Once independent, the Central American states systematically sought to join their forces, despite ideological or political conflicts and/or divisions. In that respect, the Central American regionalism never ends dying, as the main burden in the region is that states cannot regulate by themselves and are constantly caught in a tension between uniting or depending on the outside. However, the history of Central American regionalism has demonstrated that no state was actually ready to assume the costs of union, subordinating the regional projects to the flows and hazards of domestic political cycles.

Conclusion

Looking at the literature on comparative regionalism today, we found a dark corner regarding historical treatment of regional cases. However, the historical thickness of regional dynamics did not receive the deserved attention to date but insightfully consider that every actor's intervention is constrained by past norms, agreements, institutional designs, practices, attitudes, identities and so on. In 2004, Louise Fawcett proposed a new framework to study different regions. She pointed out that "more interesting is a longer view which maps the development of regionalism over time" (Fawcett, 2004, p. 430). Considering that "history of regionalism shows how regions have been defined and redefined in such selective terms", she called for a "historical turn" in regionalism studies. If we agree on the paramount importance of history and in particular the *longue durée*, Fawcett quite disappointingly limits her "longer view" to World War I. Fawcett explains that regional groupings emerged after World War I because the League of Nations was not able to offer security guarantees to all (Fawcett, 2004, p. 10). Finally, she rather intertwines her historical approximation of regionalism with the history of multilateralism. In a comparative perspective, this is not a fully satisfactory stance, as it requires us to go back much further in order to understand region building. This chapter contributes to shedding a new light on the importance of the history to understand economic or political regional behaviours.

Few attempts have been made to build upon a comparative historical perspective. An exception would be Frank Mattheis's comparative work on SADC/MERCOSUR, which measures the historical density of the regional phenomenon as a territorial construction, a product of imagined spaces and territories and a product of constructed and reconstructed boundaries (Mattheis, 2014). This chapter locates as an extension of those work and are very useful to understand other phenomena, and in particular resilience. We have demonstrated through an empirical exploration dating back to the initiating Spanish Empire that Central American regionalism has been shaped by the constitution of a progressively built-up "imagined space". This regional representation or "regional mental map" became a strategic tool for political and economic elites in order to compensate for some structural and historically constituted weaknesses of the Central American states. From the defence of sovereignty to a global economic insertion, the regional mental map has been constantly used by national elites. We provide in this chapter a long list of regional attempts, from the initial Central American Federation to the current SICA, that locate the regional concern at the core of the Central American agenda.

In a recent contribution, Daniel Bach (2016) proceeded to a similar demonstration to understand the genesis of African regionalisms. He underlined that "the establishment of colonial federations and inter-territorial services was generally followed by their transformation into Inter-Governmental Organizations (IGOs) at independence, thus contributing to the much-noted inflation of regional grouping across the African continent" (p. 13). In that respect, taking into account the paramount importance of history in the understanding of regionalisms offers fascinating perspective for comparisons. While the current comparative regionalism literature decided to focus mainly on the comparison of regional organizations, another research agenda would be studied further and, comparatively, those historical threads that have led to contemporary regionalisms in order to better understand their nature, transformations and differentiated performances.

Notes

1 El Nuevo Diario. (2009, mai 28). *A Oscar Arias le toca Presidencia del SICA*, Nicaragua. Retrieved June 21, 2019, from www.elnuevodiario.com.ni/nacionales/48802
2 The "New Laws" of 1542 were a series of laws and regulations approved by the king of Spain in November of 1542 to regulate relations between the Spaniards and indigenous peoples.
3 As the sole expedition authorized by the Spanish crown had failed, Pedro de Alvarado realized the conquest of the Central American lands and received a special title from the king (1527) of Adelantado, Gobernador y Capitán General de Guatemala. Separated from the Audience of Panama (Tierra Firme) and the Audience of Mexico, this singularity finally got institutionalized through the New Laws. For further elements on this historical sequence, see: Del Carmen Muñoz Paz (2006, noviembre). *Historia Institucional de Guatemala: la Real Audiencia, 1543–1821.* Informe final. Guatemala: Universidad San Carlos de Guatemala.
4 The "Corregimientos" had a purely administrative nature, limited to collecting the tribute of a few towns and in front of which there was a corregidor, in charge in addition to avoiding settler abuses. The "Alcaldias Mayores" were administrative-territorial minor units, in territorial extensions of "Relative wealth and special real interest, or those where, for particularities with which his conquest took place, it required direct attention from the crown" (for further details, see Flavio Quesada Saldaña, *Estructuración y desarrollo de la administración política territorial de Guatemala. En la colonia y la época independiente* (Guatemala: Centro de Estudios Urbanos y Regionales, Universidad de San Carlos de Guatemala [1983] 2005).
5 Acuerdo de Asociación entre el SICA y la Republica Dominicana, 2003, Considerando 2.
6 The Panamanian Audience had power and jurisdiction over the South American territories only until 1542. However, in 1543 the Real Audiencia de Lima was created, and Panama lost control over South America.

References

Bach, D. (2016). *Regionalism in Africa: Genealogies, institutions and trans-state networks.* London: Routledge.

Besley, T., & Persson, T. (2010). State capacity, conflict, and development. *Econometrica Journal of the Econometric Society*, 78(1), 1–34.

Braudel, F. (1949). *La Méditerranée et le Monde méditerranéen à l'époque de Philippe II.* Paris, France: Armand Colin.

Cohen Orantes, I. (1972). *Regional integration in Central America.* Lexington, MA: Lexington Books.

Dabène, O. (2012). Consistency and resilience through cycles of repoliticization. In P. Riggirozzi & D. Tussie (Eds.), *The rise of post-hegemonic regionalism: The case of Latin America* (pp. 41–64). Dordrecht: Springer.

Dabène, O., & Parthenay, K. (2017). Regionalism in Central America: An 'all-in' strategy. In J. Briceño-Ruiz & I. Morales (Eds.), *Post-hegemonic regionalism in the Americas.* New York: Routledge.

Del Carmen Muñoz, P. (2006). *Historia Institucional de Guatemala: la Real Audiencia, 1543–1821.* Informe final. Guatemala: Universidad San Carlos de Guatemala.

Fawcett, L. (2004). Exploring regional domains: A comparative history of regionalism. *International Affairs*, 80, 429–446.

García Laguardia, J. M. (1988). *La frustrada vocación federal de la región y el Proyecto de Parlamento Centroamericano.* Costa Rica: Centro Interamericano de Asesoría y Promoción Electoral.

Geertz, C. (1973). Thick description: Toward an interpretive theory of culture. In Lincoln, Y. S and Denzin . K (ed.). *Turning Points in Qualitative Research: Tying Knots in a Handkerchief, 3*, 143–168.

Lefebvre, H. (1974). La production de l'espace. *L'Homme et la société, 31*(1), 15–32.

Mahoney, J. (2001). Path-dependent explanations of regime change: Central America in comparative perspective. *Studies in Comparative International Development, 36*(1), 111–141.

Mann, M. (1993). *The sources of social power, Vol. 2: The rise of classes and nation states, 1760–1914.* New York: Cambridge University Press.

Mattheis, F. (2014). *New regionalism in the South – MERCOSUR and SADC in a comparative and interregional perspective.* Hannover, Germany: Leibniz University Press.

Parlamento Centroamericano. (2006, August). *Libro Azul del Parlacen 1991–2006, recopilación histórico-documental del Parlamento Centroamericano.* Centroamérica.

Parthenay, K. (2013). *L'intégration régionale en Amérique centrale. Une sociologie politique du changement.* Doctoral Thesis, Institut d'Études Politiques de Paris.

Parthenay, K., & Dabène O. (2019). Le régionalisme pragmatique en Amérique centrale. *Etudes Internationales, 50*(1), 95–120

Perez-Brignoli, H. (1985). *Breve historia de Centroamérica.* Colección Historia de América Latina. Madrid: Alianza Editorial.

Pierson, P. (2004). *Politics in time.* Princeton, NJ: Princeton University Press.

Pocock, D. (1972). City of the mind: A review of mental maps of urban areas. *Scottish Geographical Magazine, 88*(2), 115–124.

Quesada Saldaña, F. (2005). *Estructuración y desarrollo de la administración política territorial de Guatemala. En la colonia y la época independiente.* Guatemala: Centro de Estudios Urbanos y Regionales, Universidad de San Carlos de Guatemala.

Rouquié, A. (1992). *Guerres et paix en Amérique Centrale.* Paris, France: Éditions du Seuil.

Sanchez, R. (2009). *The politics of Central American integration.* New York: Routledge.

SE-COMISCA. (2016, junio). *XLIV Reunión Ordinaria del COMISCA, Informe de Gestión Financiera.* Tegucigalpa.

Söderbaum, F. (2016). *Rethinking regionalism.* Basingstoke: Palgrave Macmillan.

Thelen, K., & Mahoney, J. (2010). *Explaining institutional change: ambiguity, agency and power.* Cambridge: Cambridge University Press.

3 The Brazilian project of South American integration

Carlos Eduardo Vidigal

Introduction

On July 27, 1954, just weeks before the death of President Getúlio Vargas, the Embassy of Argentina to Rio de Janeiro had completed a report on the foreign and domestic policy of Brazil, commissioned by their Ministry of Foreign Relations and Worship. Despite the limited time frame for its development and the questionnaire format of the request submitted to the Argentinean chancery, then headed by Jeronimo Remorino, the report sought to provide "a permanent and organic source of information about Brazil" (MREC, 1954, p. 2). The Argentinean report was adamant in its analysis that Brazil's Itamaraty had become second only to San Martín in South American Politics.

The Argentinean embassy's review of Brazilian foreign policy was prompted by two main ideas: (a) that the greater objective of Brazil in the subcontinent was to gain leadership in South America, an objective fostered by Brazil since the Baron of Rio Branco's leadership of the Brazilian Ministry of foreign affairs (MFA) (1902–1912); and (b) that Brazil sought to support the United States in its international policy for South America, establishing a number of connections with Washington that otherwise would go against the expectations of Rio Branco but were almost certain to be an imposition from the United States. Despite having clear benefits to both countries, the possibility of overcoming the pursuit of supremacy in South America and favoring a policy of cooperation with Argentina would not have "blossomed in the minds of the successors of the Baron of Rio Branco" (Vidigal, 2009, p. 26).

Notwithstanding a few exaggerations included in the report sent to Remorino, the interpretation was on point regarding the alignment both the Dutra and the Vargas administrations upheld with Washington, on the end of the tradition of equidistance from North American policies for Latin America, and on the pursuit of a leadership policy for South America. The condition of Brazil as a South American country was highlighted by Celso Lafer in a book that details the central aspects of Brazil's international identity, a perspective that was already present, at least, since the times of Rio Branco (Lafer, 2001, p. 52). Nonetheless, it is important to distinguish the leadership role pursued since the Imperial Period, through the times of Rio Branco, and up to the post–World War II period, from the project of South American integration outlined in the 1950s and further developed in the following decade.

The Brazilian governments from 1945 to 1961 strengthened development policies, embraced ECLAC's articles for regional integration, and adopted autonomist principles according to the terms proposed by Hélio Jaguaribe (Jaguaribe, 1958). To Jaguaribe, only economic integration and a regional political coordination stemming from a mutual understanding between Brazil and Argentina would be able to reduce the dependence of the Southern Cone on North American policies. Such a change of direction has been lauded by specialized literature as a theory of Latin American autonomy, notably in the areas of history and international relations (Briceño-Ruiz & Simonoff, 2015).

This is the starting point of this chapter, which seeks to demonstrate how Brazil has outlined several projects of South American integration that altogether create a continuous line in the country's recent history. These would have constituted different individual projects if taking into account the different conjectures the country has come across over this period: (a) the independent foreign policy of Jânio Quadros and João Goulart (1961–1964); (b) the military regime (1964–1985); (c) the first period of the recent democratic period (1985–2000/2002); (d) the Workers' Party governments (2003–2016); and the new alignment with the United States (2017–2022). Nonetheless, regardless of changes in the principles guiding the foreign policy, actions in the diplomatic arena, or political ideals, a central objective has prevailed throughout this trajectory: the promotion of South American integration as an instrument for economic and geopolitical regional autonomy and Brazil's international projection.

The central argument presented herewith – of the existence of a resilient, long-term Brazilian project of South American integration – is supported by the argument that such a project has never configured itself as an instrument of domination, although hegemonic aspirations have not been absent from it. In other words, in pursuing its project of regional integration, Brazil sought to convince its neighbors of the importance and format of the integration – not always with unhindered success. Amid skepticism on the model proposed for the integration, which some regarded as having an imperialist nature, the strategy resulted in the development of a doctrine – or ideology – aimed at the beneficial integration of all.

The sub-regional integration of the Platine region and the Southern Cone, since early in the 1960s, came to be seen as one of the major historical achievements of Brazilian foreign policy. Such a resilience stemmed from the country's historical interests in its South American neighborhood, namely the clear definition of borders, the maintenance of peace, free navigation, and free trade. After the Second World War, a combination of international financial restrictions and the relative disinterest of the United States in Latin America's pro-integration ideas. Diplomatic autonomy and the diversification of commercial ties have also contributed to this integration impetus.

Independent foreign policy: autonomy and diversification

Autonomy and diversification of international relations were the main achievements following the fifteen years of frustrated attempts in seeking external financial and technological support to foster the country's development. During the construction of the Inter-American system – the Chapultepec Conference (1945), Inter-American Treaty of Reciprocal Assistance (TIAR) (1947), Organization of American States (OAS) (1948) – the focus shifted to the area of security, according to the interests of the United States, leaving the development agenda aside. Even the creation of the Economic Commission for Latin America (ECLAC, 1950), responsible for promoting discussions on the development issues faced by the countries of the region, could not bring substantial change to this scenario. ECLAC's ideas, however, would permeate the economic agendas of Latin American countries for decades and would later prove to be worthwhile.

Juscelino Kubitschek de Oliveira outlined his concerns in a letter to Dwight Eisenhower regarding the inauguration of Operación Panamericana (OPA) in the following manner: "it is time for a fundamental reversal of the policy under which this hemisphere has been comprehended and to promote an evaluation of the ongoing efforts for Pan-American ideals in all their implications" (Oliveira, 1959). The letter revealed dissatisfaction with North American policies for Latin America and urged for the topic of development to be placed at the forefront of the regional political debate, since it was one of the main pillars of Pan-American ideals. The Brazilian proposal was referred to the OAS and spurred the creation of the Committee of the 21, responsible for implementing their demands. In its first meeting, the committee dismissed the creation of a Marshall Plan for Latin America, frustrating the expectations of the Brazilian representative, Augusto F. Schmidt. In the negotiations that followed, very little progress was made until the creation of the Alliance for Progress, which, in a way, interrupted the works of the committee. The North American unwillingness to give Latin America the same treatment given to Western Europe in the post-war era was the cornerstone of the independent foreign policy ideal.

In the 1960 election campaign, Jânio Quadros announced the new policy that would guide the international area, adopting relative equidistance from disputes between the two major world powers and devoting greater attention to the Latin American region. Autonomy in the context of a bipolar order meant adopting as a guideline the broadening of relationships with all other countries, including from the communist bloc. The policy for Latin America would be implemented through the continuity and intensification of Operation Pan-America, the support to the Latin American Free Trade Association (LAFTA) integration program, and a "closer and more comprehensive" cooperation with other Latin American countries. In a way, the independent foreign policy (IFP) inaugurated a new era in the trajectory of the country's foreign policy, shifting from the tradition consolidated by Rio Branco (Doratioto & Vidigal, 2014).

The counterweight to these innovations that provided the independent foreign policy with a more conciliating and restrained tone was the recognition of "Brazil's traditional position in favor of the free world", the relationship of "sincere collaboration" with the United States "in support of the social and democratic progress of the Americas", and the "active and robust" support to the UN in the pursuit of peace and economic justice. This "Western-oriented" approach and the designation of Afonso Arinos de Melo Franco as foreign minister enabled Quadros's foreign policy to be accepted by the more conservative sectors of the national political stage.

The short term of Quadros's government, from February to August 1961, did not allow for the consolidation of IFP, although it has provided the most robust initiative to the process of developing closer relations with Argentina – the hosting of the Uruguaiana Meeting between the presidents of Brazil and Argentina's president Arturo Frondizi (1958-1962), – a process initiated still under Juscelino Kubitschek. This integration experiment, formalized by the Uruguaiana Agreements, championed political coordination under international organizations, joint assessment of regional and international politics, convergence of the economic policies of both countries, cooperation in the industrial area, improvements to bilateral trade, and military cooperation, among other dispositions.

Both the international and regional conjectures, as well as the internal political situation of both countries, did not favor the development of these initiatives. The open political crisis following the resignation of Jânio Quadros and the deposition of Frondizi in March 1962 have put an end to this approximation effort. In Brazil, notwithstanding its commitment with the continuity of IFP, the inauguration of João Goulart, conditioned to the adoption of an *ad hoc* parliamentary regime, restricted the government's capacity for action, only partially recovered with the return to the presidential system in January 1963. In addressing the possibility of an official visit by Goulart to the neighboring countries as a means of substantiating the pro–Latin American approach of the Brazilian foreign policy, the Brazilian chancery was left with very few options and ended up choosing Chile for an official visit that took place on April 22 and which was the first official visit by a Brazilian President to that country (Vidigal, 2007, p. 73).

Differently from Jânio Quadros and Afonso Arinos, the Foreign Minister San Tiago Dantas associated the IFP – at least theoretically – with the ideals of development, economic independence, representative democracy, and social reform. The most essential areas of the independent foreign policy, however, should not be overshadowed by the nearly socialist tone of Dantas's discourse, who once said that the independent foreign policy should concur for the promotion of "a social reform capable of ending the oppression of the working class by the owning class" (Dantas, 2011, p. 9). Similar to his predecessor, João Goulart's government used the independent foreign policy as a means to gain the sympathy of those at the left of the political spectrum, but the reforms he advocated, including land reform, were supposed to have taken place under the framework of a market economy. In a way, the reorientation of the principles of the Brazilian foreign policy under IFP might have been a contributing factor to nurture the alarmist discourse of the conspirators of the 1964 coup d'état.

Under the governments of Jânio Quadros and João Goulart, the Brazilian foreign policy gave more visibility to its Latin American neighbors, confirmed the possibility of starting an integration process based on a mutual understanding with Argentina, and, in the opposite direction, demonstrated the relevance of internal political processes for regional international relations and the strength of interest groups opposed to the integration. While the rivalry with a potential for conflict would continue to guide the bilateral relations to some extent, the diplomatic dialogue started to gain more relevance in regional international politics.

In conclusion, the bilateral negotiations with neighboring countries, most notably with Argentina, the challenges to the negotiation of LAFTA, and the perceived differences between Latin America and South America allowed South America to grow in importance and value. In a certain way, it is possible to affirm that whenever Brazilian authorities and negotiators mentioned "Latin America", they were often referring to "South America". This peculiarity would continue to be present in the diplomatic discourse, as it was not convenient to contrast both definitions under risk of causing an immediate negative reaction from other Hispanic neighbors.

The military regime and Latin American integration

The beginning of the military dictatorship in Brazil created a solution that allowed for the continuity of an independent foreign policy, preserving the country's position in relation to the context and values of the Cold War, allowing more freedom for foreign investments, and maintaining a discourse of alignment with the West. A closer analysis, however, shows that the foreign policy of Humberto de Alencar Castelo Branco (1964–1967) and Artur da Costa e Silva (1967–1969) maintained some of the elements introduced into the foreign policy after 1961: the agenda of economic development and the priority given to Latin American countries and sub-regional integration, in particular, physical integration. The ideal of integration had survived, but it was now under a different perspective.

Amado Luiz Cervo and Clodoaldo Bueno considered the Castelo Branco government a "step outside the cadence" of developmentalism. Although the country had surrendered to the injunctions imposed by the bipolar order and the pressures of the foreign capital, the new approach coexisted with the values of nationalism and universalism, although under a mitigated approach (Bueno & Cervo, 2015, p. 395). These values propelled the greater objective of development, a theme that was treasured by the recently installed regime. Other key aspects were the relations with Latin America, in particular South America, and the importance given to regional integration.

It is not an exaggeration to affirm that the core of the Brazilian project of South American integration was outlined by the two first military governments and further developed in the following administrations, up to the democratic period. The regional conjecture at the time, however, was not at its best: Argentina had moved away from Brazil after the coup against Frondizi in February 1962 and championed to become a Western and Christian nation; Venezuela had broken relations on April 22, 1964, based on the Betancourt Doctrine, which did not recognize dictatorial regimes; and Cuba had moved away from the United States and closer to the USSR, which, after the Missile Crisis, pushed

Washington to become more supportive of authoritarian solutions for Latin America. Amidst a challenging scenario, the Brazilian government managed to maintain both its discourse and its actions in favor of regional integration.

In his first press conference as President on May 16, 1964, Castelo Branco affirmed the independent character of Brazil's foreign policy, understood as a sovereign nation, and pondered that neutrality was not recommended at that time, criticizing the approximation with communist countries and the welfare approach of the Alliance for Progress, advocating a free enterprise policy to have a more orderly inflow of foreign capital. The general objectives of his foreign policy were outlined as part of an effort to drive economic and social development and, consequently, for strengthening the country's national power. Hence the emphasis given to disarmament, anti-colonialism, and regional integration (MREC, 1965, p. 11).

Latin American integration involved several dimensions. The relations with bordering countries would be aimed at broadening the transport and communications networks. The valuation and strengthening of LAFTA would take place through an increased exchange between the "American" countries. The Pan-American ideals should be fostered through the strengthening of OAS in the sense of restoring democratic unity in the continent. The relationship with the United States would complement the general framework, which should be developed based on cooperation and mutual understanding, as well as support to Brazil's financial and economic recovery. In this sense, the resources of the Alliance for Progress could be seen as development instruments for both Brazil and the wider Latin America.

A key aspect of the new policy of regional integration was, without question, the emphasis given to transportation and communication networks, a perspective strengthened with the inauguration of the Friendship Bridge between Brazil and Paraguay on March 27, 1965. Without mentioning it and moving in the opposite direction, Castelo Branco seemed to invoke the myth of a Brazil island – isolated from its Hispanic neighbors by the Platine and Amazon Basins – but this time seeking to connect the country to its neighbors.

In the Platine region, Brazil made an effort to maintain a cordial dialog with the Argentinean government of Arturo Illia (1963–1966), who was suspicious of the relations with Brazil and its new regime; with Uruguay, even though its government would not treat Brazilian exiles as Brasilia would expect; and with Paraguay, resuming negotiations with the government of Asunción for the exploration of hydropower in the Sete Quedas system. In some occasions, animosity persisted with Uruguay and Chile because of the alleged favorable treatment of Brazilian exiles by the Uruguayan authorities and the reformist nature of Eduardo Frei's government, whose policies raised concerns in both Rio de Janeiro and Brasilia. As for Argentina, the military coup of June 28, 1966, resulted in the rise of Lieutenant-General Juan Carlos Onganía as the President of the country, causing a relative improvement in the relations with Brazil, as both authoritarianism and a certain developmentalist approach united the two countries (Visentini, 2004). Bilateral relations, however, could not be further strengthened at the time because of disputes related to the exploration of hydropower in the Platine Rivers. Neither the long and detailed diplomatic meetings nor the signature of the La Plata Basin Treaty had been enough to overcome these shortcomings, which would persist up until the end of the 1970s (Vidigal, 2009).

In this context, the Castelo Branco government centered its efforts on a new policy for the Amazon. In 1966, Foreign Minister Juracy Magalhães, after having signed the Cataratas Act mid-year with the government of Paraguay, turned his attention to the Northern region, visiting the capitals of Amazon neighbors with the intention of promoting diplomatic dialogue and trade flows and evaluating joint opportunities in the region. The Brazilian representatives to these nations prepared extensive studies on each individual country, identifying the long route to be pursued. In the case of Colombia, for example, Juracy Magalhães visited Bogota from November 24 to 26, 1966, in a meeting that resulted in a joint communiqué with President Carlos Lleras Restrepo, where they evaluated problems related to international and regional affairs, as well as their bilateral relations. Among the convergences achieved from these conversations, they renewed their commitment to the principles of the Inter-American system, agreed that the integral development of the Amazon basin was imperative to their respective countries, and agreed on the convenience of increasing and fostering the establishment of regular transport and communication networks by air, river, and sea. They also converged on the necessity of promoting studies on the dynamization of trade and the speeding up of the LAFTA integration treaty. Similar reports were produced in La Paz, Lima, Quito, and Caracas, with the latter also concerning the "Venezuelan Guyana" and with the South America Division analyzing the situation of Guyana (MRE, 1966)

In his report on the visits to Quito and Lima, Juracy Magalhães made it clear that he was following the recommendations expressed in Castelo Branco's speech of July 31, 1964, which established as a guideline the "projection of Brazil in the American continent" as one of the "fundamental foreign policy objectives of the Revolution". According to his view, it was possible to agree on a common understanding on the problems of the hemisphere by coordinating a policy of blocs in the region while also giving full support to the "Brazilian thesis of the Americas as an inseparable whole" (Visentini, 2004, p. 32). In the context of bilateral relations, in each of the visited countries, mutual agreements were signed on the reestablishment of Mixed Commissions:

> Esteemed institutions to foster trade flows and studies on communication networks, issues that are closely connected, in particular in this region of South America. The poor condition of transport networks is a major barrier to the access of Brazilian industrialized products to the markets of the three assessed countries [Colombia, Ecuador, and Peru], and therefore these issues must be treated with priority in bilateral affairs.
>
> (MRE, 1966)

Two pieces of information, among other enlightening revelations, stand out from the report of the Brazilian foreign minister: the government's interest in leveraging the export of manufactured goods, a central element in the developmentalist approach adopted at the time;[1,2] and the concept of the American continent as an inseparable whole. The first piece of information reveals that Castelo Branco's foreign policy went beyond the "mitigated nationalism and universalism" suggested by the specialized literature (Bueno & Cervo, 2015, p. 396), pursuing the developmentalist and integrationist tradition of the 1950s. The concept of the American hemisphere as an inseparable whole played an ambivalent tactical role: while it favored dialogue with neighboring countries sympathetic to the Inter-American system, such as Colombia, it also showed Washington that initiatives such as the Alliance for Progress and LAFTA would be prioritized, which did not harm even superficially the North American interests in South America.

On the other hand, it was clear that Brasilia had directed its strategy to the South American neighborhood and started giving border countries of the Amazon region the same status as the Platine nations. The construction of an integrated South America was underway as part of Brazil's efforts to tackle underdevelopment, which simultaneously employed all instruments at its disposal to overcome the framework of hunger, unemployment, and regional inequality. The guidelines of this process were just as clear, i.e. it was the Amazon that had to be integrated into the general social and economic situation of Brazil.

It was under this perspective that, three years later, Minister Alarico da Silveira made a presentation at the Superior School of War highlighting the South American ideal of Amazon cooperation under the Brazilian "leadership and inspiration" as one of the priorities of the Brazilian foreign policy. This declaration from the minister was supported by three central arguments: (i) that the Amazon sooner or later would seek means of association; (ii) that Brazil should lead the process, guiding it according to its own conceptions about security and development; and (iii) that bilateral agreements, the starting points of this process, should follow "principles aligned with the Brazilian ideal of integration" (Vidigal, 2012, p. 72). Therefore, it was only with the Costa e Silva government and with José de Magalhães Pinto as head of the foreign ministry that Brazil further detailed its theory of South American integration.

This philosophy, translated into political-diplomatic guidelines adapted to any given circumstances, has prevailed throughout the military regime and beyond. The subsequent governments – Military Junta (1969), Emílio Médici (1969–1974), and Geisel (1974–1979) – gave sequence to this policy, each having its own specific achievements and issues to tackle. The progress of commercial negotiations with Uruguay and the signature of the Treaty of Itaipu (1973) with Paraguay were outweighed by challenges to the bilateral relationship with Argentina and frustrated a major gas deal with Bolivia, which would have involved the construction of new industries in the borders of both countries, in the Corumba municipality. The final result, however, was still very positive even in the face of hostilities coming from the neighboring countries.

Since this time, the Brazilian armed forces – most notably the army – started to consider the Amazon the most sensitive region under risk of international intervention, replacing Argentina as the major risk of conflict. In the context of the re-democratization and the beginning of the 1990s, matters of geopolitical nature were intertwined with environmental issues, as seen in The United Nations Conference on Environment and Development, held in Rio de Janeiro, 1992. Therefore, it is not a surprise that to this day, the Brazilian military remains attached to the argument of a foreign threat to the Amazon whenever deforestation or mining in the region is under discussion.

From key country to Latin American country

The relations of Brazil with other Latin American countries and, more specifically, with South American nations were stricken by the Brazilian participation in the OAS's intervention in the Dominican Republic. In the 1962 elections, the Dominican people elected the Social-Democrat Juan Bosch, a candidate of the Dominican Revolutionary Party. The new President did not care to tone down the anti-imperialist discourse that elected him and refused to adopt a discriminatory policy on the Marxists, resulting in a coup d'état supported by the United States in the same year of his inauguration, in 1963, being replaced by a junta led by Donald Reid Cabral. The public dissatisfaction with an authoritarian and elitist government added up to the frustration of sectors of the armed forces, giving rise to a constitutionalist military movement in 1965 that advocated the restitution of Juan Bosch as President. The strengthening of this movement and the removal from office of Reid Cabral caused the Lyndon B. Johnson administration to approve an intervention (Boesner, 1996, p. 220).

The North American intervention faced major backlash, igniting a civil war. Under this scenario, the OAS tried to tackle the situation, approving the creation of an Inter-American Peace Force (IAPF). Brazil not only voted in favor of OAS's intervention but also accepted being the leader of IAPF, sending to the Dominican Republic a contingent of 1,100 men, known as Faibrás. In view of these events, the Castelo Branco government started to advocate for the creation of a permanent IAPF, i.e. an OAS instrument to guarantee the collective security of the hemisphere. This decision increased the suspicion against Brasilia on the role played by Brazil in the region.

If Brazil was already considered a subservient country to the policies of Washington before the crisis in the Dominican Republic, being accused of propagating its realist theses in Latin America and promoting division in Latin American countries, after 1965, the discourse against the role of Brazil in the region grew even stronger. The country was frequently accused of keeping subrogate ties with the United States in a strategic cooperation that placed it in a privileged position to obtain economic and defense assistance. Under this scenario, Brazil started to move away from initiatives for regional integration, such as that of Perón in 1953, manifesting an ambition to become a major regional power, comprehended as a legacy from Portugal and a natural consequence of the country's natural richness, continental dimensions, and privileged position between the Southern Cone and the northern countries (Child & Kelly, 1990, p. 7). This policy would be met with severe criticism from the Argentinean diplomacy.

As a matter of fact, according to the review of the Argentinean Embassy in Rio de Janeiro, since 1964, Brazilian foreign policy started to nurture the possibility of becoming a major power, aspiration supported by its territorial dimension, demographic development, and abundant economic possibilities. Different sectors converged for this purpose, such as steel, naval construction, power supply, etc. The main consequence of this ambition was the desire to gain leadership in South America, attracting neighboring countries to its area of influence, which contrasted with the Argentinean policies and positions:

> This contrast was more rigorously observed in relation to countries which shared borders with both countries: Uruguay, Paraguay, and Bolivia. In Paraguay and Bolivia, Brazil's actions translated into a skillful economic penetration through the construction of bridges, highways, railroads and the establishment of banking institutions, seeking to free those countries from the need to use the Platine Basin for their trade activities, as their products now could be transported through the Atlantic.
>
> (MREC, 1965, p. 5)

Even if Argentina had the capacity to dissuade these three countries from using the Atlantic route by enforcing a policy of respect to free navigation in the Plata River, what was at stake was even more important. The Brazilian economic penetration in the region threatened the previously established equilibrium in the Platine region. Faced with this hostile environment, it was up to the Brazilian diplomacy to find the means for making its South American integration project less dangerous to the eyes of its neighbors.

The cordial treatment given to neighboring countries was not enough to elude suspicion of the Brazilian intentions. Itamaraty continued to benefit from its unscathed reputation of respect to public international and international organizations, defense of international treaties, pacifism, respect to the borders of neighboring countries, etc. On the other hand, the general position in favor of Washington's policies and the fact that the North American President Richard Nixon manifested in 1971 that "wherever Brazil goes, Latin America will follow" gave rise to a wave of criticism against the country, which was considered by its neighbors a "privileged satellite" of the United States. In Washington's policy of promoting the regionalization of its security policy and seeking trustworthy allies, Brazil had risen as a key country in South America. This perception would prevail up until the turn of the decade from the 1970s to the 1980s.

In the 1970s, the Brazilian project of South American integration had to tackle these and other challenges, whose epicenter was the relations with Argentina. The relations between Brasilia and Buenos Aires from 1976–1979 had as main characteristic the diplomatic efforts of Brazil in overcoming the challenges encountered since the end of the 1960s. This approximation had as main themes issues related to water resources, and it was a non-linear process. The negotiations around the Itaipú – Corpus Multilateral Treaty on Technical Cooperation, had both advancements and drawbacks and coexisted with more fluid negotiations in areas such as nuclear energy and bilateral trade.

One of the aspects that favored the Brazilian-Argentinean dialogue was the military coup of 1976, which, despite the violence with which it dealt with internal issues, presented similar points of view as the Brazilian military regime in matters of international security. Notwithstanding, the separation between state and society, stronger in Argentina than in Brazil, as the foreign policy had reached a reasonable degree of consensus in the case of Brazil, caused an erosion of the impetus for mutual understanding and led the caucus of the Argentinean military to adopt a tough position in its negotiations with Chile in relation to the islands of the Beagle Channel. As for the Argentinean obstructionism to the decision of Brazil and Paraguay to build the Itaipu Dam, it can be affirmed without much margin for questioning that it was driven by two major forces: the historical and conflicting rivalry between the two countries, nurtured by geopolitical assumptions and translated into suspicion about the growth of the power resources of its neighbor; and the realization of Brazil's preponderance in South America considering its increased economic presence in neighboring countries, whose utmost symbol was the Itaipu Dam.

Paradoxically, it was during the analyzed period that Brazil and Argentina overcame several difficulties and strengthened bilateral political and diplomatic talks in relation and due to the nature of their political regimes. From this scenario emerged the concept of mutual understanding, sustained by the lessons learned from their negotiations, even if at times they seemed to lose momentum; the progressive surpassing of old ideals and prejudices, summarized by a weakening of the diplomacy of obstruction; and the convergence of the most essential interests of both countries, embodied by the Tripartite Treaty. Such a convergence did not mean the definite overcoming of the conflictive rivalry or the prejudices and ideas associated with geopolitical thinking. It meant that a new level of bilateral relations had been achieved. In other words, the talks that took place from the 1980s are substantially different from those undertaken in previous times.

The negotiations for the signature of an Argentina-Brazil-Paraguay Tripartite Treaty (1979) to unlock the negotiations around the Itaipu Dam were the starting point for a new relationship. According to Moniz Bandeira, it was the possibility of an armed conflict between Argentina and Chile, who disputed the control of the Beagle Channel, which would have led Buenos Aires to back off. At the end of 1978, Argentina had accepted the Brazilian claims about Corpus and Itaipu, which technically meant the installation of twenty turbines in Itaipu, in line with the interests of Brazil (Bandeira, 1975, p. 260). From there, pragmatism started to set the tone for the discourses of 1980–1981, and the perspectives started to become promising again.

New negotiations held thereafter were considered "fruitful" by both chanceries in both topics of bilateral interest and in matters of regional and international relevance. As a result, several bilateral instruments were signed concerning the pacific use of nuclear energy, exploitation of water resources, the interconnection of power systems, etc. The number of agreements signed showcased the existence of a *de facto* obstruction of initiatives under bilateral dialogs, only unlocked after reciprocal presidential visits – a thesis confirmed by the visit of President Rafael Videla to Brazil in the month of August.

During the preparations for Videla's visit to Brazil, the Argentinean Ambassador Oscar Camilión proposed the following lines of action: (a) the deepening of bilateral understanding; (b) the signature of international agreements on topics of common interest; and (c) occasional agreements or adjustments on gas, oil, telecoms, and the aerospace industry (IRBr, 1980), June 24).[3] From the suggestions of Camilión, these topics were resumed in the preparatory meetings for Figueiredo's visit to Buenos Aires, and a new proposal for negotiation in several areas was drafted. Along with this process, the Brazilian ambassador Pereira de Araújo understood that the Argentinean government considered Videla's visit the appropriate occasion for exchanging instruments of ratification on the agreements signed in Buenos Aires: (a) Agreement for Cooperation on Development and the Peaceful Use of Nuclear Energy; (b) Treaty on Uruguay River; (c) Agreement on Scientific and Technological Cooperation; (d) Agreement on Animal Health; (e) Convention to Avoid Double Taxation. The first agreement on this list would have a remarkable future, resulting in an unprecedented model for bilateral cooperation in nuclear affairs, still in force today. Nevertheless, it was in the context of the Falklands War that the Brazilian authorities found the perfect opportunity to overcome the idea of being a key country to be seen as a "Latin American" country.

In 1982, with the beginning of the Falklands crisis and the subsequent war, there was a considerable deterioration of the Inter-American system, in particular when, after intense negotiations between the United States and the United Kingdom, Washington declared its support for the United Kingdom (UK). At the beginning of the conflict, Argentina invoked Article 9 of TIAR, which characterizes as aggression the unprovoked armed attack by a state against the territory, population, or armed forces of another state, as well as the invasion of the armed forces of a state against the territory of an American state. However, Argentina was the aggressor in this case, and its position was against both the OAS and the TIAR charters. Under Brasilia's perspective, it was important to try to preserve both institutions in these circumstances (Walsh, 1997). The Brazilian position, however, was acknowledged by the Argentineans.

A commendation of the positive role played by Brazil in the Falklands War from the Argentinean Chancery can be seen through the "*Reseña de la Relación Argentino-Brasileña*", drafted in 1984. According to this document, the Tripartite Agreement had settled their differences in relation to the shared exploitation of the Paraná River and enabled the establishment of new areas of understanding and cooperation "after a decade of incongruences". The presidential visits of 1980 and the presidential meetings of 1981 allowed the establishment of a continued dialogue and the signing of new agreements. On the Falklands, the document speaks for itself:

> On the subject of the Falklands, Brazil had an active role in drafting the OAS resolutions under the framework of TIAR, co-sponsoring draft resolutions adopted by the United Nations in 1982 and 1983, and maintaining a position of full support to the sovereign rights of our country over the archipelago and the pursuit of an agreeable solution to settle the dispute.
>
> (MREC, 1985, p. 3)

This way, the Falklands War became an important chapter for the development of the Brazil–Argentina dialog and an element that would allow a restart in initiatives favoring Latin American integration. The Brazilian position in face of the 1982 events created the necessary trust between the Brazilian and Argentinean militaries, establishing an important basis for military cooperation, just as in the nuclear area. The Argentinean request for Brazil to act as the country's diplomatic representative in the talks with London – a topic still hardly covered by the Brazilian historiography – is an illustration of the progress achieved in their bilateral relations. In this sense, differently from the main currents of integration literature, it was the dialog between two authoritarian regimes, in the context of a regional war, that promoted increased awareness of integration as a necessity.

In the ideological plane, it was Foreign Minister Ramiro Saraiva Guerreiro, during the government of João Batista Figueiredo (1979–1985), who drafted what would later become one of the main contributions to the "integration ideology". His starting point was as simple as his conclusion. To Saraiva Guerreiro, the country – in its complex racial and cultural formation – should make it very clear in its foreign policy where it stands, i.e. as a developing country with some importance in the international scenario. The country's history of cooperation and respect to international regulations, with firm disapproval of several types of abuse, should be reaffirmed within South America in support of regional integration and development. Developing countries from Latin America and Africa were fundamental to Brazil from an economic point of view but should not be regarded strictly as a market – "we cannot think only about plants, cabbages, and lettuces" – but should be seen as partners in the struggle towards development. Ultimately, even if Brazil eventually became a developed country, which was "our ideal", the country could not prevent itself from being culturally and politically a Latin American and an African country (Guerreiro, 1985, p. 187).

From the Southern Cone to South America

The bilateral understanding between Argentina and Brazil inaugurated a new phase in the Brazilian foreign policy for Latin America, strengthening the thesis in favor of security regionalization and economic integration. The change of government from Figueiredo to José Sarney (1985–1990) was marked by a continuity of policies, especially in relation to the Platine Basin and South America. The Sarney government was characterized by the promotion of strategic actions aimed at consolidating the country's territorial integration and the strengthening of Brazil's political and economic ties with its Latin American neighbors. Sarney understood that the strengthening of the "South American Bloc" in the global scenario required an effort from the Brazilian government for further integration with its neighboring countries (Denys, 2001, p. 249), somehow readopting the values of the preceding decades.

A meeting between Figueiredo and Alfonsín on January 9, 1985, would confirm the positive phase of their bilateral relationship. In a review of the regional conjecture, Figueiredo and Alfonsin focused on security issues and economic themes, particularly foreign debt. In the area of security, they reaffirmed their purpose to continue to pursue a more stable order in the region, whereas in matters related to Central America, whose crisis had intensified, they reaffirmed to support the efforts undertaken under the Contadora Group. In relation to the Falklands, the sovereign right of Argentina over the islands was reiterated, and Alfonsin manifested his satisfaction with Brazil's performance as representative of the Argentinean interests in London. Another relevant point was the recognition of the importance of the Treaty of Peace and Friendship recently signed between the Vatican and the Republics of Argentina and Chile through the mediation of John Paul II. On that occasion, Chile and Argentina expressed that the agreement was a realization of the efforts of both countries in seeking a peaceful solution to a complex problem, which would bring benefits to all of Latin America.

Argentina and Brazil in a way resumed the "Uruguaiana spirit" and created an environment for joint coordination on regional diplomatic issues. As for economic issues, they emphasized the topic of the foreign debt of Latin American countries, the cost it bore for each country of the region, and the necessity of seeking better payment conditions. Debt should not be allowed to hinder efforts towards development, and, in that sense, it was necessary to follow the route taken with the Quito Declaration and later developed under the framework of the Cartagena Consensus (MREC, 1985).

If in 1985 the Argentinean government still expected the birth of a "new consciousness" in the international financial powers. The Brazilian government approached Argentina with the clear goal of going beyond the phase of cooperation and starting to negotiating topics related to their integration (Bueno & Cervo, 2015, p. 452). Cervo notes that from the first moments of the 1980s, despite joint efforts in multilateral fora, regional agreements, and bilateral initiatives, the cooperation between both countries still had an experimental and opportunistic character, without the construction of a process capable of reinforcing the structural bases of the continent's autonomy. However, it should be added that in this phase, there was already a sufficiently robust bilateral background to prepare the ground, alongside the processes of re-democratization, for the agreements of 1985 and 1986.

When Sarney and Alfonsin inaugurated the Tancredo Neves Bridge on November 19, 1985, linking Foz do Iguaçu to Puerto Iguazú, along with the signature of the Iguaçu Declaration on peaceful cooperation on nuclear energy, they kickstarted a new, robust process of cooperation, starting a new chapter in the bilateral relationship of both countries. The bilateral dialog was now sufficiently mature to introduce the idea of a gradual integration towards a common market with an open admission process to other Platine and South American countries as well as the intensification of technological and scientific cooperation seeking a fundamental transformation of the economies of both countries and the perspective of an increase in the political power and capacity for negotiation of both countries through the institution of a system of bilateral consultations (Bandeira, 2003, p. 462).

In July 1986, on the occasion of the official visit of Sarney to Buenos Aires, the Brazilian President and President Alfonsín signed the Minutes for the Brazilian–Argentinean Integration, aimed at the transformation of both territories into a common economic area, which would gradually and flexibly introduce the adaptation of companies and individuals to the new legal framework and competition rules (Madrid, 2003, p. 253). The minutes established the Program for Integration and Economic Cooperation (PICE), with twelve protocols and secret agreements on atomic energy and military aviation (Bandeira, 2003, p. 463).

The bilateral negotiations, based on the dispositions of the Latin American Integration Association (LAIA), were closely followed by the governments of Uruguay and Paraguay, invited to join Brazil and Argentina in the process of integration of the Southern Cone. Undoubtedly, a political reconfiguration of the Southern Cone and of South American geopolitics was underway, along with the beginning of a process of economic integration in the region. To Bandeira, the integrationist process had the primary objective of promoting integration in the area of capital goods seeking to increase the capacity for mutual support and mutual transformation of their economies, aimed at a balanced and symmetrical development of economic and commercial relations between the countries. This marked the beginning of the process of integration, which had as a final result the signature of the Treaty of Asunción between Argentina, Brazil, Paraguay, and Uruguay, which created the Common Market of the South (MERCOSUR) on March 26, 1991.

The beginning of MERCOSUR did not create, in its first decade of existence, the favorable conditions for resuming the Brazilian project of South American integration, although the economic integration of the Southern Cone could be interpreted as a primordial step towards this process. The conceptions of Sarney and Alfonsín on the economic area of MERCOSUR, aimed not only at trade and free transit of goods but also at industrial integration, through the creation of shared production chains, and at political concertation under international fora and organizations, contributing to the integration in a broader sense. The growth sustained by the inter-bloc trade in its initial years, largely surpassing expectations and the signature of a Free Trade Agreement between MERCOSUR and Chile and a similar agreement with Bolivia, both in 1996, provided the baseline for those who believed it was possible to broaden MERCOSUR to beyond the limits of the Southern Cone. This optimism was reinforced with the approval of the Protocol of Ouro Preto (1994), which institutionalized legal personality to the bloc, with the entry into force of the Customs Union – although still at an incipient stage – in January 1995.

Amid these advancements was the rise of neoliberal governments in the region, in particular those of Carlos Saúl Menem (1989–1999) and, in Brazil, of Fernando Collor (1990–1992), Itamar Franco (1993–1994), and Fernando Henrique Cardoso (1995–2002), which created an opportunity to move from an Economic MERCOSUR to a Trade MERCOSUR, as these governments adopted economic policies inspired by the principles and values of the Washington Consensus. While the Brazilian governments kept, to some extent, integrationist purposes of neo-developmentalist and/or neo-structuralist aspirations, Menem embraced the thesis of the "reincorporation to the First World", moving away from the traditional theses of ECLAC. According to Jorge Castro's interpretation, the differences between Brazil and Argentina did not consist merely in two opposing foreign policies (autonomy versus dependency) nor in opposing assessments of the international conjecture (critical view versus acritical view). The differences stemmed from the distinct positions both countries held in relation to the United States. Whereas Brazil recognized the North American primacy and sought to maintain its autonomy for action in Latin America, Argentina would rather build a closer relationship with Washington, hoping to receive differentiated treatment in its aspirations (Castro, 1998, p. 87). Although Jorge Castro's analysis is not incorrect as to how the relations of Brazil and Argentina were shaped in relation to the United States, their internal political processes and economic policies are not of less importance.

As a matter of fact, to Miriam Gomes Saraiva, the 1990s were noteworthy for the Brazil–Argentina relations for allowing the creation and institutional consolidation of MERCOSUR, elevating interdependence to an unprecedented level in bilateral relations and reshaping, in other aspects, the project of Latin American integration. There were achievements in this period such as scientific and technological cooperation and the development of shared projects, as well as cooperation in the military area, without much progress in the sense of a shared security policy (Saraiva, 2012, p. 120). One question that arises at this point is to what extent military cooperation needs to develop in order to achieve a shared policy.

On the other hand, the mishaps between the two countries continued to be part of the landscape, as pointed out by Saraiva. The most remarkable case – whose analysis is beyond the scope of this work – was the economic policy adopted by Fernando Henrique Cardoso in the beginning of his second presidential term, which devalued the real, causing profound and negative effects in the Argentinean exports. The depreciation of the Brazilian currency caused an "invasion" of Brazilian products in the Argentinean market, deteriorating its trade balance and generating suspicion in relation to the objectives of Brasília. Fernando Henrique, in fact, sought to reposition Brazil in the framework of international finance and trade, resuming developmentalist practices and repositioning the country's foreign policy.

Following this depreciation, Fernando Henrique promoted in Brasilia the 1st Meeting of the Presidents of South America, which gathered for the first time all South American presidents to discuss topics such as politics, trade, and physical integration at continental level. In this meeting, the countries reached an understanding on the democratic clause and launched the Initiative for the Integration of Regional Infrastructure in South America (IIRSA), seeking to develop projects in areas such as energy, transportation and telecommunications. Fernando Henrique and the other South American presidents created, in their own way, the necessary conditions for resuming the dialogue on South American Integration. The developments of this meeting raised the stakes for the government of Luís Inácio Lula da Silva (2003–2010), who, under new political conditions, acted in favor of the intensification of this integration. The creation of IIRSA and the attention Fernando Henrique started to give to South American integration after five years of Brazilian "self-sufficiency" indicated that the Brazilian integration project had hibernated during the years of more intense liberal policy only to be resumed as a practical necessity. In other words, it was a proof of the resilient nature of the integration.

South American integration in the twenty-first century

When taking office as President of the republic in the beginning of 2003, Luís Inácio Lula da Silva adopted a foreign policy style of prominence in the international fora, with the creation of regional instruments for dialog and direct contact with major international leaderships. In this last aspect, Lula's administration aspired establish conversations with a pretentious equality status. As traditionally occurs in changes of government and political groups in power, more frequently in the first case, this first phase was marked by both continuities and changes, with the clear prevalence of the former, as evidenced in Lula's inauguration speech, as in the speech of Celso Amorim, his Minister of Foreign Affairs.

Lula and Celso Amorim had an extraordinary alignment of ideas and international actions promoted by the government, with guidelines that would remain up until the end of his second presidential term, with no changes to Itamaraty's command. The formulation of the government's foreign policy was under the responsibility of Amorim, Samuel Pinheiro Guimarães (Secretary-General at the MFA) and Marco Aurélio García (special advisor to the presidency for international affairs). The strongholds of their foreign policy included: (1) absolute priority given to South America; (2) the maintenance of a mature dialog with the country's traditional partners; (3) a proactive position before international organizations; (4) the shared leadership in the creation of new regional mechanisms; and (5) the emphasis given to socioeconomic development, a transversal theme in relation to all others, linked to the trajectory of the Worker's Party (PT) and the country's internal politics. The electoral and governmental alliance with the Brazilian Democratic Movement Party (PMDB) – and other base parties – were the conservative counterbalance in the face of a more active and proud foreign policy, as proposed by Amorim (2015).

The first days and months of the new government would be marked by relevant events such as the political crisis in Venezuela and the invasion of Iraq by the United States. Even before that, however, the government had pushed to the international agenda a theme until then only addressed internally.

On the occasion of his inauguration, both the press and Lula's supporters noticed that his Zero Hunger Program had not been included in his campaign program, having been immediately incorporated into his foreign policy agenda. Notwithstanding the embarrassment of the situation, the proposal of eradicating poverty in Brazil and making it an example for other countries and regions was an initiative that did not contradict the line of action adopted in the promotion of his foreign policy and reinforced the policy of approximation with peripheral countries while also pressuring countries with more purchasing power to broaden cooperation programs and giving the theme of development more density.

The high point of this program, in the international area, would be the Special Summit of the Americas, held in Monterrey in the beginning of 2004. On that occasion, the national representatives signed the Declaration of Nuevo León, with the purpose of "advancing in the implementation of measures to fight poverty, promote social development, reach an equitable economic growth and reinforce the governability of our democracies". However, after the initial excitement, the program faded with time, and hunger was obviously not eradicated in Brazil.

Another subject that occupied Lula's government in its first days was the deepening of the crisis in Venezuela, which, in April 2002, underwent a frustrated coup attempt and, by the end of that year, a lockout promoted by the company Petroleos de Venezuela (PDVSA). The political crisis in the neighboring country led the Brazilian government to participate in the creation of the Group of Friends of Venezuela, later renamed Group of Friends of the OAS Secretary-General for Venezuela, with the objective of contributing to overcome the crisis. Marco Aurélio García was designated to represent the country in this group, and his performance was criticized by the Brazilian opposition due to his sympathy for the so-called Bolivarian countries, a harbinger that would become the rule through the two presidential terms of Lula da Silva.

More than an ideological option or a party philosophy, the relations with Venezuela followed, basically, the same guidelines followed by previous governments, including those of Fernando Henrique Cardoso, who also condemned the 2002 coup and who, during the aforementioned lockout, sent a symbolic shipment of oil to Venezuela, signaling the Brazilian support to the maintenance of the order in the neighboring country. Commercial interests, participation of Brazilian companies in major construction works, and the intensification of the Brazilian project of South American integration – a topic that will be briefly covered in the following section – were similarities between the governments of the Brazilian Social Democracy Party (PSDB) and that of the Worker's Party (PT).

A third challenge was the US invasion to Iraq's territory, euphemistically called the Second Gulf War, officially in response to the terrorist attacks of September 11, 2001, which destroyed the twin towers of the World Trade Center in New York and caused major damages to the Pentagon building in Washington. The United State's government attributed the responsibility for the attack to Islamic extremist group Al-Qaeda, whose bases would be in Afghan and Iraqi territory. On the existence or not of Al-Qaeda cells in Iraqi territory, the UN Verification and Inspection Commission, led by Swedish official Hans Blix and the Organization for the Prohibition of Chemical Weapons (OPCW), then led by Brazilian official Maurício Bustani, could not find evidence of the existence of such weapons, which led the UN to deny authorization for the armed interventions in Iraq. In face of this situation, Brazil, true to its diplomatic tradition of respect to international organizations and the peaceful solution of conflicts, positioned itself against the war and in defense of the respect to international regulations.

The fight against hunger, the support to Chávez, and the position against the military intervention in Iraq would be sufficient to illustrate the more active role played by Brazil in the international scenario, in comparison with previous governments, without demerit to the projection reached by Fernando Henrique Cardoso. However, in all such cases, the Brazilian government acted following the continued guidelines of the country's foreign policy, such as autonomy, universalism, valuation of international cooperation and international institutions, defense of the rule of law, and compliance with the dispositions of public international law. These guidelines were adopted alongside the values and ideas of PT and some of its allies.

The strengthening of the relations with Venezuela and its popular and socializing regime counterbalanced the ties the party had made with conservative sectors, headed by PMDB, and the liberal economic policy. Lula and Chávez established a productive dialog early on and had great alignment in international and regional issues, mutually reinforcing their bases of internal political support. More than that, after the frustrated attempt of promoting a closer relationship between MERCOSUR and the Andean Community, the strong relationship with Caracas indicated to Brasília that the Venezuela's admission as a full member of MERCOSUR was possible. The decision of the Venezuelan government to join the bloc and request their removal from CAN, much due to political disagreements and disputes with Colombia, was in line with the Brazilian interests.

This reshaping of the Brazilian foreign policy occurred amid convergences and divergences, which, during the two Lula governments and more generally, seemed to favor much more than undermine South American integration. It is not the scope of this chapter to thoroughly address this issue, but what is worth noting is that this relative degree of political-ideological identification with the most prominent South American power of the 2000s, despite its nuances and restrictions, has favored the achievement of valuable achievements. Some of these initiatives include: still under Fernando Henrique's government, the 2nd Meeting of the Presidents of South America, which established funding for physical regional integration and the creation of the Amazon Cooperation Treaty Organization (ACTO); and, under Lula, the Trade Agreement between MERCOSUR and Peru, a similar agreement between MERCOSUR and Colombia, Ecuador, and Venezuela, the Free Trade Agreement MERCOSUR-Andean Community, and the South American Community of Nations (CASA), then replaced by the Union of South American Nations.

It would be redundant to keep drawing examples to sustain that the construction of South American integration was underway, to some extent inspired by Brazil. However, the international financial crisis and its repercussions in the countries of the region opened a new phase in this process, characterized by changes, uncertainties, and even setbacks. The economic, political, and institutional crisis in Venezuela, the impeachment/coup against President Fernando Lugo (2008–2012) in Paraguay, the presidential succession of Cristina Kirchner by Mauricio Macri in Argentina, the impeachment/coup against Dilma Rousseff in Brazil, and the challenges faced by identity projects in Bolivia and Ecuador are many of the examples of forces that have established themselves in the region, often met with a critical position and sometimes a clear opposition against the integration. This chapter, however (including the governments of Michel Temer and Jair Bolsonaro) is yet to be written by history.

Conclusion

Resilient as it is, the existence of several integration projects in South America formulated by the Brazilian diplomacy in its recent history can be considered as a single project. Altogether, the integration outlined in the Uruguaiana meeting, the policies of the military regime for both the Platine and Amazon regions, the birth of MERCOSUR, the resuming of the South American dimension of foreign policy by Fernando Henrique, and the emphasis given by Lula to South America compose the Brazilian Project of South American Integration (Pro-BIAS). It does not concern or has not concerned one single project with one specific and final form. Other than that, among the definitions of "project", one of the most common is that of a steady objective, an intent, a pursuit.

Obstacles to South American integration or even to MERCOSUR have been present since 2012, intensified by the new political orientation starting in 2017. The reasons for this derive from economic, political, and ideological aspects. Almost all of the agribusiness sector and a relevant part of the Brazilian industry have businesses with countries from outside South America, in particular the United States, Western Europe, Japan, and China. The political ties with Washington, established from the beginning of the twentieth century and deepened during the two world wars, have continued to exert remarkable influence in the recent phase of globalization. In the ideological plane, the elites – including public servants and parts of the middle class – tend to follow the values, premises, and world views imported from Europe and the United States, with prejudices against the Latin American neighbors still being a present reality. It is in this sense that values such as autonomy, universalism, and regional integration strongly depend on the internal political processes and on the current president.

Through the last seven decades, the efforts for integration of Brazil and its South American neighbors have been met with several different international conjectures and different internal political scenarios. They have been questioned by a number of actors and for many different reasons but have managed to maintain a few orienting principles and guidelines. The creation of an economic space for South America, with common norms and rules, as a means to leverage their national economies; the regional international cooperation in areas such as science and technology, where major economies hardly ever transfer any knowledge; and actions for the development of regional infrastructure are some examples of concepts that have resisted the turmoil of economic and political crises. Factors such as political instability, coups d'état, and the presence of conceptions with strong ideological approaches quite often have hindered such actions. But in a final analysis the results have been positive, which should not be considered an inconsequential optimism.

Solidarity between the Latin American and/or South American peoples, principles of autonomy and universalism, the intention of the Brazilian military to lead the integration efforts, the pursuit of a solution to the crisis of foreign debt, the neoliberal homily of economic opening as a strategy, and the integration promoted by the governments of more popular – or populist – approaches have been simultaneous and successive aspects of the regional integration, either convergingly or divergently, in times of harmony or conflict. The academic work must include among its priorities to try to balance this process, pondering what has prevailed (the lines of continuity) and what has changed over time. Establishing a hierarchy of such forces, organizing them, and providing them with form and coherence is up for interpretation.

If the Brazilian project of South American integration is still alive, it is up to its neighbors to evaluate both the hidden and explicit objectives of the country in its integration policy, as well as the reach of these proposals and their validity, by either adhering to them or not. Brazil, after all, has severe structural fragilities, such as income inequality, high levels of urban violence, high deficits in the areas of education, health, and security, oligarchical structures of power, and elites with little sense of social responsibility and citizenship. In this sense, what is the model that Brazil wants or is able to propose to its neighbors? The solution to this and other issues, as seen in this chapter, inevitably depends on collective debates and shared decisions, whose loci are the existing regional international organizations. Only then will the Brazilian project be able to move beyond its own borders and become a South American project.

Notes

1 The following paragraphs of this section refer to the same document and related reports on Amazon countries and others, unless expressly indicated otherwise.
2 At the end of 1966, Manaus hosted the 1st Meeting on Fostering Amazon Development. The objective was to finally integrate the Amazon region to the rest of the country through a broad coordination of actions involving "successful business people from other regions of Brazil", the Superintendence for the Development of the Amazon (SUDAM), the Amazon Bank, and other institutions (MRE, 1966).
3 The subsequent paragraphs were based on this document, unless expressly indicated otherwise.

References

Amorim, C. (2015). *Teerã, Ramalá e Doha: memórias da política externa ativa e altiva*. São Paulo, Brazil: Benvirá.

Bandeira, M. (1975). *Estado Nacional e política internacional na América Latina (1930–1992)*. São Paulo, Brazil: Ensaio.

Bandeira, M. (2003). *Brasil, Argentina e Estados Unidos: conflito e integração na América do Sul (1870–2003)*. Rio de Janeiro, Brazil: Revan.

Boesner, D. (1996). *Relaciones internacionales de América Latina: breve historia*. Caracas, Venezuela: Nueva Sociedad.

Briceño-Ruiz, J., & Simonoff, A. (2015). *Integración y cooperación regional en América Latina: una lectura a partir de la teoría de la autonomía*. Buenos Aires, Argentina: Biblos.

Bueno, C., & Cervo, A. L. (2015). *História da política exterior do Brasil*. Brasília: Editora da Universidade de Brasília.

Castro, J. (1998). La Argentina, Estados Unidos y Brasil: el triángulo de la década de 90. In A. Cisneros (Ed.), *Política exterior argentina (1989–1999): historia de un éxito* (pp. 83–106). Buenos Aires, Argentina: GEL.

Child, J., & Kelly, P. (Eds.). (1990). *Geopolítica del Cono Sur y la Antártida*. Buenos Aires, Argentina: Editorial Pleamar.

Dantas, S. T. (2011). *Política externa independente*. Brasília: Fundação Alexandre de Gusmão.

Denys, R. (2001). A visão estratégica. In Oliveira Bastos (Ed.), *Sarney: o outro lado da história*. Rio de Janeiro, Brazil: Nova Fronteira.

Divisão de América Meridional/Ministério das Relações Exteriores (MRE). Relatório da Viagem do Ministro das Relações Exteriores a Bogotá, Quito e Lima (24 de outubro – 1° de novembro de 1966). Confidencial. Arquivo Histórico do Brasília, Castanhos, Países Amazônicos.

Doratioto, F., & Vidigal, C. E. (2014). *História das relações internacionais do Brasil*. São Paulo, Brazil: Editora Saraiva.

Guerreiro, R. S. (1985). *O Itamaraty e o Congresso Nacional*. Brasilia, Brazil: MRE/Secretaria Especial de Relações com o Congresso.

IRBr. (1980, June 24). *Memorandum from Ambassador João Hermes Pereira de Araújo to the Secretary-General*, DAA/123, secreto-urgente. AH/MRE-BSB, memoranda, 1980, cx O-02, DTC, DTI, ERERIO, G, IRBr.

Jaguaribe, H. (1958). *O nacionalismo na atualidade brasileira*. Rio de Janeiro, Brazil: ISEB.

Lafer, C. (2001). *A identidade internacional do Brasil e a política externa brasileira*. São Paulo, Brazil: Perspectiva.

Madrid, E. (2003). *Argentina-Brasil: la suma del sur*. Mendoza, Argentina: Caviar Bleu.

Ministério das Relações Exteriores. (1996, December 6). *Boletim Informativo*, 1966.

MRE. (1966). *Memorandum to the South American Division of the Conference of Brazilian Ambassadors to Amazon Countries.* Archive, Brasília.

Ministerio de las Relaciones Exteriores y Culto (MREC). (1954, July 27). *Letra R. E., n° 888, secreta-urgente. Motivo: Informar sobre cuestionario referente a política interna y exterior del Brasil.* Caja 20, Carpeta 20. Archivo Historico, Rio de Janeiro.

Ministerio de las Relaciones Exteriores y Culto (MREC). (1965). *Brasil: Asuntos de interés susceptibles de ser tratados durante la visita de sua excelencia el Señor Canciller.* Caja: Brasil, 1958 al 1965. Producido por el Departamento de América del Sur.

Ministerio de las Relaciones Exteriores y Culto (MREC). (1984). *Reseña de la Relación Argentino-Brasileña,* secreto, lata "Brasil – Parte N.° 1", pasta "Ministro Ibáñez, 1984". Buenos Aires.

Ministerio de las Relaciones Exteriores y Culto (MREC). (1985). *Proyecto de Comunicado de Prensa para el Encuentro Presidencial del 9 de enero de 1985 en Foz de Iguazú,* lata "Brasil, 1971–1972"; pasta "Brasil, 1971–1962–68; Cuenca Plata, 180".

Oliveira, J. K. (1959). *Mensagem ao Congresso Nacional.* Rio de Janeiro, Brazil: DIN.

Saraiva, M. G. (2012). *Encontros e desencontros: o lugar da Argentina na política externa brasileira.* Belo Horizonte, Brazil: Fino Traço.

Vidigal, C. E. (2007). Relações Brasil-Bolívia (1973–1974): o gás e a geopolítica regional. *Cena Internacional, 9*(2).

Vidigal, C. E. (2009). *Relações Brasil-Argentina: a construção do entendimento (1958–1986).* Curitiba, Brazil: Juruá.

Vidigal, C. E. (2012). A Integração Sul-Americana como um Projeto Brasileiro: de Uruguaiana às Malvinas. In FUNAG (Ed.), *A América do Sul e a integração regional* (pp. 63–78). Brasília: FUNAG. Retrieved from http://funag.gov.br/biblioteca/download/939-America_do_Sul_e_a_Integracao_Regional_A.pdf

Visentini, P. F. (2004). *A política externa do regime militar brasileiro.* Porto Alegre, Brazil: Editora da UFRGS.

Walsh, M. (1997). *A atuação do Brasil frente à crise das Malvinas/Falklands (1982).* Brasília, Brazil: Universidade de Brasília.

4 Diplomats and technocrats in the construction of Latin American regionalism

Autonomy and development as variables

José Briceño-Ruiz, María Antonia Correa Serrano and Enrique Catalán Salgado

The resilience of Latin American regionalism is explained by both systemic and agential factors. The action of economic, social and political actors throughout Latin American history helps to understand why the idea and practice of regional integration and cooperation have persisted despite diverse crises. The diplomats and the technocrats of international institutions have played a crucial role in that process. By using a Braudelian approach of *longue durée*, this chapter analyzes the political actions and the initiatives promoted by these two categories of actors.

Diplomats have been critical in the promotion of regionalism in Latin America. By diplomats we understand not only the formal attaché, ambassadors or consuls, but also the ministers of foreign affairs. Similarly, ministers in special missions were important in the promotion of regional unity. In this sense, pundits like Gomez Hoyos (1969) argue that even the young Simón Bolívar acted as a diplomat for Venezuela when he visited the United Kingdom with Andrés Bello in 1810, to promote the independence of the Spanish American territories. What is true is that since the early years of independence, diplomats such as Pedro Gual and Joaquín Mosquera in Colombia; Lucas Alamán, Juan de Dios Cañedo and Manuel Crescencio Rejón in México; and Manuel Corpancho and José Gregorio Paz Soldan in Peru, promoted initiatives of regional unity. Afterwards, other diplomats, such as Manuel Montt in Chile, Vicente Quesada and Roque Sáenz Peña in Argentina or Jose Maria da Silva Paranhos Junior (known as Barão of Rio Branco) in Brazil, also promoted regional initiatives. Even figures non-traditionally associated with idea of regional unity, like Diego Portales in Chile or Domingo Faustino Sarmiento in Argentina, in certain periods of their political life also had diplomatic functions and favored regional initiatives. In the 20th century, Osvaldo Aranha in Brazil, Gabriel Valdés Subercaseaux in Chile, Dante Caputo in Argentina and Celso Amorim in Brazil followed the tradition of Latin American diplomats committed to promoting regionalism. A particularly interesting case was that of Juan Carlos Puig, a prominent Latin American scholar in the field of International Relations that developed a theorization about political autonomy and its link to regional integration. Puig was briefly Ministry of Foreign Affairs during the government of Hector Cámpora in Argentina in 1973.

International technocrats have also been important in furthering regional integration and cooperation. Since the emergence of international organizations in the late 19th century, but especially in the first half of the 20th century, international technocracy has contributed to the design of regional public policies. In the case of Latin America, the creation of the United Nations Economic Commission for Latin America (ECLA)[1] was a milestone in the advancing of the idea of Latin American regionalism. Raúl Prebisch was a leading figure in that process by furthering the proposal of a Latin American Common Market. In diverse ECLA publications, Prebisch designed the project of the common market as executive secretary of that institution. Felipe Herrera is also considered a key actor in fostering of the regional ideal. Herrera was the first president of the Interamerican Development Bank (IDB) in 1959 and from that institution supported ECLA's projects of Latin American integration, including sub-regional initiatives. In the case of Central American integration, a Mexican scholar, Victor Urquidi, made proposals similar to those of Prebisch. Urquidi was working at the ECLA's Mexican bureau in the late 1950s and early 1960s, where he influenced the design of the Central American Common Market (CACM). We can also mention Sebastián Allegret, a Venezuelan diplomat who served as Secretary General of the Latin American Economic System (1983–1987) and later on as Secretary General of the Andean Community (1997–2002). Another important actor was Juan Mario Vacchino, an Argentinean academic and technocrat. He was a professor of the National University of La Plata in Argentina and moved to the Universidad Central de Venezuela during his political exile since the mid-1970s and early 1980s. Later, Vacchino also became general secretary of the Latin American Integration Association (ALADI[2] in Spanish), director of the Institute for the Integration of Latin American (INTAL in Spanish) and the secretary of development of the Latin American Economic System (SELA in Spanish). Prebisch's commitment to regional integration was followed by other ECLA experts, such as Gert Rosenthal, also a ECLA general secretary, that in the 1990s adapted the concept of open regionalism (originally from the Asia Pacific region) to the Latin American context.

As suggested in this chapter, both diplomats and international technocrats have been significant players in the promotion of Latin America. There is no place here for an in-depth analysis of all the diplomats and technocrats mentioned. For that reason, we have selected three diplomats and three technocrats. To follow the logic of a long-term historical analysis, we have chosen a diplomat of the early decades of independence: the Mexican Lucas Alamán; the second one is the Barão of Rio Branco, the Brazilian Minister of Foreign Affairs in the first twelve years of the 20th century. Afterwards, we examine the political action of the Argentinean Dante Caputo in the 1980s, concerning the reactivation of regional cooperation and integration in Latin America. In the case of technocrats, we choose three figures in the promotion of economic regionalism in Latin America: Raúl Prebisch, Víctor Urquidi and Felipe Herrera.

Diplomats and their efforts for regional unity

Lucas Alamán (1792–1853), a contemporary of Simón Bolívar, lived the most critical moments in the conformation of the Latin American countries and their struggle for independence. He believed that in that difficult context, regional unity could be one of the best tools for the defense of those countries. Alamán witnessed the birth of the continental emancipation, where everything had still to be done. America (the whole continent) was a territory with independent but impoverished nations, a continent whose nations were being inserted into the world market mainly as suppliers of raw materials.

The ideas of continental union promoted in Colombia by Bolivar and in Mexico by Alamán shared similarities. Simón Bolivar was without doubt the main promoter of regional unity. His country, Colombia, was in fact the result of the unification of the former Royal Audiencia of Quito, the Viceroyalty of New Granada and the Captaincy General of Venezuela. Later, he proposed a Federation of the Andes, including current Peru and Bolivia. However, Bolivar also wanted closer links to the new Hispanic American countries, as expressed in the letter of Jamaica (1815) and in his plan to convene an anfictionic Hispanic American congress in Panama (1926). Alamán had similar ideas and believed that the former Spanish colonies were the natural family of the Mexican nation (Herrera, 2013, p. 173). For that reason, he fostered in 1823 the signing of an Agreement of Perpetual Union, League and Confederation between Mexico and Colombia (Vazquez, 1991, p. 547). At that moment, other initiatives emerged, such as the Notes on a Treaty of General Confederation among all the American Republics made by Francisco Severo Maldonado (1823), a project of a military confederation of all the American republics. The United States and Mexico would play a leading role in that initiative, and the permanent headquarters of the confederation would be in Cuba, "from where the liberating military forces would depart to all points occupied or threatened by enemies conjured against the human species" (Hernández Jaimes, 2016, p. 23). Another important antecedent was the proposal of Juan de Dios Mayorga in 1823, much more political than military. He projected the convening of a continental congress to discuss issues such as mutual recognition, border delimitation and relations between the new states. The utmost goal was to create a "Perpetual Alliance" that would guarantee continental defense but also regional and internal peace (Hernández Jaimes, 2016, p. 23).

Alamán developed his own political and economic vision of continental integration. Since it was evident that the new nations shared important cultural similarities derived from their common colonial past, it was natural that the Hispanic-Americanism constituted an historical identity. In 1825, in a speech in the Mexican congress, Alamán asserted (quoted by Hernández Jaimes, 2016):

> The naturalness, the uniformity of interests and the cause that sustain all the countries of America that has shaken off the yoke of Spain, link them in a such a way that one can say even if they are divided and exist several

government centers, they constitute a single compound of homogeneous parts. These circumstances make their relations be closer and the setbacks and prosperity of one of them cannot be indifferent to the others and that all they are willing to help each other to achieve the object to which all uniformly are in the track.

(p. 24)

Thus, Alamán joined the efforts fostered in the south of the continent by Francisco de Miranda and Simón Bolívar, who pursued, under their own visions, the same ideal of continental unity. In fact, Alamán strongly supported the Mexican participation in the Congress of Panamá in 1826. In a speech at the Mexican congress, he asserted that the meeting in Panamá "was the basis of a real family pact that make one of all the Americans, united to defend their independence and liberty and foster trade and mutual interests" (quoted in Vazquez, 1991, p. 555).

After failure of the Congress of Panamá, Alamán attempted on different occasions to convene a new Hispanic America Congress. Thus, in 1832 Alamán appointed Manuel Díez de Bonilla to a diplomatic mission in Colombia and Central America and Juan de Dios Cañedo, in Peru, Chile and Brazil. The goal of those missions was to organize a new Congress to promote the integration of the "family" (namely, the Hispanic American nations and Brazil) and establish common positions in issues such as the signing of the peace with Spain, the adoption of concordats with the Vatican, promotion of trade, security and defense and the solution of conflicts (Vázquez, 1991, p. 557). In other words, the idea was the creation of mechanisms of political cooperation among the new American states. There were obstacles to this cooperation. One of them was the political distrust due to differences about government systems. Mexico and Brazil had initially opted for a monarchy, which was contrary to the predominant republican tendency across the region. Moreover, the geographical dimension of the Mexican empire and its economic possibilities as one of the main former Spanish colonies also caused concern in the rest of the Hispanic American countries (Vázquez, 1991, p. 546). Despite these factors, the need for unity to prevent a recapture from the European powers was the criteria that prevailed.

Under this idea, some of the first integration proposals contemplated a continental union of the whole Americas, including the United States of America (USA). However, it should be noted that as a preventive response to US expansionism, Alamán was always opposed to inviting this country to the regional initiatives that he was furthering. For Alamán, the USA had to be kept away. Hence, one of his first tasks as Minister of Foreign Affairs (1823–1825; 1830–1832) was the total recognition and respect of Mexican borders. He rejected any violation of Mexican territory and observed closely the US and Russian settlements in California. He also prevented a possible annexation of Guatemala by the USA (Galeana, 1992, p. 59). Alamán insisted in his writings and political speeches that neither the European powers nor the United States should be included in a continental union. He argued that their mercantile and political interests were opposed to those of the Hispanic American republics, and therefore, those external powers were more determined to hinder the union than to promote it. In consequence, the convening of a Congress should "only consult the peculiar interests of this group of Republics born of the old Spanish colonies; interests that have nothing in common with those of the other powers and, consequently must be regarded with absolute exclusion of all of them" (Cancillería Mexicana, 1831 as cited in Hernández Jaimes, 2016, p. 26). Alamán had also his own ideas about economic development and promoted the creation of a Hispanic American economic community based on bilateral trade agreements, like that subscribed with Colombia in 1823.

Concerning economic development, Alamán recognized the importance of mining and especially the relevance of industry for the economic growth, and therefore, he founded the Banco de Avío to promote investment and industrialization (Potash, 1953). However, industrialization and economic sovereignty were goals difficult to achieve for a country in economic and political turmoil such as Mexico, which also began its independent life with a huge amount of debt with different big powers.

Alamán also promoted the creation of a large Hispanic-American market that would give these countries the opportunity to strengthen their industries by linking and complementing them. This would allow the states to achieve economic growth under better conditions of equality than if they were directly integrated into the world market, where there was not opportunity for fair competition and where asymmetric exchanges would take place. The defense of commercial preferences for the Hispanic American countries in the negotiation of treaties was also a priority during his administration as Minister of Foreign Affairs. However, Alamán considered that that strategic foreign trade would require an effective solution: high tariffs had to be imposed on imports. According to Hernández Jaimes (2016), for Alamán:

> foreign trade with restrictions should be the means to achieve the main objective of the Latin American economies: industrialization and economic sovereignty. A policy of relatively high tariffs would provide the necessary resources to modernize the machinery for production, while protecting national productions. Likewise, it should be established the bases for a Latin American market in which an increasing amount of production of member countries was located.
>
> (p. 30)

Two positive results were expected from this strategy: the first was to obtain resources to modernize the country and the second one was to provide the necessary protection for the burgeoning national industry (Bernecker, 1988; Yañez López, 2015).

This diagnosis was correct, and one can find even some reminiscences of this in the ideas that ECLA and Prebisch would propose a century later. However,

Alamán's trade integration project could not be carried out due to what Hernández Jaimes (2016) calls the "commercial cosmopolitism", namely, the hegemony of the ideology of economic liberalism among the economic elites that led them to reject protectionist measures.

The growing rise of Hispanic-American nationalisms and the disputes over territorial boundaries, which led to a turbulent century with several wars, ended up with any possibility of integration until the twilight of the 19th century. At that moment, new initiatives were proposed but under the hemispheric leadership of the US and Pan-Americanism, different from those promoted by Lucas Alamán during his life.

Another diplomat who deserved to be analyzed is the Barão of Rio Branco (1845–1912). He became a diplomatic principal actor in those years of the impulse of Pan-Americanism on the eve of the 20th century. Rio Branco is a controversial figure when analyzing Latin American regionalism. It is well known that as defender of Brazilian monarchy, he subscribed to the idea of Brazil as "an island", a country in which "order and progress" prevailed and where civil war, political instability and *caudillism* did not exist throughout the first decades of independent life. This made Brazil different from its South American neighbors, and Rio Branco wanted "to differentiate Brazil from its neighbors vis-à-vis European countries and United States" (Doratioto, 2000, p. 133). Rio Branco also promoted close relations with the United States in a way that the US scholar Bradford Burns (1966, XX) described as an "unwritten alliance". As part of this, the Brazilian diplomat supported Pan-Americanism and even was favorable to the United States' President Theodore Roosevelt's corollary to the Monroe Doctrine. The corollary allowed the US to intervene in certain countries when the national governments were not able to guarantee order and prevent civil unrest. The Barão considered that countries which were able to guarantee order and stability should not be concern about a possible US intervention. When the Argentinean expert in internationell law Luis María Drago proposed the so-called Drago Doctrine,[3] to reject the use of force to collect debts, the Barão did not subscribe to that idea (Bueno, 2012). Finally, the Brazilian decision to order three battleships from the United Kingdom in 1905 caused an arms race with Argentina and Chile. In the case of Argentina, Estanislao Zeballos, the Minister of Foreign Affairs, strongly rejected the Brazilian plans and accused the government in Rio de Janeiro of a hostile policy (Bengoechea, 2007; Garay, 2012).

Thus, at first glance it seems that the Barão was not a promoter of regionalism in Latin America. He always thought that it was an illusory alliance or confederation of Hispanic American countries as proposed throughout the 19th century. In consequence, he did not approve the Brazilian participation in those initiatives. In a dispatch sent to Alfredo de Morais Gomes Ferreira in 1905, the Barão asserted that "the so-called league of the Hispanic American Republics to confront the United States is unrealistic thinking, because of the impossibility of agreement between peoples in general separated from each other, and it is even ridiculous, given the known weakness and lack of resources of almost all of them" (Rio Branco quoted in Bueno, p. 271).

Rio Branco was favorable to Pan-Americanism, namely, the regional project designed in Washington, firstly through the Monroe Doctrine and afterwards through the Pan-American Congress held in 1889–1890 in Washington (Burns, 1964). The Barão believed that Brazil could share with the US a leadership in promoting the Pan-American ideal. For that reason, Brazil organized the Third Pan-American Congress in Rio in 1906. Some experts such as Rubens Ricupero (2000) consider that the Barão aimed at "multilateralizing" the Monroe Doctrine. Celso Lafer argues that Brazil did not interpret the Monroe Doctrine as a US unilateral policy but rather as part of international law in the American continent. In consequence, its implementation should be made through the cooperative actions of the principal republics. For Lafer, "the multilateral interpretation of the Monroe Doctrine as a constituent part of the Brazilian policy doctrine entailed a controlled rolling over U.S unilateral interference based on its premise of 'manifest destiny'" (Lafer, 2009, p. 105).

Notwithstanding these facts, we subscribe to the belief that, realizing or without realizing it, the Barão was a promoter of regionalism in South America. Firstly, he resolved an issue that was important in the region in the 19th century: the delimitation of borders. Thus, during his tenure as Minister of Foreign Affairs, Brazil signed agreements with most of its neighbors. Beyond this, the Barão was particularly interested in the stability and autonomy of South America in general and the Southern Cone in particular. In this scenario, the "unwritten alliance" had limits, as it was shown for example for the Brazilian rejection of the US attempt to "internationalize" the Amazon River basin. Another issue was the conflict about the province of Acre. This had been a territory in dispute among Bolivia, Peru and Brazil, but in 1902, the Bolivian government granted a special concession to the Bolivian Syndicate, an Anglo-American company to control de production of rubber in Acre. The Brazilian government perceived this as a US intervention in South America that could not be tolerated. After a series of diplomatic maneuvers, the Brazilian diplomacy succeeded in abrogating the concession, and Acre was eventually annexed to Brazil (Garay Vera, 2008). Similarly, when Panama declared its independence from Colombia, to a large extent as a result of US interventionism to build and control the Panama Canal, the Barão proposed to Argentina and Brazil a joint recognition of the country. In other words, the Barão's Pan-Americanism had limits.

Furthermore, Rio Branco strongly believed in the Southern Cone as a particular geopolitical region in the Western Hemisphere. Conversely to ideas widespread in certain Argentinean circles in those years, the Barão was not interested in imposing a Brazilian hegemony in South America or being a sort of South American delegate of the US. Conversely, as the Brazilian historian Alvaro Lins (1965) argued, Rio Branco's view on South America aimed at setting up a regional equilibrium against any non-regional imperialist dreams or hegemony projects. Francisco Doratioto (2000, p. 133) claims that Rio Branco's plan was "a South America geopolitical space of Brazilian leadership, in consensus with Argentina, not imposed and without expansionist or interventionist purposes". Despite the naval crisis and the difficult relations with Zeballos, Rio Branco wished to maintain with Argentina and Chile a policy of cordial intelligence. The idea was not to isolate Argentina but to convince leaders in Buenos Aires that political stability, peace and security only could be achieved through cooperation among the three countries. Thus, in a letter sent to the plenipotentiary minister of Brazil in Buenos Aires, dated November 22, 1904, Rio Branco suggested the creation by the three main countries of South America (Argentina, Brazil and Chile, ABC) of a legal instrument that would promote peace and order in the region. This idea was shared by Julio Argentina Roca, the Argentinean President who favored the joint action of the so-called ABC Triangle. The Barão let it be known in different occasions his view to Argentinean ambassador in Rio de Janeiro, Manuel Gorostiga "on the desirability and necessity of a permanent agreement between Brazil and Argentina to maintain peace in the region" (Rio Branco quoted in Doratioto, 2000, p. 134). As Cloadoaldo Bueno points out, for Rio Branco "the friendship between the three nations would not only maintain balance and prevent of intervention of one of them in Republics of lesser expression, but it would also leave Brazil more comfortable in the sub-regional context" (Bueno, 2012, p. 281).

The project did not prosper to a large extent due to the naval arms race crisis and the differences with Zeballos. The incident known as "telegram no. 9", a denunciation by Zeballos of the decoding of a Rio Branco telegram to the Brazilian legation in Chile, in which alleged hostile intentions of Brazil towards Argentina were revealed, had an impact in any rapprochement between both countries. Rio Branco authorized the divulgation of the real content of the telegram, and as a result of such divulgation, it was demonstrated that Zeballos' allegations of a Brazilian hostility were false. Conversely, in the telegram the Barão asserted: "I always saw advantages in a certain intelligence between Brazil, Chile and Argentina, and I sometimes recalled its desirability" (Rio Branco quoted in Doratioto, 2000, p. 140).

Afterwards, Puga Borne (Chilean Minister Foreign Affairs) and Lorenzo Anadón (Argentine Representative in Santiago) drafted on October 20, 1907, a treaty to regulate relations between the ABC countries. The draft written by Puga Borne and Anadón, although it contemplated the rule of immigration and the adhesion of other countries, was a military alliance and even foresaw a "discreet equivalence" in the naval forces of the three nations (Bueno, 2012, p. 281). With the rise to power of Roque Saénz Peña in Argentina in 1910, the regional scenario changed. Saénz is known for his motto: "Everything unites us, nothing separates us", when he described the Argentinean–Brazilian relationship. He believed that the South American peace might be achieved only based on a firm understanding between the Argentinean and Brazilian governments. He also thought that a political co-ordination between both countries could counterbalance the US in the region (Doratioto, 2000, p. 141). As a result, Saénz put an end to the naval arm race by proposing to Brazil a "gentlemen's agreement" according to which both countries would give up building a third battleship.

This was the origin of the project of the so-called ABC Treaty, an important precedent of regional cooperation in Latin America. The treaty was eventually signed in 1915, after Rio Branco's death in 1912. Even if the 1915 treaty is not exactly based on the same premises of the 1909-draft (Vidigal, 2016), the creation of an Argentina–Brazil–Chile entente was a recognition of the initiative and efforts made by Rio Branco. The ABC Treaty was not eventually ratified by the Argentinean government. However, it is difficult to deny the importance of the ABC treaty as one the first initiatives to create a space of political dialogue, cooperation and joint action of South American countries. It is worth mentioning that the ABC Treaty had been preceded by the joint diplomatic mediation of Argentina, Brazil and Chile in the crisis between Mexico and the United States in 1914. The Niagara Falls meeting in Canada was a common initiative of three Latin American countries to avoid a military conflict in the continent Small (2009). Similarly, the ABC was an effort to influence the politics of the Western Hemisphere. There are contrasting views on this issue. Conduru (1998) has explained quite properly those views, in a paper written in 1998. For Conduru, experts such as Clodoaldo Bueno and Rubens Ricupero believed that the idea of an ABC entente did not involve an anti-US strategy. Conversely, the ABC treaty would be a complement to the bilateral rapprochement to the US promoted by Rio Branco. Luiz Alberto Moniz Bandeira, by contrast, considered that the ABC was an initiative to impede the US and European expansionism in South America (Conduru, 1998, pp. 70–79). It is not the goal of this chapter to examine such debate. What it is clear is that the ABC proposal was one of the first attempts to create a regional space for political dialogue and cooperation in South America.

Six decades later, an Argentinean diplomat helped in the relaunch of regional economic integration in South America. Dante Caputo was the minister of foreign affairs in the government of Raúl Alfolsín (1983–1989) in Argentina, and his role in the political rapprochement with Brazil is recognized in both the academic and political spheres. Certainly, Alfonsín was a decisive politician in this process. He believed in the need for an improvement of the relations with Brazil as well as a relaunch of Latin American regional integration and cooperation. Caputo was a close Alfonsin ally in promoting that idea.

The political context in those years was difficult throughout the region. The previous decade was characterized by the proliferations of coup d'état in South America and civil wars in Central America. Democracy was mostly absent in the region: only Costa Rica and Venezuela were consolidated democracies. Despite recurrent elections, Colombia and Mexico were contested democracies due to the political violence in the former case and the hegemony of a single party (the Partido Revolucionario Institucional, PRI) in the latter. The beginning of the 1980s did not foresee radical changes in the situation. The rise to power of President Ronald Reagan in the United States meant support for the anticommunist dictatorships in South America and the rejection of left-wing guerrillas in El Salvador and Guatemala. Reagan was also a fierce opponent to the Sandinista revolution in Nicaragua and furthered an increased interventionism by financing an armed opposition known as the *Contra* and mining Nicaraguan harbors. To make matters worse, the so-called debt crisis began in 1982, when the Mexican secretary of finance, Jesús Silva Herzog, declared that Mexico was not able to pay its debt. This announcement was replicated in many Latin American capital cities that were not also able to service their debts. That was the beginning of what ECLC described as a "lost decade" in Latin America, with economic recession, hyperinflation and instability as the rule. Finally, the Argentinean military government decided in April 1982 to recover the Malvinas Islands, which were under British control. This led to a war that showed the weakness of the Inter-American system of defense when Argentine invoked the Inter-American Treaty of Reciprocal Assistance (known in Spanish as TIAR), but the US decided to support the United Kingdom.

That was the complex scenario that Alfonsín had to deal with at the beginning of his administration. A first issue to be considered was the debt crisis. Most of the Latin American countries had been trying to find a solution by promoting unilateral negotiations with the banks. Caputo believed that regional action should be pursued. A first step in this direction was to convince Brazil to be part of a regional strategy. In a visit to Brazil to meet President João Batista Figueiredo in 1984, Caputo took the opportunity to raise the issue. He described that meeting as "tense". Figuereido had been a colleague and friend of the Argentinean dictator Jorge Videla, who was being judged in Argentina when Caputo was in Brasilia. Thus, the meeting was difficult until the moment Caputo mentioned the problem of the external debt. At that point, Figueiredo reacted by saying, "This situation is unbearable, intolerable. We must join forces to solve that problem because they are stealing us" (Figueiredo quoted by Caputo, 2015, p. 131). This had a dual positive effect. On the one hand, it meant a consolidation in a political rapprochement with Brazil that had begun even in the dictatorial era, when both countries signed a treaty to resolve the conflict in Itaipú[4] in 1979, and continued with the Brazilian support to Argentina during the Malvinas war. On the other hand, with Brazil on board, Argentina was able to deploy a diplomatic strategy to join other Latin American countries in the search for a regional solution to the debt crisis. The result was the so-called *Consenso de Cartagena* (Cartagena's Consensus), a mechanism established in 1984 to coordinate positions in the renegotiation of debts with international banks. The mechanism was established in a summit of ministers held in the Colombian city of Cartagena with participation of the most indebted countries of the region (Caputo, 2015). Certainly, the consensus failed to promote a common negotiation between the international banks and the Latin American debtors, but it was a step in the relaunch of the political cooperation in the region.

Another step had been given in Central America with the aim to find a regional peaceful solution, stop Reagan's interventionism and put an end to the military conflicts in El Salvador and Nicaragua. Colombia, Mexico, Panama and Venezuela had established the so-called Contadora Group in 1983 with the goal of achieving a democratic and peaceful solution to the crisis. A key element of the strategy was to balance the US interventionism in Central America by promoting a Latin American solution to the crisis, in which the European Union would play a crucial role through the San José Dialogue. However, the relative power of Contadora member countries was weak in the Latin American context. Mexico and Venezuela were indeed regional powers, but the construction of an alternative solution to the crisis implied the involvement of major Latin American countries: Argentina and Brazil. The Argentinean government and Caputo himself understood the importance of the issue, and diplomatic actions were displayed to support Contadora's action. This led to the creation of the Grupo de Apoyo (the Support Group) by Argentina, Brazil, Peru and Uruguay in 1984. The Support Group coordinated its diplomatic actions with Contadora and isolated the US strategy of a military intervention in Central America. Afterwards, the members of the Contadora Group and the Support Group joined in the Rio Group, created in 1999. This was another example of Latin American political regionalism.

In the sphere of economic integration, Caputo was a crucial player in the rapprochement between Argentina and Brazil that eventually would lead to the creation of MERCOSUR. As Caputo recognized himself, President Alfonsín was really committed to the idea of overcoming the differences that had divided Argentina and Brazil for decades. He also believed that both countries should work together in the defense of their young democracies (Caputo & Sábato, 1991, p. 198). The way to achieve those objectives was by promoting closer economic ties. Caputo also credited for the idea of integration with Brazil and he emphasized that the creation of a democratic community in the Southern Cone to a large extent depended on the political cooperation and economic integration between Argentina and Brazil (Gardini, 2005, p. 410). Alfonsín commissioned Caputo to start diplomatic talks with Brazil even before the democratic transition in this latter country. By quoting Brazilian Foreign Minister, Saraiva Guerreiro, Gardini mentions that during an informal meeting with Guerreiro in December 1983, Caputo was 'very disposed to a practically immediate integration', but the Brazilian minister warned him about the difficulties and the degree of effort and patience that such an operation required' (Gardini, 2005, p. 410). The rest of the story is very well known: the negotiations to foster economic integration began in 1984, and President Alfonsin and Sarney met in Foz de Iguaçu in November 1985 to launch the bilateral integration between Argentina and Brazil. Afterwards, the Bilateral Program of Economic Integration (known in Spanish as PICE) was approved, and it began a process of economic integration that led to the incorporation of Uruguay and Paraguay and, eventually, to the establishment of MERCOSUR in 1991.

Technocrats and economic integration in Latin America

Prebisch, Urquidi and Herrera are examples of "defiant bureaucrats". Although they worked in international institutions that were created by nation-states, they promoted goals that in many case were beyond the objectives of the organizational bureaucracies to which they belonged. These "defiant bureaucrats" find mechanism to challenge the mainstream views (Rivarola Puntigliano & Appelqvist, 2011, p. 32). The defiant bureaucrats managed to link local (national) values and interests with international institutions and a systemic outlook, but as Rivarola Puntigliano and Appelqvist assert:

> At the regional institutional level, it was more evident that "defiance" was not just a matter of intellectual work and new theoretical perspectives. Institutions and actors were here more influenced by a geopolitical framework that expressed demands from peripheral areas. In this way, the "defiant bureaucrats" and the regional entities became transmission belts for geopolitical demands from countries with a weaker voice at the international level.

> (p. 51)

Prebisch, Urquidi and Herrera are without doubt Latin American examples of "defiant bureaucrats".

Raul Prebisch (1910–1986) is probably the most important economist in Latin American history. His contribution to regional economic integration was initially during his tenure as general director of the Executive Secretariat of ECLA, from 1949 to 1963. This objective also was fostered when he was Secretary-General of the United Nations Conference for the Development (UNCTAD) (1964–1968). Afterwards, he returned to ECLA where he became responsible for the ECLA Review in the 1970s, an academic platform to divulge his approach to development and regionalism.

Prebisch and ECLA's approach to regional economic integration was related to a view of the international economic system divided into center and periphery. As professor of Political Economy at the University of Buenos Aires (1925–1948), Prebisch emphasized that the underdevelopment of Latin America could be explained as a result of its relationship with the central countries and its role in the international division of labor as exporters of primary goods and importers of manufactures. These ideas were systematized in the document "The Economic Development of Latin America and its Principal Problems", published by ECLA in 1949, a critique of the development theories elaborated in the industrialized countries at that time, which argued that development would spontaneously extend to the entire periphery of the world economy. Prebisch played a critical role in the elaboration of that document, in which for the first time ECLA presented the famous dichotomy of the world economy between center and periphery, resulting from the uneven spread of technical progress. According to Prebisch, the core countries were the main beneficiaries of technical progress generated since the industrial revolution. The products of the center experienced an increase of their value in the world markets rather than a price reduction due to improvements in productivity. Increased productivity at the center caused a rise in the income of producers and workers, generating an equitable distribution of the technical progress. However, new technologies in the periphery, mostly imported, were concentrated in the export sectors that specialized in commodities. As a result, "increased productivity in the periphery itself has been lost to the centers. The masses living in the periphery consequently find themselves in a vicious circle of low productivity and low savings" Frankenhoff (1962, p. 191).

The technological gap between center and periphery produced a persistent imbalance in the commercial exchange that Prebisch described as a deterioration in the terms of trade. Prebisch observed that since the 1860s to the years before World War II, the price ratio was constantly moved against primary production. This process of "deterioration in the terms of trade" accounted for the detriment in the price ratio between primary goods and agricultural goods that occurs despite a further technical progress of the former compared to the latter.

The solution proposed by Prebisch was the industrialization of Latin American countries with the goal to obtain a part of the benefits of technical progress and to progressively improve the standard of living of the population. For Prebisch, the development of a competitive and consolidated industrial sector would allow achieving a dynamic and autonomous development that would be less vulnerable to external factors. For Prebisch, the development of a competitive and consolidated industrial sector would make the Latin American countries less vulnerable to external factors. As José Antonio Ocampo argues: "industrialization was initially seen as the main way of changing the production structure, 'spreading technical progress' and import substitution as its main instrument" (Ocampo, 2001, p. 24).

When Prebisch and ECLA formulated their strategy of import substitution industrialization (ISI), some countries had already begun the process of industrial development in response to the Great Depression of the 1930s and World War II. As Bielschwosky (2009, p. 175) asserts, industrialization "spontaneously progressed" without the support of development policies. However, this incipient industrial development had a feature that raised doubts about its viability: the process was developed within an uncompetitive national framework that led to the establishment of inefficient factories. This limited competitiveness of the new industries derived from the narrowness of national markets in which they were being developed. This did not allow the periphery benefiting from the technical progress and contributed to the increasing deterioration in the terms of trade (see ECLA, 1950). Hence there was a need to move forward in a process of regional integration to advance a selective import substitution process in the framework of a common market. "Integration would make it possible to carry through import substitution on a regional or, at least, a sub-regional basis, instead of a purely national one" (Alexander, 1990, pp. 19–20). Experts such as Aggarwal, Espach and Tulchin (2004, p. 23) point out that "the work of Raúl Prebisch and other, promoted the creation of a protected regional markets in order to nurture local industrialization through economies of scale and reduce dependency on imports from the United States and Europe".

Therefore, it is valid to argue that the cornerstone of Prebisch's and ECLA's approach to regional economic integration was the creation of a regional common market to allow an efficient regional industrialization (Briceño-Ruiz, 2017). Although Prebisch did not reject free trade, he considered that trade liberalization should be functional to the broader objective of promoting industrial development. The Latin American common market was conceived as a mechanism to foster free trade of goods produced in the nascent regional industries as well as a space in which the new industries would learn to compete and, once matured, would be able to compete in the global markets Briceño-Ruiz (2017). This approach was broadened in the 1960s and 1970s, when Prebisch was general secretary of the Conference of the United Nations Development Program (UNTACD). His interest in regional integration as a mechanism to solve the center–periphery dichotomy was complemented by demands for increased trade openness in favor of the Third World, which was accompanied by a growing concern on the need to promote exports (Prebisch, 1964, p. 60).

The Mexican Víctor Urquidi (1919–2004) was also a promoter of economic integration in the region. His interest in economic integration is explained by his training as an economist and by his professional work at the World Bank from 1947 to 1949. As director of the ECLA sub-regional headquarters in Mexico City, he promoted the creation of the Central American Common Market. In his approach to regionalism, he left aside the political integration. Latin Americas was disarticulated in the 1950s and 1960s both by the problems between the countries and by the interference of US companies in the region. Then, political integration was not a realistic goal for him, even if the Central American countries were seeking to achieve that objective for decades, and they had established the Organization of Central American States (ODECA) in 1952. Urquidi and ECLA opted for promoting the idea of industrialization as a mechanism to further economic integration.

Urquidi believed that economic integration was a mechanism to achieve development, but he considered that disparities among Latin American countries made difficult the success of such a strategy at the regional level. Hence, Urquidi opted for promoting sub-regional integration between countries whose differences were minor, as was the case of the Central American states. According to Urquidi (1998), the idea of Latin America as a single region, at least in a strict economic sense, was not easy to achieve at that moment. Similarly, for him, an imitation of the European model, which was always shown as the archetype to be followed, was unrealistic due to the differences that existed among the Latin America and the Caribbean countries. In his words:

> With reference just to the most important economic and social facts, and taking into account both the degree of industrialization and the extent of social cohesion, it is evident – and this is shown by the recent analysis of ECLAC itself – that the internal disparities of the region, namely, among the 34 countries that formally compose it, have considerably increased. From this point of view, these inequalities are very deep and are difficult to overcome – unlike the convergences of the members of the European

Union – and it means, basically, that the general recipes that are often offered from outside to the region do not have a possible application in all of our countries.

(p. 117)

Thus, Urquidi's proposal of economic integration was based on the definition of strategic sectors that could be opened to international trade and become drivers of productivity and employment, with a high intervention of the state. In consequence, he rejected the traditional argument of international trade is a generator of development and made a rupture with the classical theory of economic integration, as Prebisch had also done. For Urquidi, the way trade and productivity are linked has an impact in the accumulation of capital, in the income of the export sector and the state income received by taxes from the business sector. In his view, "If these revenues are transferred to the development of other domestic sectors capable of substituting imports, in the long term it would be possible to diversify the external sector and increase exports. However, this depends on the structural flexibility, the evolution of the country's infrastructure, the institutional capacity to achieve these transfers and the necessary investments" (Urquidi, 2005, p. 24). Thus, by creating a CACM, it was expected that these countries could overcome the differences in their economic structure.

Then, economic development was a crucial goal in Urquidi's approach to regional integration. This strategy was implemented between the 1950s and 1980s, after which Central America entered a cycle of economic liberation and neoliberalism that characterized Latin America in the 1990s. As a result, the Latin American economic regional regionalism in general, and the Central American one in particular, was reformed and adapted to a logic of insertion into the global economy and the promotion of closer link with extra-regional powers. Once again in Urquidi's words: "Regional and sub-regional integration have never been too solid or show spectacular results, it has been weakened and, in certain periods, has ceased to act as auxiliary instruments for trade development and investment. In conditions of crisis, some of these integrations practically disappeared" (Urquidi, 1998, p. 120).

Felipe Herrera Lane (1922–1996) is another example of a technocrat devoted to promoting regional unity in Latin America. Herrera was Chilean and throughout his life encouraged the political, economic and cultural unity of the Latin American countries. In this sense, he was different from Prebisch and Urquidi, who were mainly involved in the promotion of economic integration. Herrera believed that Latin America was a nation, a divided nation, and therefore culture was a crucial variable to achieve regional unity.

Herrera was the minister of economy of Carlos Ibañez, a pro-integration president who supported the creation of a new ABC Treaty, as proposed by Juan Domingo Perón in the early 1950s. Later, he was chief executive of Central Bank of Chile and executive director of the International Monetary Fund (Pinedo, 2009, p. 164). Despite this link with international institutions not always favorable to regional economic integration, Herrera never abandoned his ideas about the need to establish closer relations among the Latin America countries. These ideas were advanced when he was appointed as the first Director of the IDB in 1960. In the IDB, he created the Institute for the Integration of Latin America (INTAL) in 1965, which became a research center for the study and divulgation of economic integration in Latin America. Herrera described the IDB as the "Bank of integration", "more than a bank", as Pinedo (2009, p. 168) argues, because the Bank should play a role in economic and intellectual leadership in supporting the institutional strengthening, financing of development projects and the economic, social and integration. Thus, Herrera subscribed to the model of regional economic integration to consolidate industrialization designed by Prebisch and ECLA. These words of Prebisch (1986) allow us to see his coincidences with Herrera:

> If we aim to integrate ourselves as vigorous and egalitarian participants with the rest of the world economy, we must transform our economic relations with foreign countries at the root and this basically implies modifying the structure of our international trade, incorporating increasingly industrial products in the total of our exports (. . .) Faced with this huge challenge that our countries are addressing, the question is raised in terms of whether each one can do it separately or if, on the contrary, the vigorous integration of everyone's efforts is indispensable. (. . .) The answer is obviously affirmative in the second approach, because in the case of Latin America, integration will not only be a posterior manifestation of technical progress and the elevation of development levels, but it is a *sine qua non conditio* to achieve such superior levels.
>
> (pp. 201–202)

This text shows that Herrera ratified one of the ECLA's premises, namely, that the way Latin America had been inserted into the global arena needed to be modified and that industrialization was required. Like Prebisch and ECLA, he believes that that task would be done better through a regional effort instead of individual action of each state. Such ideas were ratified based on the experience of LAFTA. Herrera favored this process, and even if he considered that the regional initiative had shortcomings, it was better than the bilateralism that predominated before LAFTA. However, he had reasons to criticize that regional bloc. Despite LAFTA, Herrera (1967a) described Latin America like an "archipelago" of isolated economies. In his words:

> Among these economic islands we have established in recent years, in the case of LAFTA, the bridges of trade liberalization; but we already see that, in order to create a dynamic flow of intra-regional exchange, we need more advanced integration policies that are expressed in a mechanism that encourage and oriented large investments in regional infrastructure and industries conceived according to an expanded regional market.
>
> (p. 218)

This notwithstanding, Herrera went well beyond Prebisch and ECLA when analyzing Latin American regionalism. For him, even if economic integration as a mechanism to achieve development was important, it was not enough. In other words, Latin American regionalism was much more than economic integration. This is in the basis of his idea of Latin America as a "grand broken nation" ("*una gran nación desecha*" in Spanish). Herrera clearly noted that regionalism in Latin America is not something that began with ECLA's proposals of a Latin American Common Market but with the ideas and proposals of Latin American leaders and thinkers, in particular Simón Bolivar, but also Andrés Bello and Eugenio María de Hostos (Herrera, 1983a; Herrera, 1967c, pp. 158–178). In *América Latina Integrada*, a book written by Herrera in 1967, the author asserts: "The Latin American nation is not a fictitious entity. Underlying at the root of our modern states, it persists as a vital force and profound reality" (Herrera, 1967b, pp. 47–48). This nation had been divided after the wars of independence. The idea of a single nation implies common values and views of the world and, of course, a similar language and religion; but above all the idea of a nation implies a common identity: a Latin American identity (Herrera, 1983b).

If Latin America is a single nation, there must be a "Latin American nationalism", a continental Latin American nationalism. As the nation is broken, divided, mechanisms to reunify it must be furthered, and regional economic integration is certainly one of them, but not the only one. Thus, Herrera promoted the cultural integration of Latin America. In this sense, he wrote in 1983: "The Latin American being has its own connotation through its intrinsic force towards permanent cultural integration" (Herrera, 1983b, p. 13). This would be achieved by promoting regional policies on culture and education, one example of which was the Andrés Bello agreement subscribed in 1970 in the framework of the Andean Pact. Herrera also supported political and economic cooperation, in particular the creation of the SELA in 1976 (Herrera, 1986). Even proposed the political integration of Latin American countries. This was a bold proposal due to the importance of sovereignty for many Latin American leaders. Nevertheless, he asked: "is premature and utopian to consider at this time the need to work for the political integration of Latin America?", and responded that, "we resolutely believe not; we are convinced that political integration is an imperative that we cannot continue to neglect" (Herrera, 1967b, p. 53). And he concludes:

> Latin America needs to carry out its deed of political unity, not only because through it, it will be able to give content and effectiveness to economic integration and common well-being, but also because that collective achievement will bring about the creation of spiritual forces that will allow to consolidate the beliefs in our cultural values and to avoid that the expressions of this continent are only copy of foreign concepts.
>
> (Herrera, 1967b, p. 53)

For all these reasons, it is not an exaggeration to consider Felipe Herrera as a leading figure in the promotion of regionalism in the 20th century in Latin America.

Explaining diplomats' and technocrats' political action: autonomy and development as variables

Autonomy and development have been described as two factors that explain the resilience of Latin American regionalism (Rivarola Puntigliano & Briceño-Ruiz, 2013). If one analyzes the political action of both diplomats and technocrats, it is easy to observe their influence on regional integration. The long-term historical analysis allows confirming that throughout Latin American history, autonomy and development have been behind the regional initiatives. The six cases that have been examined in this chapter allow us to confirm such an assertion.

Autonomy was clearly a variable considered by Alamán, Rio Branco and Caputo in three different periods of Latin American history. After the struggle for independence, the new fight for the new Latin American nations was not only being sovereign nations but also autonomous ones. That seemed to be difficult to achieve. Spain had abandoned the American continent, but other imperial powers, in particular France and the United Kingdom, began to display their diplomatic strategies to influence in the decisions of the states. Irregular credits, unfair trade agreements or demand for special treatment of the citizens (from France and the UK) in the new nations allowed to glimpse an asymmetric pattern of relations between Latin America and the main global powers. By the same token, the Mexicans were the first ones to realize that the US would not be a brother of an "American family of nations", as the separation of Texas in 1836 and the expansionist war in in 1846–1848 demonstrated. Filibusterism in the 1850s and open interventionism in the 1890s and 1900s evidenced the US pretensions of hegemony in the Western Hemisphere.

Those facts were perceived by Alamán and explain his Family Pact. He rejected the signing of unequal trade agreements that some Latin American countries, like Argentina, Brazil and Colombia, had signed with the UK. He found that pattern of trade the replication of colonial bonds that had to be eliminated. That is the reason why he fostered the creation of an embryonic economic community through the signing of trade agreements. As analyzed, the Family Pact had a political dimension expressed in instruments of common dialogue with Spain and the Vatican or the creation of mechanisms to resolve the border disputes among the Hispanic American countries. In the case of Rio Branco, there was also a commitment to creating regional mechanism such as the ABC treaty to deal with issues such as political instability or peace and security. These were embryonic attempts at regional cooperation in South America. It is true that Rio Branco believed in Pan-Americanism and fostered closer relations with the US, but as described in this chapter, that commitment had limits, as expressed in the rejection of the internationalization of the

Amazon River or the crisis in Acre. It is important to highlight that mechanisms such as the ABC treaty were promoted in a moment in which the Latin American idea had lost vitality in terms of institutionalization of cooperation. Although at the beginning of the 20th century, thinkers such as José Enrique Rodó, José Martí or Manuel Ugarte furthered "Latin America" as an idea to unify the former Spanish and Portuguese territories, in the continental political scenario, Pan-Americanism had prevailed since 1889. Hispanic American congress as those held in Lima in 1846 and 1865 or Santiago in 1856 were not convened anymore. The Pan-Americanism, under the aegis of the US, had become the institutional framework through which the Latin America countries where met. The ABC treaty was a first attempt to break with the hegemony of Pan-Americanism by gathering Argentina, Brazil and Chile, at that moment the richest countries in South America. The aim was for the ABC to have a single voice in regional affairs, even vis-à-vis the US, as the Niagara Falls mediation demonstrated. A similar situation would take place six decades later in a quite different regional and global context. When Alamán proposed the Family Pact, the US was not the main concern, but Spain, the UK and France. In the Rio Branco era, the US was already an emerging global power. In the 1980s, the US was a superpower in conflict with the Soviet Union and led by Reagan, a strong anti-communist president convinced that Latin America was the back yard of the US, in which external forces had to be expelled. Similarly, regionalism was weakened in most of the sub-continent. Even if initiatives such as the Andean Pact or the CACM had shown some progress in the 1970s, the debt crisis and the military conflict in the isthmus had affected them. In the Southern Cone, the military dictatorships in Argentina, Brazil, Chile and Uruguay had no interest in regional integration and cooperation. That was the context in which Caputo (led by Alfonsín) began to deploy his diplomatic action. He was a crucial actor in promoting the "Support Group" that strengthened the power of the Contadora Group to balance the interventionist policy of Reagan in Central America and would lead afterwards to the creation of the Rio Group. Caputo also furthered the Cartagena Consensus to deal with the debt crisis. Even if this initiative failed, it was an attempt to create a Latin American space for dialogue and concertation in a critical issue for the region at that moment. Last but not least, Caputo fostered the bilateral integration with Brazil, putting aside decades of misunderstanding between both regions and eliminating hypothesis of conflict. This certainly meant an increasing bargaining power for both countries. The final result was the creation of MERCOSUR, a space of economic integration, defense of democracy and join action in trade issues, as expressed in the negotiations with the US in the framework of the Free Trade Area of the Americas (FTAA) process and the negotiations with the EU. Thus, if we see a line of time in the actions of Alamán, Rio Branco and Caputo, we can perceive that the search for an increasing of room to maneuver was a goal behind their diplomatic actions. Autonomy is then a factor that explains their proposal, and it allows us to consider it as a factor to account for the resilience of regionalism.

Development has been another variable present in the political actions of diplomats and technocrats. Alamán is a peculiar case because, as we have seen, he was concerned about the autonomy of the new republics, but he also gave importance to development. His interest in promoting industrialization in Mexico and his proposal of a development bank (el Banco de Avio) show that for him, his country (and maybe Hispanic America) was not doomed to be a producer of raw materials. For him, industrialization had to be fostered, and the creation of a web of trade agreements provided a market for some of those productions. Thus, it is not an exaggeration to describe Alamán as one of the beginners of the "industrialist tradition" in Latin America, continued later by Alejandro Bunge, Raúl Prebisch, Felipe Herrera, Aldo Ferrer and Helio Jaguaribe, among others. Prebisch and Herrera continued that tradition in the 20th century. Both are interesting examples of scholars who theorize about economic development and economic integration at the same time as they were international civil servants in international organizations such as the International Monetary Fund, ECLA, IAD and UNTADC. From those positions, they promoted concrete actions to advance regional initiatives. Prebisch is without a doubt a leading figure; we can describe his as a "life devoted to regional integration and development". His original theoretical contributions and his concrete actions to promote a Latin American common market made him a reference. And, as beforehand explained, for Prebisch, economic integration was a tool to achieve economic development. Herrera subscribed to those ideas and also highlighted the importance of industrialization in the frame of regional market and the need of an institution to finance it. That was, for him, the IAD. Thus, development has been a variable considered by these actors when promoting their regional initiatives. This is a factor that must be consider when analyzing the resilience of regionalism in Latin America.

Conclusions

This chapter shows that both diplomats and technocrats have promoted regionalism in Latin America since the early years of independent life. This long-term historical analysis demonstrates that the resilience of regionalism in that part of the world, to some extent, is the result of their political action. Actor behavior in global affairs is conditioned to the opportunities and constrains of the international system as well as the domestic politics. Agents behave in the context of systemic-structural forces. They are not slaves of those forces, but neither can they evade their action. The action of Latin American diplomats and technocrats was not an exception of this premise.

The six actors analyzed in this chapter acted in different historical contexts. These actors reacted to situations in the international system that put their states at stake, but they also perceived the internal backwardness both economic and institutional of their nations. These factors impeded a consolidation of their nations as autonomous players in the world scenario and also maintained a situation of fragility and inequality as a result of the lack of economic development. Most of them witnessed structural changes in the international system as the consolidation of UK imperialism and later the emergence of the US as a global power in the early 1900s, the Cold War and its end in the 1980s. In all those different contexts, they believed that regionalism was an option for Latin America. They understood that regional integration and cooperation could be a mechanism to promote autonomy and development. The political action of technocrats and diplomats analyzed under a long-term historical approach allow demonstration of that argument.

Diplomats were mostly concerned with autonomy. Alamán is a controversial figure in Mexican history due to his conservative ideas, but it would be a historical injustice to ignore his contribution to the formation of the regional idea in what would be known later as Latin America. His concern about the US expansionism or his criticism to the signing of unequal trade agreements evidenced that external threats were on the basis of his convictions on the need of regional unity. It is true, he never used the expression "autonomy", but his political and economic ideas are clearly related with the goal of widening the room to maneuver of the young Hispanic American states. Rio Branco was also a controversial figure due to a so-called unwritten alliance with the USA and his views on the Monroe Doctrine, but it is difficult to deny that in his own way, he fostered a diplomatic rapprochement in South America. He was mostly concerned with achieving the stability in South America without foreign intervention, namely, without the intervention of extra-regional powers. Similar to Alamán, Rio Branco never used the category "autonomy", but his proposals such as the ABC clearly had goals that can be described as "autonomist". This was also the case of Caputo, who managed a complex scenario of a weakened Latin America after the era of dictatorships and in the middle of the debt crisis and civil war in the 1980s, where autonomy seemed to be quite weak, but he believed in regional solutions. The Cartagena Consensus, the Support Group to Contadora (that would lead to the Rio Group) and the bilateral rapprochement with Brazil, the initial step towards the creation of MERCOSUR, are regional mechanisms that Caputo helped to create.

The same argument is valid when referring to Prebisch, Urquidi and Herrera. They were clearly cases of "defiant bureaucrats" who were politically committed to improve the economic situation of Latin American countries, in particular economic development. They were concerned on how to transform economic integration into a mechanism to achieve the economic development of Latin America. Prebisch is without doubt a leading figure in establishing a link between economic integration and development. In fact, as argued in another paper (Briceño-Ruiz, 2017), Prebisch's approach to regional economic integration is an original Latin American contribution to the debates on the issue that, in some aspects, challenged the mainstream. Urquidi and Herrera followed Prebisch's ideas but made their original contributions. Urquidi, for example, understood that the economic heterogeneity of Latin America did not allow establishing a common market including all the countries. For him, Central American countries should first further their regional unity, and afterwards, they should enter into a Latin American common market. Herrera was an outstanding figure that successfully combined the political, economic, historical and cultural analysis to explain the need for regional unity. This was materialized with concrete political actions when he was at the IDB in the 1960s.

All these actions of these political actors (diplomats and technocrats) maintained regionalism alive, despite the crises and setbacks. They made regionalism resilient. And their actions were linked to two goals that the Latin American countries have been seeking for decades: autonomy and development.

Notes

1 ECLA is known in Spanish as CEPAL (Comisión Económica para América Latina), but we prefer to use the English acronym ECLA.
2 LAIA (Latin American Integration Association) is the acronym used in English when referring to ALADI, but it is not very well known. In cases similar to ALADI or when referring to institutions of blocs that don't have an English acronym, we use the Spanish ones.
3 The Drago Doctrine refers to a principle proposed by the minister of foreign affairs of Argentina (1902–1903), Luis María Drago. The doctrine was announced as a Latin American response to the threat of military intervention of Great Britain, Germany and Italy in Venezuela to collect debts. The doctrine asserts that "The public debt cannot occasion armed intervention nor even the actual occupation of the territory of American nations."
4 The Itaipú is a dam built in the Paraná River, the border between Brazil and Paraguay. Argentina contested the construction of the dam because it could alter the flow of the Paraná River. This created diplomatic tensions between Argentina and Brazil in the 1970s.

References

Aggarwal, V. K., Espach, R. H., & Tulchin, J. S. (2004). *The strategic dynamics of Latin American Trade*. Stanford: Stanford University Press.

Alexander, R. J. (1990). Import substitution on in Latin American retrospect. In J. L. Dietz & D. J. V. Dilmus (Eds.), *Progress towards development in Latin America. From Prebisch to technological Autonomy* (pp. 15–28). Boulder, CO and London: Lynne Rienner Publishers.

Bengoechea, T. F. (2007). José María Da Silva Paranhos, Barón de Río Branco. Culminación de una exitosa política de límites. *Épocas, 1*, 125–143.

Bernecker, W. L. (1988). Foreign interests, tariff policy and early industrialization in Mexico 1821–1848. *Ibero-Amerikanisches Archiv, 14*(1), 61–102.

Bielschwosky, R. (2009). Sixty years of ECLAC: Structuralism and neo-structuralism. *CEPAL Review, 97*, 171–192.

Briceño-Ruiz, J. (2017). Raúl Prebisch and the theory of regional economic integration. In M. Margulis (Ed.), *The global political economy of Raúl Prebisch* (pp. 79–95). Abingdon: Routledge.

Bueno, C. (2012). Rio Branco e a política internacional de sua época. Barão do Rio Branco. In M. Gomes Pereira (org.), *Barão do Rio Branco: 100 anos de memória* (pp. 253–290). Brasília: FUNAG.

Burns, E. B. (1964). Rio Branco e a sua política externa. *Revista de História, 58*, 367–381.

Burns, E. B. (1966). *The unwritten alliance: Rio-Branco and Brazilian-American relations*. New York: Columbia University Press.

Caputo, D. M. (2015). *Un péndulo austral: Argentina entre el populismo y establishment.* Buenos Aires: Capital Intelectual.

Caputo, D. M., & Sábato, J. F. (1991). Perspectivas de la integración política económica continental. La integración de las democracias pobres: oportunidades y peligros. *Estudios Internacionales, 24*(94), 194–208.

Conduru, G. F. (1998). O subsistema americano, Rio Branco e o ABC. *Revista Brasileira de Política Internacional, 41*(2), 59–82.

Doratioto, F. F. M. (2000). A política platina do Barão do Rio Branco. *Revista brasileira de política internacional, 43*(2), 130–149.

Economic Commission for Latin America (ECLAC). (1950). *The economic development of Latin America and its principal problems.* New York: United Nations Department of Economic Affairs.

Frankenhoff, Ch. A. (1962). The Prebisch thesis: A theory of industrialism for Latin America. *Journal of Inter-American Studies, 4*(2), 185–206.

Galeana, P. (1992). Lucas Alamán y Escalada. In Secretaría de Relaciones Exteriores (Ed.), *Cancilleres de México* (pp. 57–75). México: Instituto Matías Romero de Estudios Diplomáticos.

Garay, C. (2012). Las carreras armamentistas navales entre Argentina, Chile y Brasil (1891–1923). *Historia crítica, 48*, 39–57.

Garay Vera, C. (2008). El Acre y los asuntos del Pacífico: Bolivia, Brasil, Chile y Unidos, 1898–1909. *Historia, 41*(2), 341–369.

Gardini, G. L. (2005). Two critical passages on the road to MERCOSUR. *Cambridge Review of International Affairs, 18*(3), 405–420.

Gomez Hoyos, R. (1969). Bolívar, primer diplomático de la libertad americana. *Boletín Cultural y Bibliográfico, 12*(3), 5–33.

Hernández Jaimes, J. (2016). La metrópoli de toda la América. Argumentos y motivos del fallido hispanoamericanismo mexicano, 1821–1843. *Estudios de Historia Moderna y Contemporánea de México, 51*, 19–36.

Herrera, F. (1967a). *El desarrollo de América Latina y su financiamiento.* Buenos Aires: Águila.

Herrera, F. (1967b). *América Latina integrada.* Buenos Aires: Losada.

Herrera, F. (1967c). *Nacionalismo Latinoamericano.* Santiago de Chile: Editorial Universitaria.

Herrera, F. (1983a). Vigencia de Bolívar. *Integración Latinoamericana. Atenea (Concepción), 44*, 37–57.

Herrera, F. (1983b). Aspectos culturales de la integración latinoamericana. *Integración Latinoamericana, 8*(79), 12–22.

Herrera, F. (1986). *América Latina: Desarrollo e Integración.* Santiago de Chile: Editorial Emisión.

Herrera León, F. (2013). Lucas Alamán, estadista y artífice de las misiones por un "Pacto de Familia". *Revista Mexicana de Política Exterior, 97*, 167–190.

Lafer, C. (2009). Brazil and the world. In I. Sachs, J. Wilheim, & P. Pinheiro (Eds.), *Brazil: A century of change* (pp. 101–119). Chapel Hill, NC: The University of North Carolina Press.

Lins, A. (1965). *Rio-Branco (O Barão do Rio Branco): biografia pessoal e história política.* São Paulo, Brazil: Companhia Editorial Nacional.

Ocampo, J. A. (2001). Raúl Prebisch and the development agenda at the dawn of the twenty-first century. *CEPAL Review, 75*, 23–37.

Pinedo, J. (2009). Felipe Herrera y su proyecto de integración latinoamericana. Apuntes para una biografía intelectual. *Revista Universum, 24*(1), 162–180.

Potash, R. (1953). Alamán y el Banco de Avío. *Investigación económica, 13*(4), 499–511.

Prebisch, R. (1964). *Towards a new trade policy for development. Report by the Secretary-General of the United Nations Conference on Trade and Development.* New York: United Nations.

Ricupero, R. (2000). *Barón de Rio Branco.* Buenos Aires: Nueva Mayoría.

Rivarola Puntigliano, A., & Appelqvist, Ö. (2011). Prebisch and Myrdal: Development economics in the core and on the periphery. *Journal of Global History*, *6*(1), 29–52.

Rivarola Puntigliano, A., & Briceño-Ruiz, J. (Eds.). (2013). *Resilience of regionalism in Latin America and the Caribbean: Development and autonomy*. New York: Palgrave.

Small, M. (2009). *The forgotten peace: Mediation at Niagara Falls, 1914*. Ottawa: University of Ottawa Press.

Urquidi, V. L. (1998). Hacia una perspectiva para la Cepalc en el siglo XXI. *Estudios Internacionales*, *31*(121–122), 115–123.

Urquidi, V. L. (2005). *Otro siglo perdido. Las políticas de desarrollo en América Latina (1930–2005*. México: Fondo de Cultura Económica.

Vázquez, J. Z. (1991). El Pacto de Familia. Intentos mexicanos para la integración hispanoamericana 1830–1847. *Revista de Indias*, *51*(193), 545–570.

Vidigal, C. E. (2016). Río Branco, los tratados de ABC y la construcción de la Potencia Cordial. In I. Matus Matus & G. Aranda Bustamante (Eds.), *A 100 años del ABC: desafíos y proyecciones en el marco de la integración regional* (pp. 35–53). Santiago de Chile: CESIM-IEI-. Retrieved from https://observatoriolegislativoyparlamentario.files.word press.com/2016/09/100-ac3b1os-abc.pdf

Yañez López, L. M. (2015). Breve presentación historiográfica en torno a dos directrices del pensamiento económico de Lucas Alamán. *Tiempo Económico*, *29*(10), 7–80.

5 The military and Latin American integration

Andrés Rivarola Puntigliano

Introduction

There is a persistent view of Latin American military as anti-popular, pro-oligarchic, or subordinated to imperial designs. There are indeed good reasons for this. The military forces have often played a role in such issues as *praetorianism* and human rights violations, contributing to the perception of Latin American democracies as feeble and dominated by military-supported elites and autocratic *caudillos*. However, this view can sometimes be overly general and ignores the fact that Latin America also has a long and rich democratic history, hosting some of the oldest republics of the modern world, and serves as an "extraordinary laboratory for examining democratic movements, ideas, and institutions" (Drake, 2009, p. 1). The military has played a part in these developments as well. During different periods, military forces have been key agents behind progressive initiatives, deeply connected to popular demands. These have often had anti-oligarchic, anti-imperialist, pro-democratic, socialist and development-oriented agendas (Rouquié, 1987). A tenet of this chapter is that ideas concerning regional integration and of military forces supporting these notions have, to a great extent, been related to this line of action. Hence, the military can be regarded as one of the agents that might explain the 'resilience' of regional integration in Latin America.

As addressed here, military forces have many times been connected to regional integration through macro-regional geopolitical and nationalist visions. I will refer to this as the 'geopolitics of integration'. This can be expressed in different ways. In some cases, military-supported projects have had a close discursive connection to the *pueblo* concept, implying a closer attachment to social movements and macro-nationalist projections such as the *Patria Grande* (Great Fatherland). In others, there might be a more authoritarian position taken. As pointed out in this study, there have been cases in which the geopolitics of integration and development were pursued through authoritarian means: sometimes in confrontation with what at various points has been referred to as the *pueblo* (popular sector social movements), and at other times seeking a closer connection. *Pueblo* or not, the main goal of this chapter is to address the notion that the military have been an important and, in some cases, even a key agent concerning the promotion of regional integration. The relevance of the armed forces in Latin American societies and political structures gives this study a particular importance. After all, the military still represent one of the most popular institutions in the region, currently, with substantially higher support than political parties, the government or congress (Latinobarómetro, 2015, p. 7; Pion-Berlin & Carreras, 2017).

The first section of this chapter places our theme of study, military and regional integration, within the broader field of analysis of civil–military relations in Latin America. The aim is to place my object of study within the framework of broader analysis on the role of the military in Latin America. In the second section, the study turns to a historical exploration referred to as the 'soldier and the *pueblo*', which aims to explain and understand the roots of what here is called 'popular geopolitics'. The following section turns to an analysis of the geopolitics of integration and development, with examples of the different directions mentioned. This will be outlined in greater detail in the sections related to more specific analysis of cases from different Latin American countries.

Analysing the military in Latin America

An important dimension in the analysis of armed forces in Latin America is concerned with the dimension called 'civil–military relations'. During the 1960s, research along this track focused on military regimes and political interventions. One example is the work of Robert Putnam, who highlighted two important issues: that social mobilization "clearly increases the prospects for civilian rule" and that "economic development seems to encourage, rather than to inhibit, military involvement in politics" (Putnam, 1967, p. 107). Putnam was particularly puzzled about the latter point, which was later taken up in Guillermo O'Donnell's study of the military regimes during the 1970s, in which he referred to the concept of 'bureaucratic-authoritarianism' (BA). According to O'Donnell (1978, p. 6), BA should be seen as a pattern of domination that corresponds to a stage of transformations in the mechanisms of capital accumulation of society. Such changes were, in his view, "part of the 'deepening' process of a peripheral and dependent capitalism characterized by extensive industrialization".

With the wave of democratization in Latin America during the 1980s, research became more concentrated in the institutionalization of civilian control over the military and the insertion of the latter into a democratic system. Criticism of O'Donnell's model was tendered, particularly to what was seen as a misleading appearance of uniformity, regarded as "inadequate to propose a relationship between economic development and political change" (O'Brien & Cammack, 1985, p. 6). One of the specific issues that was pointed out was inconsistency in understanding the variety of cases and outcomes. A good example was the contrasting cases of Chile and Brazil. While the latter strengthened its pre-coup state-led developmentalist orientation and had a (comparatively) much less repressive regime (Stepan, 1988), the former consolidated a neo-liberal oriented technocratic structure linked to high levels of violence. Another example could be found in the differences in degrees of technocracy and market-oriented reforms in Chile and Uruguay (Rivarola Puntigliano, 2003).

O'Donnell himself was aware of the shortcomings of the original model due to tensions that he later saw in the BA state. According to him, behind its *façade*, BA was subject to contradictions and dilemmas, arising from its difficulty to legitimize itself (O'Donnell, 1979, p. 286). At the core of the tension was its contradiction in aiming to "[statize] the idea of the nation", at the same time as it suppressed citizenship with a "prohibition of appeals to the *pueblo* and to social class as basis for making demands for substantive justice" (O'Donnell, 1979, p. 294). A visible element of this contradiction was to foster a denationalization of civil society in favour of international capital through the armed forces, "the most nationalistic and least capitalistic of the state institutions" (O'Donnell, 1979, p. 301).

This situation was highly confrontational within the armed forces themselves. While all agreed on an appeal to the 'nation' for supreme justifications related to security, there were dividing lines between those upholding appeals to the *pueblo* and social inclusion and those upholding status based on traditional structures and alignments to foreign powers. The sector more clearly aligned with regional integration is to be found within the first group, which sought changes in the subordinated position of their countries along a geopolitics of integration and development. That is the case of armed forces supporting and promoting national developmentalist projects with strategic goals linked to industrialization and autonomy. In some cases, they sought a closer alignment to popular movements and democratic-oriented political structures. As explained further in what follows, in terms of pro-integrationist and development-oriented strategies, there were at least three differences between various armed forces: (a) those linking their doctrine to 'popular' social movements, (b) those following an authoritarian developmentalist model, and (c) those taking an intermediate position.

A review of the literature on civil–military relations shows that these 'developmentalist' and pro-integrationist forces are often neglected, particularly those upholding a democratic and popular developmentalism. When mentioned, these are usually inserted under the label of 'populism', epitomized by Juan Domingo Perón (1895–1974) and the Justicialist movement in Argentina. Taking this vantage point, scholars such as Kacowicz (2000) see Latin American geopolitics as related to a pernicious, aggressive and expansionary strand that is related to the 'organic state', revisionism and revanchism (p. 96). In Kacowicz's opinion, a change from these 'pernicious geopolitical perspectives' became more dominant through more cooperative geo-economic perspectives that gained force after the formation of the Common Market of the South (MERCOSUR) in 1991.

While sharing the view that there was a change during the 1990s, compared to the heyday of military rule during the 1970s and 1980s, I disagree with the way in which 'geopolitics' is described. Scholars such as Jack Child (1979, 1985) present a more nuanced view of the different lines of thinking and action among the armed forces. Yet even Child described the action of military such as Perón's as 'aggressive', in search of a 'greater Argentina' (1979, p. 96). Perón might have sought a 'greater Argentina' but, as outlined in what follows, it was within the framework of South American geopolitical integration and of the greater regional nationhood of a Latin American *Patria Grande*. In sum, there were (and still are) Latin American military forces that are pro-oligarchic, anti-popular or 'despoilers of democracy' (Diamint, 2015, p. 14), but civic–military relations have also been formulated as a kind of "brotherhood between the armed forces and the people" (Diamint, 2015, p. 112). As suggested in this chapter, this is generally related to a 'geopolitics of development', in which the relation between development, integration and the idea of national and even continental '*pueblo*' are central components.

The soldier and the pueblo

Civil–military relations can be thought of as having three dimensions: (a) government–military relations, (b) broader military–state relations, and (c) civil society–military relations. With regard to the *pueblo*, the focus is on the last dimension. A deeper understanding of the role of the military in Latin America needs to go beyond Samuel Huntington's (1957) focus on 'soldier and state' (or government) by analysing what scholars, such as David R. Mares (2014, p. 218), see as the "key role of society in civil–military relations". In Mares's view, the degree of functions and prerogatives given or taken by the military are largely dependent on acceptance and accountability from the civil society. In accordance with this dimension, I introduce the concept of *pueblo* because it has been often framed in this way by sectors of the armed forces themselves.

A conceptualization of *pueblo* is more complex than simply translating the word as the English word 'people'. In dealing with the military, the idea of the *pueblo* needs to be related to a form of *raison d'être* of the military, which is the defence and, at some point, the embodiment of the 'nation'. There is also an interesting historical origin of the concept of pueblo. According to the Spanish philosopher José Ortega y Gasset, the concept of *populus* had its origin in Rome, where it was used to call the citizens ready for war or what the French in 1790 would call 'a nation in arms'. Thus, *populus* would mean "all the citizens together in front of danger" (Ortega y Gasset, 1966, 159).

Some equate the idea of *pueblo* to 'populism'. Yet 'populism' is a rather unclear concept, often used in a pejorative way, treating populism as synonymous with different forms of authoritarianism. As Francisco Panizza (2008, p. 83) has pointed out, as in all other logics that are part of the democratic imaginary, if pushed to its extremes, populism might be incompatible with democracy. Rather, as Panizza adds, the compatibility between populisms and democracy depends on specific articulations of populist, liberal and republican logics. This is not the place to go into great detail on this debate. Rather, my aim here is to understand the leverage of the idea of the 'popular' or *pueblo* among the armed forces and in their relation to national-popular expressions. In relation to regional integration, the idea of the *pueblo* has, in some cases, acquired a regional dimension. This is, for example, the case of visions from sectors of the Catholic Church, which promote Latin America as a geopolitical nation, the home of a united *pueblo* with common ideas of development, anti-imperialism, Christianity and solidarity (Rivarola Puntigliano, 2019, p. 3). The 'geopolitics of integration' is an outcome of this.

In the case of Latin America, the 'commitment' of military forces towards this line of thinking has been motivated 'for the people' or 'with the people' to take hold of the state and use resources for the promotion of issues as 'development', 'autonomy' and (sometimes) 'democracy'. At some moments in time and in places, these elements are joined together; in others, we find only the first two. Yet for almost all cases, this line of action has implied a more positive stance towards regional integration. A starting point to understand this can be found in a historical perspective that, as Alain Rouquié (1987) rightly points out, "is required if we are to overcome partisan mythologies" (p. 39).

According to Rouquié (1987, pp. 43–44), the history of Latin American military can be divided into three phases: (1) the 'professionalization' of the military, just after the achievement of independence, (2) the creation of national armies, generally under the command of ruling classes, and (3) the modern armed forces, along the line of modernization of states throughout the 20th century. This is a good periodization, but it lacks an earlier phase related to the very inception of armed forces in the war of independence. Rouquié does touch upon this, however, when he says that "to speak about the state in Latin America, it is necessary to consider the role of the army" (1987, p. 38).

Going back to the pre-independence, by the early 19th century, the Spanish American colonies (Brazil followed a different path) were mostly defended by a few detachments of the army of the mother country, blocking local born *criollos* to become higher officers. An important part of the defense forces were though in the hands of local militias, which served to assure the maintenance of internal order. Between 1759 and 1808, the danger of British military actions changed this situation, with the Spanish crown reinforcing its garrisons on the basis of local recruitment, "allowing native-born *criollos* to the officers' ranks in the army" (Rouquié, 1987, p. 45). The incorporation of militias with local-born soldiers and officers was actually a common pattern in all American colonial territories, and part of these forces made the base of the new post-independence national armies.

In the case of Iberian-American lands, non-white people made up much of these forces, and this group also represented a majority of the population. In some cases, ambitious agendas of social inclusion and economic reforms were promoted within the new armies. In the case of the Spanish-speaking regions, there were also ideas of a common 'continental' union (Ramos, 1968, pp. 16, 26). The search for unity in the armies of José de San Martin, Simón Bolívar and Bernardo O'Higgins represented a regional 'national scope' that could be called, using Octavio Ianni's formulation (1988, p. 17), a 'fifth frontier nationalism'. These 'Libertadores' even created a Freemasonry lodge called *Logia Lautaro* to coordinate common efforts in the continental struggle against the Spanish empire.

It is, however, important to remember that, during the wars for independence, royalist forces also recruited troops within the popular classes. Yet the side that finally attracted the broadest sectors of society was that of the *Libertadores*, although they later lost their ability to influence to local oligarchies and foreign interests. In the case of the Spanish-speaking countries, this contributed to the fragmentation of the former empire into separate republics. Hence, after the end of the independence period, the initiatives to form larger confederations of states within the former Spanish territories were set aside by processes of fragmentation that led to the construction of new nation-states, which, to a great extent, still exist. The military played a pivotal role as a consolidating force of the new states, embodying the role of a nation-building institution.

Brazil took a different path, maintaining the monarchic system as well as withholding territorial unity. It did, however, exhibit a pattern of development similar to that of all other new Latin American states throughout the 19th century, that is, (a) export-driven economy, (b) export of raw materials, (c) export concentration to few markets, outside Latin America, (d) oligarchic domination, (e) strong income and ethnic inequalities and (f) weak states. The last point is particularly interesting, since as Rouquié (1987) maintains, "one cannot analyse military power in Latin America without speaking of the state, indeed of a particular form of the state, that of dependent societies" (p. 35). This kind of state contains what Rouquié identifies as a Latin American paradox, that is, "when the productive classes and capitalist elites never fail to manifest an aversion to state control and intervention, however slight, despite the fact that those sectors owe everything to the power of the state" (p. 37).

During the second half of the 19th century, both states and (particularly) the military went through a deep process of modernization and professionalization. Here, the military played a twofold role, reinforcing weak state structures as well as becoming the venue for a process of social mobility and class conflict. New social and, in some cases, 'ethnic' groups became more influential and used the army to challenge the *status quo*. The professionalization efforts during this period were assisted by contracted instructors from European countries and the United States, the latter exerting greater influence in Central America and the Caribbean (Nunn, 2001, p. 16). In the case of European influence, a great deal of Spanish and Portuguese remained, although it was increasingly replaced by French- and German-inspired systems. In the case of the French, there was an important emphasis in the civilizing mission of the army, along with the moral and cultural mentorship of "France's grand *mission civilizatrice*" (Nunn, 2001, p. 20).

In relation to regional integration, an interesting influence was that of German, due to its implications in the idea of *pueblo* and continentalist political geography. During the 1880s, in countries such as Argentina, Bolivia and

Chile, German officers were "contracted to teach, administer, organize, train and write up codes according to their standards that in turn were spread to other countries; as is the case of Chilean experts training Ecuadoreans, Colombians and Salvadorans" (Nunn, 2001, p. 16). An important textbook of German military formation was Colmar Freiherr von der Goltz's *Das Volk in Waffen* (a nation in arms), which stressed relations between the 'people' (*Volk*) and their army. As Nunn explains, based on lessons learned about mass mobilization and mechanization during the Franco-Prussian War, Goltz's book presented an encompassing vision of state, nation and army as an organic whole. According to this view, national security could only be ensured if people were able to serve the interests of the state when needed. In other words, a kind of permanent popular force should always stand ready in case of conflicts (Nunn, 2001, p. 19). This interpretation of an inclusive national ideal of defense would become a challenge to Latin American societies. To a great extent, this view was impregnated with oligarchic civilizatory ideals, marked by neo-colonial doctrines of 'scientific racism' upholding that "national populations could – and should – be whitened over time, through immigration and intermarriage" (Chasten, 2011, p. 219).

As Nunn pointed out, the new military professionalism was regarded as "the willingness and propensity to provide solutions to a country's problems – economic, political, social – based on a military ethos. . . . sometimes called mentality" (2001, p. 15). At times, this 'ethos' found connection with the forces upholding ideas of the 'people'. When mixed with Latin American ideas of nationhood and geopolitical projection, the notion of the 'people' shifted towards embracing the integrated multitudes of Latin American states. This macro-regional nationhood become also identified with the notion of *Patria Grande*.

In these cases, the armed forces encouraged officers to pay attention to domestic affairs by linking 'national security' to the construction of an 'organic whole'. In Latin America, this process would become clearer by the end of the 19th and early 20th centuries, with the crisis of liberalism and the emergence of the concept of 'development', as linked to autonomy and progress. Here, the emerging notion of 'development' acquired two key elements: industrialization and regional integration. When this expanded to military forces, their interpretation of 'development' became connected to another central notion, that of 'nation'. As will be outlined in greater detail, this connection evolved into what can be labelled as the 'geopolitics of development', which had as an outcome in the 'geopolitics of integration'.

Regional integration and the 'geopolitics of development'

Until World War I, the dominant economic model in Latin America was liberal and free trade oriented. The state kept, in general, a low profile concerning production-oriented policies, and both political and economic life were often controlled by export-oriented elites, linked to primary goods. With the breakdown of the international economic system due to the two world wars and the severe depression of the 1930s, this model became exhausted, creating deep social and economic instability across Latin America. One of the solutions to this crisis was concerned with overcoming patterns of subordination towards industrialized countries and giving a stronger and more active role to the state. When the issue of industrialization gained importance in the debate on how to overcome (what were increasingly regarded as structural) weaknesses, two elements appeared: the need to control national resources and the creation of regional markets for locally produced goods, with preference for industrial goods.

This affected the interests of those sectors that had traditionally benefitted from (a) free trade–oriented policies and exports of raw materials, (b) converging interests with non-regional powers and markets supporting this model and (c) control over weak state organizations, financial resources and reduced policies of income distribution. By the early 1920s, many people had joined new political parties and movements claiming to promote economic, political and social change. Within this mass, we find a new social group of first- or second-generation immigrants seeking opportunities, improved conditions and social recognition. They had found themselves increasingly disconnected from local elites and their ideals of nation-state and social order. In many countries, the armed forces were a venue for these people, with their concerns with national transformation. One reason for this was the important commitment of military sectors to the progress of industrialization, where the development of a national arms industry and the state's control over strategic natural resources (such as those related to energy) were regarded as being central to progress. Indeed, the 'economic problem' was a fundamental political problem, with "foreign capital under increasing suspicion and 'planned economies' an increasingly attractive substitute to free-trade models as a way to overcome underdevelopment" (Johnson, 1962, p. 114).

During the post-war period, 'development' became an established concept, together with more advanced analysis and policies related to economic and social planning. The creation of the United Nations Economic Commission for Latin America (CEPAL in Spanish) in 1948 was a major step in this direction. For the first time, Latin America had an intergovernmental organization that represented the region as a whole and was establishing common objectives. Industrialization was a central aim, but it was dependent on regional integration.

CEPAL's experts understood very early that the promotion of efficient industries depended on economies of scale, on strengthening a regional market, on finding synergies in the use of natural resources and on promoting common investments in infrastructure. Early on, CEPAL was committed to assisting in the creation of a Central American common market. During the 1950s, the commission was actively engaged in the promotion of a Latin American common market. To present its argument, CEPAL used a modern economic approach known as 'structuralism' (Prebisch, 1950). The military, among other sectors of society, were inspired by these ideas but they also added other issues such as geopolitics and the nationalist dimension. That was embedded in the new package of ideas that became known as 'developmentalism' (Sikkink, 1991).

'Development' was here linked to the concept of 'autonomy', bringing in dimensions such as foreign policy and defence. This package of ideas has had a strong influence on the armed forces, which, at least since the early 20th century, have increasingly "identified themselves with industrialization. In fact, the technical skills of the military personnel have made them the bearers of modernity as represented by industrialization. Officers have become increasingly concerned with what they consider to be the military liabilities involved in dependence upon more industrially advanced countries for war material" (Johnson, 1962, p. 121).

The commitment of the armed forces along this line became increasingly outspoken and influential, since many political leaders during the mid-20th century were part of the military. Perón was one of the most important and influential of these leaders throughout the region during the 1950s, but there were other high-ranking military/politicians who this applied to as well, including Chilean president (General) Carlos Ibáñez del Campo (1927–1931, 1952–1958), Guatemalan president (Captain) Jacobo Árbenz (1951–1954) and Bolivian president (Colonel) David Toro (1936–1937) and his platform of 'military socialism'. A deeper outline of some of these names and their roles in regional integration comes in what follows. What is relevant here is to outline the differences of the armed forces across the region, between those whose geopolitics of development were democratic and those who were 'authoritarian'. Most of those from the first group had a popular connection, with a closer attachment to popular social movements. Within the second group, one could find a further subdivision between those seeking a closer popular connection and those with an elitist attachment to the geopolitics of development.

To the popular side, one could add names such as Colonel Marmaduke Grove (later a democratically elected candidate)[1] who, for a short period, installed a socialist republic in Chile. Also relevant to this discussion is the leader of the so-called *tenente* revolt in Brazil, Lieutenant Luís Carlos Prestes (1898–1990), who later served as the general-secretary of the Brazilian Communist Party. Finally, more recently, one could also highlight the founder and leader of the Uruguayan left coalition, *Frente Amplio*, General Liber Seregni (1916–2004), who always followed a popular and democratic path. On the 'authoritarian' side, we have the Brazilian military, which ruled the country between 1964 and 1983. In an intermediate position between 'popular' and 'authoritarian' is the case of the Peruvian military during the 1960s and 1970s, in particular with regard to President (General) Juan Velasco Alvarado (1968–1975) and his minister of foreign affairs, (General) Edgardo Mercado Jarrín (1968–1971).

To be sure, all these different currents were in favour of regional integration, and all supported 'development'-oriented agendas that were inclined towards a 'geopolitics of integration', that is, a geopolitical outlook viewing regional integration as a relevant and sometimes central issue of the development and foreign policy agenda of a country. Linked to this, they shared a view of industrialization and active state involvement as key elements for development. The same was true concerning a more autonomous foreign policy, although with greater limitations in those cases promoting 'authoritarian' geopolitics of development. One important difference between these approaches was related to the social composition of reform movements, where the 'popular' joined ranks with social movements to challenge openly national and foreign oligarchic groups. It is also in this 'popular' and social-oriented group where regional integration outlooks might fall into the 'fifth frontier' national identity, such as *Patria Grande*. There is no room here to expand on this, but some cases from different countries will be presented in the next section.

The case of Brazil

In the case of Brazil, it is important to have in mind that in 1889, "the republic was born through a military coup", not a revolution (de Moraes, 1991, p. 48). After a prolonged and atrocious war with Paraguay (1864–1870), the Brazilian military pursued a thorough process of transformation. On the one hand, this meant following a professionalization path, which implied the strengthening of meritocracy, beyond former (imperially linked) class hierarchies. It also meant new and closer interactions between social classes and groups, as well as a national spirit, decoupling officers from local attachment dominated by subnational oligarchies. Along these lines, the army became both a driving force for the abolition of slavery (from which the mass of Brazilian soldiers fighting Paraguay had been recruited) and republicanism.

Later, the army was one of the sectors of society in which socialist ideals gained strength. An example was the well-known military revolt of the 1920s led by Prestes. Even if the majority of the armed forces did not follow Prestes's radical line, it became part of a movement of national transformation. The German ideas were very relevant here, particularly those concerned with the elaboration of new national ideals, linked to development-oriented goals aiming for internal and external geopolitical consolidation. Much of this package of ideas was produced within the emergence of what could be called a Brazilian geopolitical school, created initially by civilians and later followed by the military.

Among the leading names behind the formulation of this school, we find prominent national intellectuals such as João Pandía Calógeras (1925 /1998), Everardo Backheuser (1948) and Mario Travassos (1947), who mixed geographic (spatial) dimensions with historical outlooks, politics and the economy. In the 1930s, there was a first specific linkage to geopolitics in the work of Backheuser, a Brazilian geologist. Drawing on north European geopolitical thought, he focused on the issue of national unity and occupation of space, recommending the internal consolidation of national space with a central role of the state Backheuser (1948). An important step towards the national and regional projection of Brazil was the work of Travassos during the 1930s, which strongly emphasized a 'continentalist' geopolitical outlook (1947). This would soon become a central part of later Brazilian strategic projections from the military and successive civilian governments during the first half of the 20th century.

The 'continentalist' approach can be interpreted in different ways. There were and still are groups that see it in terms of a Brazilian hegemony, a projection of the country as a global power, over and beyond its neighbours. There are also those who see the 'global projection' as being intertwined with different forms of regional integration. As shown elsewhere, Brazilian foreign policy has had a mixture of both sides, with shifting predominance (Rivarola Puntigliano & Briceño-Ruiz, 2017). In the case of integration-oriented positions, it has become more clearly formulated since the emergence of national-popular governments, from the presidency of Getulio Vargas (1930–1945, 1951–1954) to the military coup of 1964. There was, however, a continuity in many of the ideas linked to the geopolitics of development and integration throughout the military regime until its end in 1983.

The Brazilian regional vision has been dominated by a South American scope, even if there has also been room for a Latin American dimension (Preuss, 2011). The military have, however, been more concentrated in the South American framework, as formulated in early geopolitical texts, with emphasis in seeking (South American) geographical 'nodes' or promotion of 'exchange areas' in frontiers (de Meira Mattos, 1977, pp. 111–112). There was also a call for nested regional and global dimensions of convergences (do Couto e Silva, 1955). Even if the issues of 'march to the east' and 'continentalism' are mostly referred to by and with regard to Brazil, during the period of military rule, there were pro–integration-oriented policies, as was the case of a proposal for a customs union with Argentina in 1967, the Amazon's treaty in 1978 and the creation of the Latin American Integration Association (LAIA) in 1980 (Rivarola Puntigliano & Briceño-Ruiz, 2017).

After the end of the military regime, this was followed by the path that was forged through the creation of the Common Market of the South (MERCOSUR) in 1991, followed later by the Union of South American Nations (UNASUR) in 2008. A preamble of MERCOSUR was the collaboration between the Argentinean and Brazilian military forces during the Malvinas/Falklands War in 1982. Industrialization was regarded as a key issue around these regional integration initiatives. Particularly from a Brazilian and Argentinean perspective was where the military were particularly interested and involved in the arms industry. One of the most important documents in relation to regional integration was the white book on national defence (Ministério da Defesa, 2012), where it was stated that:

At the regional level, especially in South America, the relationship between foreign and defence policies must be strong in order to foster and expand integration to empower South American action in the international arena.

It should also be an aggregating factor in enabling the interaction of neighbouring governments in order to prevent threats to the peace and security of the region.

(p. 52)

A new institution in which regional integration, national foreign policy and the armed forces converged was UNASUR's Defence Council. This could be regarded as a 'window of opportunity' to open up dialogue between South American military forces and defence sectors, becoming a platform for different forms of coordination, such as the joint participation at the Misión de Estabilización de las Naciones Unidas en Haití (MINUSTAH); the creation of the combined Chilean-Argentinean peace force, *Cruz del Sur,* or the mixed engineering units of Chile-Ecuador and Argentina-Peru (Comini, 2010, p. 18).

To be sure, conceptualization and reference to 'continentalism' and a 'march to the west' (Ministério da Defesa, 2012, p. 22) still appear in the white book. Contrary to discourse during the military period, integration is not referred to here as a nested cooperation facing non-Western enemies (the communists) or as a footnote in relation to a Brazilian-centred South American space. Rather, South American integration is presented in this document as a strategic objective for Brazilian foreign policy (Ministério da Defesa, 2012, p. 37). The armed forces were part of this; yet more research is needed to determine to what extent this is so and to reveal the internal contradictions concerning these strategies that were elaborated upon by the government at that time. With the more recent shift of power, during the administration of Jair Bolsonaro (2019–), Brazil has been retreating from many of the regional organizations mentioned. Yet one of those who are setting limits to this line of action is the vice president, General António Hamilton Martins Mourão.

The case of Argentina

Another particular case presented in this study is Argentina. As previously mentioned, after the popular origin of the Argentinean army, during the independence period, the army became part of the national oligarchic project. Its role was to combat the enemies of the 'liberal' order, benefiting trading companies based in the city of Buenos Aires and oligarchic export-oriented interests in the agro-food sector. The 'enemies' were, for example, the militias of *gauchos* that grouped in so-called *montoneras* to fight against the armies from Buenos Aires. These *montoneras* were mainly backed by forces opposing free trade-oriented policies and centralization of power in Buenos Aires. There were popular interests here, often led by local oligarchies predominant outside Buenos Aires. With modernization, the export boom of the mid-19th century and the Paraguay war, these local oligarchies united with Buenos Aires, segmenting what is today the Argentinean republic.

The basis of a more modern and professional army was set during the presidency of Julio Argentino Roca (1880–1886, 1898–1904). Contrary to the former line of action that allowed and sometimes even actively sought territorial fragmentation, Roca pursued a strategy of consolidation and expansion of national territory, even if this might mean an aggressive takeover of large territories controlled by indigenous communities. This implied a closer interaction with Brazil, segmented, among other things, by the Brazilian-Argentinean alliance in the war against Paraguay (1864–1870). This was not about integration, but it was a step forward in consolidating areas of interaction and common viewpoints in neighbouring countries.

During the first decades of the 20th century, in which there was a crisis of the free trade–oriented agro-food export-led model, there were new political cleavages and shifts within the Argentinean armed forces. The presidency of Hipólito Yrigoyen (1916–1922, 1928–1930) was a result of these new changes, whereby the Argentinean political system took a major shift towards increasing state involvement and expanding social rights. Within the military forces, visions were still dominated by perceptions of strategic priorities favouring Argentinean insularity. One example is the influential writing of one of the pioneers in Argentinean geopolitics, Admiral Segundo R. Storni. In the early 1900s, Storni presented a vision of Argentina turning towards the sea and being socially and geographically insular in respect to the rest of the continent (Storni, 2009, pp. 28–29). This was a logical position concerning the special trade link that Argentina had had for decades, in particular with Great Britain. Nevertheless, Storni recommended a very friendly position towards neighbouring countries. To protect Argentinean foreign trade, there was, in his view, a need for solidarity and common support from all the American nations: on the one hand, close friendship with Brazil and Uruguay, and on the other, friendship with Chile and Peru as well (Storni, 2009, pp. 91–92). The idea here was not only about having a good neighbourhood but also, as in the case of Chile or Uruguay, of a 'political union' (Storni, 2009, pp. 91–93).

Yet 'insularity' predominated during a time of military intervention in Argentinean politics during the 1920s and '30s. During this period, 'insularity' was accompanied by a hostile position towards the Argentinean labour movement, which had harsh repression as a result. With the new global economic context, the breaking of traditional trade ties with Europe and the crises of liberal models, new positions gained strength within the armed forces. Inspired and informed by German models, as well as ideas related to industrialization and inclusive national thinking, younger military officers desired new structural changes. Among the German models, there are, e.g., Colmar Freiherr von der Goltz's book *Das Volk in Waffen*, which was used in the education of young Argentinean officers. As explained by Nunn (2001), Goltz's: "[n]ineteenth-century treatise stressed relations between the people and their army, making it clear that national security could only be ensured if the populace were able to serve the interests of the state when needed. An entire nation in arms might be needed in future conflicts, and some kind of permanent force should stand ever ready" (pp. 18–19).

Young officers were also inspired by Latin and Ibero-American models and ideals, as well as, in all likelihood, by the *tenentista* movement in Brazil and other military movements across Latin America (see what follows). The same is true for economic ideas concerning state-led promotion of industrialization, customs unions and other kinds of developmental and nationalist proposals. Among these younger Argentinean officers, we find people such as Enrique Carlos Alberto Mosconi. Coming from a family of Italian immigrants, Mosconi was both military officer and engineer. He was highly committed to the policies of reform during the period of Yrigoyen's administration and promoted industrialization and the nationalization of Argentinean natural resources, becoming the first president of the national oil company, *Yacimentos Petrolíferos Fiscales* (YPF). Mosconi travelled tirelessly to communities in Latin America, spreading his ideas throughout the region. These influenced the creation of national companies in such countries as Bolivia, Uruguay and Brazil, where this line of action was also gaining strength during the presidency of Vargas (Ramos, 1968, p. 83).

Mosconi is a good example of the growing importance of the sectors of the army, pursuing a new policy, which saw industrialization as being linked with an alliance with popular sectors. For this reason, he did not support the anti-popular repression from the other strand of the army, which favoured an oligarchic-supported military regime. Even if the anti-popular force held power throughout the 1930s, the end of Argentina's advantageous position in the British-dominated export-led model increased the internal contradictions of the Argentinean society. These fuelled tensions within the armed forces, with the increasing influence of the nationalist *Grupo de Oficiales Unidos* (GOU), which finally led to a new coup and a reorientation of Argentinean policy. Even if anti-communism and pro-industrialisation policies were uniting elements within this group, there was a motley crew of positions: from anti-popular right-wing nationalists to those influenced by socialist ideals seeking national alliances where popular sectors gained central importance.

From the latter group emerged a new dominant leader, General Juan Domingo Perón, who won the democratic election of 1946, supported by sectors of the army in alliance with social movements. Perón advocated a national project on a strong platform of national inclusion, giving a stronger role to the state, industrialization and nationalization (with emphasis on arms production and technology). Another pivotal dimension of this strategy was 'regional integration'. On this issue, Perón and his followers were attracted to a current of thinking that saw a closer intertwinement with the region as an alternative path to foster development.

Regional integration was at the centre of Peron's geopolitical project. It involved, first, a national Argentinean integration and then a South and Latin American regional integration. Perón took his integration proposals to a more ambitious level, speaking of a United States of South America, which was regarded as the geopolitical node of further Latin American integration. This direction required, at the national level, a strategic alliance between the army and the people. At the international level, the conformation of an Argentinean-Brazilian axis would be the central node of South American and Latin American integration (Perón, 2007). The Argentinean nationalism was here inserted in a broader regional nationalism, of the *Patria Grande*, with South American integration as a proximate geopolitical goal.

However, Perón could not eliminate social tensions and structural imbalances in the declining Argentinean economy, leading to economic slowdowns and political turmoil. That was the case of the mid-1950s, when the unity of the army was broken, leading to a coup against Peron's democratically elected government, with subsequent repression of the labour movement and other social forces. Those military members seeking to foster regional integration and, to some extent, a closer relation to the *pueblo* did, however, not disappear. In fact, they came back to power during the brief return of a developmentalist government led by the democratically elected Arturo Frondizi (1958–1962). Among the influential advisors of this governments, we find General Juan E. Guglialmelli, who was director of the *Escuela Superior de Guerra* and of the *Centro de Altos Estudios* and later secretary of the *Consejo Nacional de Desarrollo* (CONADE) during the presidency of Roberto Levingston (1970–1971). Being one of the most important members of the Argentinean geopolitical school, Guglialmelli distanced himself from some of the earlier positions of Admiral Storni. In Guglialmelli's view, Argentina should definitely shift its position from one of peninsular insularity to what he called a 'continental vertebration'. In his view, there were two types of frontiers, the 'internal' (national) and the 'peripheral'. According to his view, the latter (for Argentina, the Southern Cone) was a core political unit in the path towards a united Latin America (Guglialmelli, 1979, p. 22).

Ideas concerning *Patria Grande* linked to the need of industrialization were again a central element. The same was true for those from other leading Argentinean geopoliticians such as Colonel José Felipe Marini, who was an enthusiastic promoter of the line of autonomy, which in his view implied a search for the *Patria Grande*. Marini was perhaps the first to speak of a Latin American 'geopolitics of integration' (Marini, 1987).

Other cases

The case of Chile is interesting and contradictory. A good example is the role of Carlos Ibáñez del Campo. He was, initially, an ally of Marmaduke Grove, who led a fraction of the military that installed a brief Chilean socialist republic in 1925 (Thomas, 1967, p. 26). Later, Ibañez shifted between democratic and authoritarian positions, with both repression of and alliances with popular movements and left-wing–oriented forces, sometimes aligning with traditional oligarchies, at other times confronting them. He was a developmental nationalist, who strongly inclined towards industrialization, a leading role for the state, and regional integration. One step clearly in this direction was signing the Treaty of Lima in 1929, whereby Chile agreed to return the Tacna Province (which had been seized during the War of the Pacific) to Peru. Another was the close interaction with Perón, with regard to the so-called new ABC (Argentina, Brazil and Chile) initiative.

Ibañez shared many of Perón's strategic views concerning South American integration, joining with Brazil but within the framework of greater integration of the Spanish-speaking countries, to counter against the geopolitical size of Brazil. In this regard, Ibañez advocated a 'Union of the South', in line with his minister of finance, Felipe Herrera; he was also surely influenced by the political economy writings of scholars such as the Argentinean Alejandro Bunge, who had outlined the creation of a South American Customs Union (Piñeiro Iñiguez, 2010, p. 546; Bunge, 1940). Of course, as was the case for all Latin American armed forces, the split concerning integrationist policies also existed in Chile. Yet the support towards developmentalist policies was maintained during the 1960s, where Chile was a leader concerning regional-oriented initiatives. The Chilean initiative to create a United Nations Economic Commission for Latin America (ECLA) in 1948 (with its main office in Santiago de Chile), was an early move in this direction. Later on, the Chilean state was a driving force in the creation of the Andean Pact in 1969. However, the anti-popular and regionalist countermovement came from the armed forces themselves, during the administration of General Augusto Pinochet (1973–1989).

In Bolivia, Toro's 'military socialism' had opened the door for state-led policies and closer relation to neighbouring countries. Measures such as the nationalization of petroleum concessions were inspired by Argentinean policies (Klein, 1965, p. 44), which also might have inspired the formation of the military political organization called Radepa (*Razón de Patria*). Radepa was a kind of Bolivian *tenentismo*, advocating inclusion, nationalization and anti-imperialism. This was symbolically important because it was a showcase for a new alliance between *pueblo* and armed forces. All this was also in line with initiatives for regional integration at the time, followed by the later Revolutionary Nationalist Movement (*Movimiento Nacionalista Revolucionario*, MNR) that took Víctor Paz Estenssoro (1952–1956) to the presidency.

Regional integration was also a key element behind the reform policy of Guatemala, which started after 1945 and strengthened during the presidency of Colonel Jacobo Árbenz (1951–1954). It was through the leadership of Árbenz and others in his administration that ECLA was incorporated into plans for Central American integration, perhaps the commission's first inroad into what later came to be one of its central issues: regional integration. The case of Perú is also a relevant case concerning the military. The commitment for regional integration was strong in this country. A central element along this line was the creation of the American Popular Revolutionary Alliance (*Acción Popular Revolucionaria Americana*, APRA) under the leadership of Victor Haya de la Torre during the 1920s.

APRA was probably the first political party to clearly establish Latin American integration as a central issue in its political agenda. Haya de la Torre was a devoted 'continentalist', with close relations and networks across Latin America.

This was the case, for example, with movements such as FORJA (*Fuerza Orientadora Radical para la Joven Argentina*) in Argentina, which was very influential behind the scenes of Perón's and the armed force's ideological positions, particularly regarding regional integration and the notion of *Patria Grande*. Although under Haya de la Torre's leadership, APRA never attained power, the influence of its ideas were highly pervasive, even influencing those who opposed Torre, including the military regime of Velasco Alvarado (1968–1975). This came down to the government opposing popular democratic forces, such as APRA, but incorporating many of its points in its own agenda. The strategic thinking of General Edgardo Mercado Jarrín played an important role here, making Perú a staunch supporter of regional integration. This country was, for example, a founder and strong promoter of the Andean Community, with a particularly relevant role after Chile withdrew from the organization in 1976.

Many more military commanders could be added to the list. There is, for example, the case of the former Mexican president (Brigadier General) Lazaro Cárdenas (1930–1940), whose government accentuated a Latin American-oriented line of action, together with developmentalist and social inclusive policies. Although not being part of a government, it would also be important to mention here the founder and leader of the Uruguayan left coalition, *Frente Amplio*: General Liber Seregni (1916–2004). He was a staunch supporter of regional integration and a key political force behind Frente Amplio's acceptance of Uruguay's incorporation into MERCOSUR in 1991. This line was later fervently adopted by President José Mujica (2010–2015), a member of the Frente Amplio and with good connection to the armed forces on this matter. In this case, there was also outspoken support for the idea of *Patria Grande* and continental regionalism. In the case of the armed forces, the relevance of the region and common regional defense initiatives were clearly marked in the Governments' official documents (Presidencia de la República Oriental del Uruguay, 2014). Important also to remark that the, by then Commander in Chief of the Military forces, General Guido Manini Rios (2015–2019) has now become an influential political leader advocating the importance of *Patria Grande*, regional integration and the influence of the pro-integration philosopher Alberto Methol Ferré (Manini Rios 2019, pp. 40, 61).

Finally, a word here about a military leader who was probably most active in creating policy in favour of regional integration during recent years. I refer of course to Lieutenant Colonel Hugo Chávez Frías, president of Venezuela between 1999 and 2013. This is a more modern case of a popular geopolitics of development. The outlook pursued by Chávez was drawn from a long tradition of ideas and action among Latin American military. In the case of Venezuela, the nationalist advocacy of the national hero Simón Bolívar was linked to the ideas of Latin American *Patria Grande*. Along this line, the political movement led by Chávez and the Venezuelan military forces created a new 'socialist Bolivar', with ideals of social inclusion and income distribution. This was, in turn, connected to principles of 'autonomy', through the rejection of foreign 'imperial' dominance as well as with proposals for 'development' related to industrialization and infrastructure. The Venezuela project forged strong bonds with militaries in Ecuador, Bolivia, Cuba and Nicaragua, within the collaboration framework of the regional integration organization Bolivarian Alliance for the Peoples of Our America (*Alianza Bolivariana para los Pueblos de Nuestra América*, ALBA), originally created in 2004 by the governments of Cuba and Venezuela. After the death of Chávez in 2013 and the deep economic and political crisis of the country since then, all regional initiatives have been severely curtailed, if not directly dismantled.

Conclusion

Regionalist-oriented initiatives among military forces have had different political alignments in different countries and periods of time. As addressed in this chapter, the origin of armed forces in the region was linked to frameworks of action and identities that went beyond the boundaries of current nation-states. These armies were also marked by their popular attachment, with an important role for multi-ethnic militias. During the consolidation of the new Latin American states, the armed forces played a central role, sometimes being the only organization grouping people from the whole country and the bearer of a national idea that was practically non-existent in the rest of society. This period saw an increasing professionalization of the armed forces and their detachment from popular sectors. The armed forces increasingly became a force for modernization, which generally meant to serve the interests of national oligarchies linked to export-led commodity models and foreign powers.

Yet the armed forces, due to their composition, maintained links to popular sectors as well as to officers, who were often recruited from social groups outside established elites. When the liberal oligarchic system of commodity-led exports had broken down by the early decades of the 20th century, new modernizing models appeared. One of the core ideas concerned the need to find alternatives to primary goods dependence, which would lead to industrialization. During the 20th century, this position became known as 'developmentalism'. One of the core issues of developmentalism was to compensate small markets and vulnerabilities in terms of autonomous policies, with regional integration. I refer to this as the 'geopolitics of integration', something that implies a line of action that often clashes with traditional elites and their support groups, often to be found among foreign powers. In some cases, the military integration projects carried a 'socialist' label. In some, there was more authoritarian developmentalism, something linked to the 'people', and in others not. Independent of this status, this chapter intended to show that the Latin American armed forces have been and still are an important source of resilience concerning regional integration.

Note

1 Marmaduke Grove was later founder of Chile's Socialist Party, presidential candidate at the 1932 elections and senator for the Popular Front coalition, which won the presidential election with candidate Pedro Aguirre Cerda.

References

Backheuser, E. (1948). *Curso de Geopolítica Geral e do Brasil*. Rio de Janeiro, Brazil: Gráfica Laemmert Limitada.

Bunge, A. (1940). *Una Nueva Argentina*. Buenos Aires, Argentina: Editorial Guillermo Kraft Ltda.

Calógeras, J. P. (1998). *A Política Exterior do Imperio*, 1925, *1*. Brasília, Brazil: Senado Federal.

Chasten, J. Ch. (2011). *Born in blood & fire: A concise history of Latin America*. Chapel Hill, NC: University of North Carolina.

Child, J. (1979). Geopolitical thinking in Latin America. *Latin American Research Review*, *14*(2), 89–111. Retrieved from www.jstor.org/stable/2502880

Child, J. (1985). *Geopolitics and conflict in South America: Quarrels among neighbours*. New York: Praeger.

Comini, N. (2010). El rol del Consejo de Defensa de la UNASUR en los últimos conflictos regionales. *Nueva Sociedad*, *230*, 14–22.

de Meira Mattos, C. (1977). *A Geopolítica e as Projeções do Poder*. Rio de Janeiro: Livraria J. Olympio Editora.

De Moraes, J. Q. (1991) [1941]. *A Esquerda Militar no brasil: da Conspiração Republican á Guerrilha dos Tenetes*. São Paulo, Brazil: Siciliano.

Diamint, R. (2015). A new militarism in Latin America. *Journal of Democracy*, *26*(4), 155–168.

Do Couto e Silva, G. (1955). *Geopolítica do Brasil* (2a. Edição., pp. 100–187). Rio de Janeiro, Brazil: Livraria José Olympo.

Drake, P. W. (2009). *Between tyranny and anarchy: A history of democracy in Latin America, 1800–2006*. Stanford: Stanford University Press.

Guglialmelli, J. E. (1979). *Geopolítica del Cono Sur*. Buenos Aires: El Cid Editor.

Huntington, S. P. (1957). *The soldier and the state: The theory and practice of civil-military relations*. Cambridge, MA: Harvard University Press.

Ianni, O. (1988). A Questão Nacional na América Latina. *Estudos Avançados, São Paulo*, *2*(1), 5–40. Retrieved from www.revistas.usp.br/eav/article/view/8474/10025

Johnson, J. (Ed.). (1962). The Latin-American military as politically competing group in transitional society. In J. Johnson (Ed.), *The role of the military in underdeveloped countries* (pp. 91–130). Princeton: Princeton University Press.

Kacowicz, A. M. (2000). Geopolitics and territorial issues: Relevance for South America. *Geopolitics*, *5*(1), 81–100. https://doi.org/10.1080/14650040008407668.

Klein, H. (1965). David Toro and the establishment of "military socialism" in Bolivia. *The Hispanic American Historical Review*, *45*(1), 25–52. https://doi:10.2307/2510530

Latinobarómetro. (2015). La Confianza en América Latina 1995–2015, 20 años de Opinión Pública Latinoamericana. *Latinobarómetro*. Banco de Datos en Línea, Santiago de Chile. Retrieved from www.latinobarometro.org

Manini Ríos, G. (2019). *Vengo a Cumplir*. Montevideo: Artemisa Editores.

Mares, D. R., & Martínez, R. (Eds.). (2014). *Debating civil-military relations in Latin America*. Brighton: Sussex Academic Press.

Marini, J. F. (1987). *Geopolítica Latinoamericana de la Integración*. Buenos Aires: Editorial Humanitas.

Ministério da Defesa. (2012). *Defense White Paper/Livro Branco de Defesa Nacional*. Brasilia, Brazil: Ministério da Defesa. Retrieved from www.defesa.gov.br/arquivos/estado_e_defesa/livro_branco/lbdn_2013_ing_net.pdf

Nunn, F. (2001). Foreign influences on the South American military: Professionalization and politicization. In P. Silva (Ed.), *The soldier and the state in South America: Essays in civil-military relations* (pp. 13–37). New York: Palgrave.

O'Brien, P., & Cammack, P. (1985). *Generals in retreat: The crisis of military rule in Latin America*. Manchester: Manchester University Press.

O'Donnell, G. (1978). Reflections on the patterns of change in the bureaucratic-authoritarian state. *Latin American Research Review, 13*(1), 3–38. Retrieved from www.jstor.org/stable/2502640

O'Donnell, G. (1979). Tensions in the bureaucratic-authoritarian state and the question of democracy. In D. Collier (Ed.), *The new authoritarianism in Latin America* (pp. 285–318). Princeton, NJ: Princeton University Press.

Ortega y Gasset, J. (1966). *Una Interpretación de la Historia Universal*. Madrid: Revista de Occidente.

Panizza, F. (2008, December). Fisuras entre Populismo y Democracia en América Latina. In A. Rivarola Puntigliano & A. Garcé (Eds.), *Latin America: Left, right or beyond? Stockholm review of Latin American Studies* (Vol. 3, pp. 81–93). Stockholm: Institute of Latin American Studies, Stockholm University.

Perón, J. D. (2007). *Los Estados Unidos de América del Sur*. Buenos Aires: Corregidor.

Piñeiro Iñiguez, C. (2010). *Perón. La Construcción de un Ideario*. Buenos Aires: Siglo XXI Editora Iberoamericana.

Pion-Berlin, D., & Carreras, M. (2017). Armed forces, police and crime-fighting in Latin America. *Journal of Politics in Latin America, 9*(3), 3–26. https://doi.org/10.1177/1866802X1700900301

Prebisch, R. (1950). *The economic development of Latin America and its principal problems*. New York: United Nations.

Presidencia de la República Oriental del Uruguay. (2014, April). *Política de Defensa Nacional. Un Uruguay Integrado a la Región y Abierta al Mundo*, D/3578. Montevideo, Uruguay.

Preuss, O. (2011). *Bridging the island: Brazilians' views of Spanish America and themselves, 1865–1912*. Madrid: Iberoamericana Vervuert.

Putnam, R. (1967). Toward explaining military intervention in Latin American politics. *World Politics, 20*(1), 83–110. https://doi:10.2307/2009729

Ramos Abelardo, J. (1968). *Ejército y Semi-Colonia*. Buenos Aires: Editorial Sudestada.

Rivarola Puntigliano, A. (2003). *Mirrors of change: A study of business associations in Chile and Uruguay*. Stockholm: Institute of Latin American Studies, Stockholm University.

Rivarola Puntigliano, A. (2019). The geopolitics of the Catholic Church in Latin America. *Territory, Politics, Governance*. https://doi:10.1080/21622671.2019.1687326

Rivarola Puntigliano, A., & Briceño-Ruiz, J. (2017). *Brazil and Latin America: Between the separation and integration paths*. Lanham, MD: Lexington Books.

Rouquié, A. (1987). *The military and the state in Latin America*. Berkeley, CA: University of California Press.

Sikkink, K. (1991). *Ideas and institutions: Developmentalism in Brazil and Argentina*. Ithaca, NY: Cornell University Press.

Stepan, A. (1988). *Rethinking military politics: Brazil and the Southern Cone*. Princeton, NJ: Princeton University Press.

Storni, S. R. (2009) [1916]. *Intereses Argentinos en el Mar* (2nd ed.). Buenos Aires: Armada Argentina.

Thomas, J. R. (1967). The evolution of a Chilean socialist: Marmaduke Grove. *The Hispanic American Historical Review, 47*(1), 22–37.

Travassos, M. (1947). *Projeção Continental do Brasil* (4th ed.). São Paulo: Companhia Editora Nacional.

6 Latin America and the Caribbean

From geopolitics to geopoetics

Liliana Weinberg; Translated by
Ana Laura Magis Weinberg

A chronicle of an integration foretold

I would like to begin, as a tribute to my father, the Argentinian thinker Gregorio Weinberg, with these words of his that seemingly anticipated the relationship between integration and resilience: "Let us interrogate which are the reasons that have led unity of origin to result in a diversity of destinies, and which have caused diversity of developments to demand a unity of destinies" (1982, p. 240).[1]

When discussing integration policies, economic or political dimensions have prevailed, but any integration initiative should be rooted in a cultural dimension. Traditional conceptions of culture have relegated this dimension to little more than legacy or heritage; by doing so, they have underscored the past. However, culture has newly been understood as a way of life, a significant experience, or a creative resource (as critics such as Raymond Williams, Clifford Geertz, and Stuart Hall have noted). Thus understood, culture has now become open to both present and future. We might consider that culture is at the core of Latin American integration, bringing past, present, and future together in the social experience and providing resilience in integration.

The idea of culture also allows us to bring together individuals, local and social groups, and national and transnational entities in order to consider Latin American traditions, assumptions, and experiences as a whole in the light of long-term processes and broad spatial approaches. Inasmuch as we can associate culture with creative imagination, we can observe a relationship between 'instituting' and 'instituted' elements – in Cornelius Castoriadis's terms (1975/1989). We should also keep in mind that creative imagination operates at both a singular and a collective level. Given that culture includes tradition and legacy as well as creation and imagination, we can understand cultural integration as a phenomenon in which resilience becomes essential. In the literal sense, resilience can be considered as the desire to maintain and increase cultural dynamics and to preserve that which has been acquired and to elaborate new contents. However, in a more figurative manner, resilience could be regarded as a way of understanding culture in the long term, with a future perspective and in creative and imaginative terms (taking into consideration, of course, that there will always be a multiplicity of meanings and an openness of the idea of *future*).

There is a special field, the creative and imaginative one including literature and the arts, that has called the attention of many integration projects. We agree that in order to approach cultural integration, it is necessary to consider the relationship between concrete projects and generous and creative perspectives. We also need to consider the specificity of these projects, because it is only from their very specificity that they can contribute to integration. We have to understand these projects not only as resources but also as imaginative contributions to integration. In a wider sense, they generate a geopoetics of regional integration that links territory, language, and experience in order to create new imaginary worlds. Latin America and the Caribbean may be seen as 'integrational designations' in that they connect concrete components with their own potentialities; they are summary of preexistent facts that are interpreted with a future and imaginative perspective - they are as much projects as they are potentialities. They look towards the future, creativity, and imagination, just as culture and integration do.

New specific initiatives arise from the field of arts and literature that converge with these projects of cultural integration. This coincides with the fact that the concept of culture itself has had various changes and redefinitions. Early characterizations of culture, starting with Edward Tylor's foundational definition in *Primitive Culture*, 1871 (2016), understood it as a set of knowledges, capabilities and habits acquired within a society. Newer and more modern definitions have shifted their focus to encompass symbolic and creative elements as well.

Beyond recognizing the importance of culture as a subject, there is much left to do. As the Brazilian Mónica Allende Serra, founder of "Arte Sin Fronteras" (ASF, Art Without Frontiers), wrote between 2002–2003:

> The development chart seems to be based only on economic factors, leaving in the shadows, for those who measure with numbers the advances of integration, the cultural aspects which are sometimes responsible of social balances and imbalances that may give or deny support to economic achievements. The enhancement of the idea of an integral growth of the countries is based on a pluralistic standpoint of development, rejecting a fragmented interpretation of reality and suggesting that all its social, economic and cultural aspects should be situated in the same level of importance. In the light of this outlook, ASF considered that if efforts of every sector are brought together and if this initiative comes from artists, this goal could be reached in the medium-term. Likewise, it is necessary that a permanent effort of debate is born from civil society in order to keep diagnoses up to date and to discuss how to place culture as a priority to governments, highlighting it as the instigator of public policies of any kind.
>
> (Allende Serra, 2002–2003, para. 8)[2]

We should reconsider definitions of culture according to their implicit dimensions of past, present, and future. There are many characterizations that emphasize the element of acquisition, of inheritance: since its inception, culture has been dependent on the past. There has now been a progressive shift towards conceptualizing culture as the possibility to influence and transform the present and also the possibility of performatively influencing the future. The concept of resilience itself has a strong temporal and operative sense and seems to encompass the dimensions of past, present, and future inasmuch as it implies a sense of inheritance and actuality as a project, program, and proposition. This can only be understood by considering a social recognition of the idea of future, which is itself connected to the notion of a never-ending horizon, an active and creative openness towards a time beyond the present. It is from this point that some of the great contemporary specialists that have made interesting contributions to the study of culture and public policies in this matter, such as George Yúdice (2009), propose to see it in an operative and open sense as 'a resource' that could habilitate the possibility of extending itself to other fields, different from integration policies: "The premise that culture pervades all areas of human life -from the conventional anthropological perspective of symbolic reproduction of collective and personal identity, to broader understandings of culture's role in economic growth, governance and security- is today a worldwide commonplace" (Yúdice, 2009, p. 110). George Yúdice also mentions that:

> As should be clear, current understandings and practices of culture are complex, located at the intersection of economic and social justice agendas. Culture is undergoing a transformation that "already is challenging many of our most basic assumptions about what constitutes human society" (Rifkin 10–11). Today, it is nearly impossible to find public statements that do not recruit art and culture either to better social conditions through the creation of multicultural tolerance and civic participation or to spur economic growth through urban cultural development projects and the concomitant proliferation of museums and other venues for cultural tourism. I raise the complexity of the understandings and uses of culture, not as the basis for the rejection of the desirability of instruments and practices that ensure cultural diversity and cultural rights. On the contrary, they are needed ever more in a context in which traditional cultural foundations become porous and crumble, along with legal and political foundations. This said, there are two poles around which most uses of culture cluster: on the one hand, the anthropological understanding, which prioritizes values, worldviews, symbolic reproduction, etc., and on the other hand, the creative element in culture which provides the leading edge in innovation and economic growth in the knowledge and information society. The first pole has been more important in the development of cultural rights, particularly of indigenous peoples, minorities and women, while the second has been at the forefront of creative industries and creative cities projects.
>
> (pp. 114–115)

I consider that envisioning integration as a project can only be possible if done from a perspective of future and attending to the specificity of each of its components. Therefore, literary and artistic practices are not just any other cultural component and should not be reduced to the commercial endeavors of the cultural industry. These practices should be regarded in their specificity and their capacity to imagine possible scenarios and value systems.

Inspired by Gabriel García Márquez, we can refer to a "chronicle of an integration foretold"; and, according to this notion, we can consider literary and artistic works, and particularly the essay, as the practice of "critical imagination" (Paz, 1970/1994, p. 269). Essays have been very generous spaces of intellectual and artistic endeavors. They adopt long-term perspectives and a wide territorial, cultural, and imaginative perspective as much as they represent and perform the transition from geopolitics to geopoetics. In other words, many Latin American thinkers and writers managed to transform and surpass a restrictive consideration of the geographic or even telluric influences on international politics and policies.[3] They tried to offer a more creative and imaginative conception and recreation of the territorial and geographical dimensions through literary texts.[4] In this way, they offer original ways of conceptualizing historical periods and broader cartographies. As the editors of this volume state, they help "to identify long-term processes" as much as "to identify some of the intellectual mechanisms" that led to "a resilience of regional integration" that can be "studied within a broader geographic and continental framework, as well as within a long-term time span, as this allows for the identification of processes".

Our America is an essay ("*Nuestra América es un ensayo*")

Colombian intellectual Germán Arciniegas declared in 1963 that "Our America Is an Essay". Indeed, there is a strong relationship between the history of the essay and the history of America. The New World of the essay is strongly connected to essaying (or experiencing) the New World. European contact with the New World drew attention to a new sphere of social life, a sphere that from Montaigne on began to be recognized as one of "habits". This cataloguing of customs (Voltairean *moeurs*) would evolve into what was later identified and defined by Edward Tylor as 'culture'. It is no coincidence that the essay emerged at the same time as news of contact with America started circulating throughout Europe, and it is no coincidence that, after Montaigne, Bacon, and Locke began to think about "habits" in the light of colonialism, another phenomenon whose name, as Terry Eagleton showed, is derived from the same root as the word "culture": colonialism (2000, pp. 2–13). Other characteristics of the genre associate it with the New World. Freedom of composition, openness, and its inclusive, dialogical, and permeable quality allow the essay to incorporate new elements and motifs in an open reflection that owes much to the idea of an unattainable, never-ending horizon – the result of exploration and discovery brought about by oversea voyages.

The Latin American essay assimilated several components. First, it inherited Enlightenment and French Revolution thinking. In fact, Latin American essays were inspired by contraband ideas (which arrived despite colonial Spain's censorship) proceeding from European Enlightenment, in the tradition of Voltaire and Rousseau. These ideas gave rise to critical and rebellious thinking in our continent (since Voltaire examined in a more open and explicit manner the tension between the abstract thinking subject and the criticism of *moeurs*). Walter Mignolo observed that in Latin America, the essay was derived not from Montaigne's hermeneutical nor Bacon's epistemological lines but from Voltaire's strong ideological influence (1984, pp. 45–61). Second, the Latin American essay inherited the Anglo-Saxon modern tradition of journalism and political debate, which opened the possibility of the circulation of ideas and the education of the citizens. This was particularly manifested in the political and scientific essays that started in the English colonies in North America on the eve of declaring their independence. Third, following another Hispanic American tradition, the Latin American essay also has its roots in a line started by figures such as Miguel de Unamuno or José Ortega y Gasset: understanding cultural functions as the identitary keys of nationality and their connection to the region. Lastly, the Latin American essay inherited, from Romanticism and Nietzsche, the idea that art is a fundamental space where the individual connects to their culture. Eagleton writes:

> Culture is a form of universal subjectivity at work within each of us, just as the state is the presence of the universal within the particularist realm of civil society. As Friedrich Schiller puts it in his *Letters on the Aesthetic Education of Man* (1795): Every individual human being, one may say, carries within him, potentially and prescriptively, an ideal man, the archetype of a human being, and it is his life's task to be, through all his changing manifestations, in harmony with the unchanging unity of this ideal. This archetype, which is to be discerned more or less clearly in every individual, is represented by the State, the objective and, as it were, canonical form in which all the diversity of individual subjects strives to unite.
>
> (Eagleton, 2000, p. 13)[5]

This passage from Schiller is crucial for understanding some aspects of Latin American thought. For several Latin American intellectuals, the notions of individual, group, and state became intrinsically interconnected. Domingo Faustino Sarmiento, who was a Romantic Liberal on the eve of Positivism, introduced the dichotomy 'civilization–barbarism' - a brilliant contraposition that could be strategically applied to the individual, the group, and the state. 'Barbarism' is an earlier state, in both a temporary and an evolutionary sense, that points both to the wild aspects that precede submission to the civilizing regulations of society and state. All these currents of thinking converge and are combined and recombined in different ways, with different emphasis in the work of the great Latin American essayists, whose texts we would like to re-read from the perspective of integration.

Essays have also assisted to the intellectual self-configuration of our great thinkers, and they have served as the foundation of their actions in the public sphere. There are countless instances of Latin American thinkers also functioning as essayists. In the territory that would become Venezuela, educator Simón Rodríguez and civilizer Andrés Bello were both mentors to Simón Bolívar. Further south, the aforementioned Sarmiento used essays as a platform for his project, while Francisco Bilbao's writings gave way to his coining of the term 'Latin America'. In Cuba, José Martí found a strong connection between culture, "nuestroamericanismo" (our-Americanism), and integration. In the twentieth century, essayists played a key role in contributing to concrete cultural and integrationist policies, including editorial, educational, and journalistic projects.

Culture, literature, and the arts have contributed greatly to envision and strengthen ties to each other as a continent and even to conceptualize and imagine Latin America as a single entity. The possibility of thinking of Latin America as a whole was addressed in various essays, but many of them (which were originally letters, speeches, or articles) were themselves destined to weave links between creators and intellectuals that allowed them to think and imagine inter-American networks.

In the nineteenth century, when literature had become a discourse of discourses, writing started to generate an Americanist narrative. This narrative would, after the Independence, turn towards the national and would eventually start to open, little by little, to new perspectives of a supra-national reach that were nurtured by the printed word. And in the twentieth and twenty-first centuries, when new modes of expression and new technologies amplify and multiply the possibility of intercommunication, the need to return to a sense of cultural integration becomes even stronger.

Hereafter, we will discuss some of those great moments of productive and programmatic reflection that have been able to more wholly manifest the creative and imaginative sense of human beings and their culture. As Simón Rodríguez said, "*O inventamos o erramos*" ("We must either invent or fail"). Those great moments of contact between the particular experiences of the great critical thinkers in Latin America and the cultural world have given way from geopolitics to geopoetics – a place where culture, territory, and imagination converge to build a new notion of Latin America.

From geopolitics to geopoetics

Simón Bolívar's "Letter from Jamaica" (Bolívar, 1815) was a geopolitical meditation that considered at the same time our identity and our integration:

> It is a grandiose idea to think of consolidating the New World into a single nation, united by pacts into a single bond. It is reasoned that, as these parts have a common origin, language, customs, and religion, they ought to have a single government to permit the newly formed states to unite in a confederation. But this is not possible. Actually, climatic differences, geographic diversity, conflicting interests, and dissimilar characteristics separate

America. How beautiful it would be if the Isthmus of Panamá could be for us what the Isthmus of Corinth was for the Greeks! Would to God that someday we may have the good fortune to convene there an august assembly of representatives of republics, kingdoms, and empires to deliberate upon the high interests of peace and war with the nations of the other three-quarters of the globe.

(Bolívar, 1815, p. 39)

Bolívar speculated on the elements that Latin Americans have in common:

It would be easier to have the two continents meet than to reconcile the spirits of the two countries. The habit of obedience; a community of interest, of understanding, of religion; mutual goodwill; a tender regard for the birthplace and good name of our forefathers; in short, all that gave rise to our hopes, came to us from Spain. As a result there was born principle of affinity that seemed eternal, notwithstanding the misbehavior of our rulers, which weakened that sympathy, or, rather, that bond enforced by the domination of their rule.

(Letter from Jamaica, para. 5)

Here we can already trace America conceived as a unity. Bolívar also considered the idea of legitimacy and the need of recognition for Latin America and Latin Americans in the global stage. By setting his sights on the never-ending horizon, Bolívar envisioned a future free state made possible by the revolutionary wars for independence.

When the fight for political independence started to give way to the fight for intellectual autonomy, other strategies were implemented. Proper to Latin America are the ways these strategies took shape: education projects that went hand in hand with editorial projects. In this context, Andrés Bello's and Juan García del Río's *Biblioteca Americana* and *El Repertorio Americano*, as well as Juan María Gutiérrez's anthology titled *América Poética*, started a movement towards the continent's cultural integration by circulating literary texts from all over America. Popularizing a series of texts signified drawing a map that went beyond national spaces, effectively building a Latin American library.

As a precedent to the conception of Latin America as a unit, that is, as a precedent to a geopoetics that would enable us to think of Latin America as a whole, we must turn to José Martí (1891) and the aptly titled "Nuestra América":

The pompous villager thinks his hometown is the whole world. As long as he can stay on as mayor, humiliate the rival who stole his sweetheart, and watch his nest egg grow in its strongbox, he believes the universe is in good order. He knows nothing of the giants in seven-league boots who can crush him underfoot, the battling comets in the heavens which devour the worlds that lie sleeping in their paths. Whatever is left in

America of such drowsy provincialism must awaken. These are not times for lying comfortably in bed. Like Juan de Castellanos' men, we must have no other pillow but our weapons – weapons of the mind, which vanquish all others. Fortifications built of ideas are more valuable than those built of stone. No armored prow can smash through a cloud of ideas. A vital idea brandished before the world at the right moment like the mystic banner of Judgment Day can stop a fleet of battleships. Nations that remain strangers must rush to know one another, like soldiers about to go into battle together.

("Our America," para. 1)

Voyages, letters, different forms of sociability, the establishment of artistic and intellectual networks, the exchange of publications, the organization of editorial projects, and the circulation of newspapers and journals – all have been fundamental for generating a sense of regional belonging that will itself feed our integration. Hence the importance of the printing press, periodicals, cables and telegrams, the post, trains, steamboats, as well as different forms of communication and intercommunication that spread in the twentieth century, from radio and recorded sound to television and the internet.

As the nineteenth century marched along and the twentieth century approached, the expansion of school systems and public libraries was also central for generating a sense of belonging and for expanding the readers' horizons, at the same time as the region underwent a profound demographic change brought by immigration and internal migration - the arrival of new populations and the shift from countryside to city changed the social and the cultural face of many Latin American countries.

A shift came in the first decades of the twentieth century. Inspired by the Mexican Revolution (1910), the University Reform (1918), and working-class protests (and the new ideas that circulated along with them), a new wave of Latin American intellectuals came about. These thinkers (such as José Vasconcelos, Pedro Henríquez Ureña, Alfonso Reyes, José Carlos Mariátegui, Daniel Cosío Villegas, and many others who promoted literacy and education) were in effect the great strategists of Latin American cultural integration. Many of them were at the head of publishing projects such as Fondo de Cultura Económica, collections such as "Tierra Firme", or great cultural journals that, just as *Repertorio Americano, Amauta, Cuadernos Americanos, Orígenes* or *Sur*, made through their circulation networks of integration through imagination.

Certain continental texts, such as José Enrique Rodó's *Ariel* or José Ingenieros's *El hombre mediocre*, had a rapid circulation and reception and helped articulate the concerns of cultural integration that were already present in the Latin American collective mind that Alfonso Reyes would call 'inteligencia americana'. Certain literary movements such as Modernism, which had a great presence throughout the whole continent, came to signify a "synchronization" of our watches to the time of the wider world (Rama, 1982).

Decades later, a new literary phenomenon came to re-unify Latin America: the *boom*. In his Nobel acceptance speech titled "La soledad de América Latina" ("The Solitude of Latin America", 1982), Gabriel García Márquez said:

> Latin America neither wants, nor has any reason, to be a pawn without a will of its own; nor is it merely wishful thinking that its quest for independence and originality should become a Western aspiration. However, the navigational advances that have narrowed such distances between our Americas and Europe seem, conversely, to have accentuated our cultural remoteness. Why is the originality so readily granted us in literature so mistrustfully denied us in our difficult attempts at social change? Why think that the social justice sought by progressive Europeans for their own countries cannot also be a goal for Latin America, with different methods for dissimilar conditions? No: the immeasurable violence and pain of our history are the result of age-old inequities and untold bitterness, and not a conspiracy plotted three thousand leagues from our home. But many European leaders and thinkers have thought so, with the childishness of old-timers who have forgotten the fruitful excess of their youth as if it were impossible to find another destiny than to live at the mercy of the two great masters of the world. This, my friends, is the very scale of our solitude.
>
> (The Solitude of Latin America, para. 9)

While some had interpreted the "boom" as an "extraterritorial" or "deterritorialized" conception of Latin American imagination, García Márquez re-situates our solitude in a geopolitical perspective that spawns a geopoetic perspective by which this literary movement proves to be historically tied to territory.

The laureate concludes with an optimistic affirmation about the power of literary imagination:

> we, the inventors of tales, who will believe anything, feel entitled to believe that it is not yet too late to engage in the creation of the opposite utopia. A new and sweeping utopia of life, where no one will be able to decide for others how they die, where love will prove true and happiness be possible, and where the races condemned to one hundred years of solitude will have, at last and forever, a second opportunity on earth.
>
> ("The Solitude of Latin America," para. 11)

The essay in the mainland

In the early decades of the twentieth century, the weaving of the networks that would truly connect Latin America began under what was then called "la hora americana" (or "the American hour", as was mentioned in the manifesto titled "La juventud argentina de Córdoba a los hombres libres de Sud América,

1918, p. 1). The essay followed suit in what I have named "the essay in the mainland",[6] where the genre was consolidated as a form that could give voice to the intellectual activities in Latin America, fundamentally supported in the historical-cultural axis. This is a moment in which the old concept of *Kultur* gave way to a new anthropological concept of culture, which displaced the old and deterministic concept of race. In this case, the essay went hand in hand with the consolidation of new models that made identity be an element both instituting and instituted.

From the 1940s to the 1960s, the essay became a fundamental space for articulating the culture-literature dichotomy – a dichotomy where both terms feed into and justify each other, and in which the concept of culture operates in two levels at the same time. The essay is also linked to the possibility of thinking of a cultural identity, in a confluence of sense that strongly places culture and literature in mutual relation (González Echevarría, 2001, p. 15).

In this era the notion of culture as spiritual patrimony in the hands of a *cultivated* elite progressed to an anthropological concept of culture as way of life and collection of material and symbolic goods. The concept of culture is therefore used to overcome and suture the contradictory spaces that arise from nationalistic visions in favor of a nascent *Latin Americanism*.

The mid-forties constituted a moment of singular importance for rethinking Latin American critical tradition through the essay, a genre that turned into a symbolic place of mediation between thought and action for our intellectuals. Books such as Mariano Picón-Salas's *De la conquista a la independencia: tres siglos de historia cultural hispanoamericana* (1944) and Medardo Vitier's *El ensayo americano* (1945) were brought into direct dialogue with one another by Alfonso Reyes's editorial project Tierra Firme. The vision of Reyes (who famously defined the essay as "a centaur of genres") is captured by how Picón Salas started his book: "To Alfonso Reyes – great humanist, great writer – in memory of the many conversations where he in his clarity defined and made our shared hope in America both rule and learning" (p. 15).[7]

In 1963, Germán Arciniegas published "Nuestra América es un ensayo". This text confirms the possibility of establishing a strong relationship between Latin American culture and the essay, both supported by the cornerstone of the history of America, in a discourse conducted by the intellectual sector that perceived itself as embodying "the American intelligence". This Colombian writer is also one of the representatives of university reformism, which sought Latin American integration. Arciniegas was one of the first to recognize the Atlantic experience, itself an expansion on the Mediterranean model, which authors like Pedro Henríquez Ureña always considered their great fore-model: if the Roman Empire expanded towards the Mediterranean, giving way to a series of nations that have survived its fall with strong cultural connections, the same can be said of Latin American nations after the fall of the Spanish Empire. This emphasis on a shared historical experience was also present in Picón-Salas (1944/1994, p. 15): "How is the Hispanic American culture forged, what spiritual ingredients lead to it, which European forms are modified on contact with the New World and which sprout from the mestizo spirit - these are the questions I want to answer in this essay on cultural history".[8]

During these two decades books, and culture were made into a means for integrating and modernizing society. This era came to signify advances but also contradictions. On the one hand, the public space was expanded and strengthened, and a generous map of books and periodical circulation was traced, which took into consideration the expansion of urban middle-class readers and aspired to build a virtuous circle of book-school-library-citizenship. Through the practices in the public space of our intellectuals, essays, culture, and representations began to respond to the demands of social representativity.

Thus, the essay went hand in hand with the modernizing model of state, but it also went through problematic places and contradictions in a model that was based on the axis of continental Hispanic America, and that, although it saw itself as inclusive, did not achieve its desired opening to Brazil, the Caribbean, and the United States and Canada. The essay did not fully integrate regions, cultural and social experiences, and population sectors that were later described as subaltern: the mostly criollo and middle-class intellectuals threw aside "la visión de los vencidos" ("the vision of the defeated", a phrase coined by León-Portilla in 1959) and included it only by aestheticizing the experience of rural, first nations, and afro-descendent populations. For a long time, most of the great Caribbean intellectuals would see their own reality as part of the larger "mainland". This "mainland" interpretation of Latin America left many actors behind and also excluded the decolonization processes that the extra-Western world was going through at that time. Furthermore, it was not sufficiently open to new literary vanguards (we should note the exceptions of those writers that were in fact conscious of the larger literary movements, such as José Carlos Mariátegui, Fernando Ortiz, Oswald de Andrade, Gilberto Freyre, or Aimé Césaire).

The Cuban essay, which for a time was connected to the hegemonic vision from "the mainland", started to turn from 1940, the year when *Contrapunteo cubano del tabaco y el azúcar* by Fernando Ortiz was published. This book was the basis of a new type of dialogue between literature and anthropology, as well as a new form of conceiving the relationship between the Caribbean and other regions of the world. Decades later, Antonio Benítez Rojo would begin to talk about *La isla que se repite* (1989) in a foundational text that introduced new conceptions and operations to the interpreting of an insular world that up to that point had been subsumed to the continental model.

Among the essays of the last decades, which have taken up the challenge of thinking of Latin American culture as a whole, we find Carlos Fuentes's *El espejo enterrado*, published in 1992 by Fondo de Cultura Económica. Once more, the stone that corners discourse is the possibility of thinking of a historic-cultural future for the whole region in which art and literature have a role of the utmost importance.

Another example, closer to us in time, is that of Colombian writer William Ospina, who in his 2010 "El dibujo secreto de la América Latina" ("The secret sketch of Latin America") attempts to restore a vision of the whole, in this case after the certainties of "the mainland", and it is here that the possibility of the existence of Latin America is proposed as an enigma, a secret map, that now has to take into account plurality and diversity:

> Since the time when Bolívar wrote his "Carta de Jamaica", a fundamental task of this continent has been the dialogue between unity and diversity. We would be lying if we said that our America is one: there is evidence of its plurality everywhere [. . .].
> And I am not only speaking of the extraordinary geographical and bio-logical diversity but, into it and about it, of diversity of peoples and their cultures, or of something even more suggestive, the many undisputed nuances of one vast continental culture.
>
> (Ospina, 2010, p. 36)[9]

Ospina writes about a continent characterized by intermingling and novelty, to the point that although "almost nothing is native to our continent", everything can be celebrated as "original":

> there is one common feature of Latin-American culture and it is that noth-ing in it could be described today as absolutely native, except maybe for those peoples from the Amazon that have never been in contact with any-thing different. In other regions of the world, until not so long ago, one could talk about purity, of pure races, of uncontaminated languages. Mixes here started very early, not to reach the undifferentiated but to produce in every case truly new things. Let's say that in our continental culture almost nothing is native, but everything is original.
>
> (Ospina, 2010, p. 37)[10]

From the sixties and the Cuban Revolution onward, the essay will have to enter into conversation with social sciences and discourses about the Third World. Gustavo Guerrero (2014) has shown how the work of Car-los Monsiváis and Néstor García Canclini opened new forms of interpret-ing Latin American culture, in that they proposed to "insert the name of 'Latin America'" in the global dialogue" (p. 73). The *boom* of Latin American literature was also of great importance to bring Latin America to the foreground of universal culture. The essayists concerned with defin-ing Latin America now had to grapple with a new phenomenon, coming from Latin American narrative, that since the imagining of Macondo was reconfigured into "a certain interpretation of Latin American culture as a totality unified around the telling of our difference, whose foundation is magical realism".[11] Around this time, both the studies of Latin American culture started to appear alongside the newly founded cultural studies - to borrow Mabel Moraña's terminology, studies *from* Latin America and stud-ies *about* Latin America.[12]

Other fundamental components are the shifts in the educational panorama, the transformation of readership and reading habits (themselves modified by new technologies), and, in particular, changes of the publishing practices and the expansion of cultural industries. Guerrero (2009) warned of "the lack of spaces for mediation" and the existence of "an oversaturated space, segmented, confusing", with a strong geographical dispersion and problems of circulation and distribution of books at a continental level (p. 25). We witness a fragmentation of processes and the emergence of "segmented landscapes" (p. 25). At the same time, "the idea of a panorama as a whole disappears definitely", and there emerges "a pluralist model for thinking of the universality without the totality of societies that will come" (p. 28).

Nowadays, we are experiencing the general shift from an interpretative model based on the temporal axis to a model based on drifting through space, as well as the aspiration to an all-encompassing and comprehensive view based on an ample concept of culture, on emphasizing contradictions, fragmentations, and bottlenecks. It is here that the strong presence of figures such as "maps", "atlases", "cartographies", "itineraries", etc. comes in - figures that translate this new conception of place, both real and imagined.

In the current crisis of the concept of Latin America and the possibility of articulating culture-literature-identity in a system of mutual implication, which is related to the change in the roles of intellectuals, book culture, and the appearance of new communication technologies, there have also been new proposals to understand ourselves as a community of destinations. Many of our essayists are dedicated to envisioning new scenarios and realities. Such is the case of the Brazilian sociologist Renato Ortiz (2000), who talks about not one but several "Latin Americas".

Archipelagos of relationships

The aforementioned *Contrapunteo cubano del tabaco y el azúcar* is both a synthesis and a turning point in the evolution of a conception of Latin America whose symbolical axis was "the mainland" to a conception centered around insularity and the recognition of the specificity of the Caribbean experience. Ortiz's proposal, influenced by folklorist Lydia Cabrera, studied historical, cultural, social, economic, and political components of Cuba through his use of two figures whose counterpointing will define the history of this island: tobacco and sugar. These are two objects that are based both in literature and in economics, since they operate simultaneously as characters and commodities (Coronil, 2010). In this text, Ortiz introduces the revolutionary concept of 'transculturation', which allows him to capture a new and much wider look, more dynamic and ubiquitous, than the concept of 'acculturation' (the processes that allowed for cultural contact). The notion of 'transculturation' has long been accepted, since it was incorporated to the intellectual tradition in Latin America through Mariano Picón-Salas and Ángel Rama, who applied it towards explaining literary phenomena. It was also recuperated and enriched by cultural and postcolonial studies, starting by Mary Louise Pratt's applying it to the study of "contact zones" (1991). But Ortiz also marked the way to the recognition of popular culture and Afro heritage. In this interpretation style, as playful as it is dynamic, the concepts of counterpointing and transculturation are already forewarning a notion that will also be fundamental as one of the contributions of Caribbean thought: that of the "poetics of relationships" (1997). It was Martiniquan poet and philosopher Édouard Glissant who posed in a very original manner the necessity to invent a "poetics of relationships", based not on the one-directional Atlantic model but in a model with the Caribbean as archipelagos of relationships (Glissant, 1990).

In the opening text for an exhibition of the work of Lydia Cabrera and Édouard Glissant, we can read:

> The official stories of national, ethnic, and historical identity are no longer convincing. The idea of a "culture" as hermetic and transhistorical has always been problematic, but today these constructs have been fatally weakened by an array of turbulent forces and a global process of creolization. For some, this has led to a choice between two unsatisfying options: on the one hand, a culture of globalization marked by anomie and exploitation, and on the other, a return to an imaginary state of ethno-cultural purity. In this exhibition we propose to look back, not toward an idealized past, but to two figures of the twentieth century from the Caribbean archipelago, a region where many of our current political conditions have already been anticipated and experienced. Lydia Cabrera and Édouard Glissant were highly aware of the erasures and stagnations of creolization, a subtle and unstoppable movement common to all humans - and indeed, to all life. For Cabrera and Glissant, thinking beyond narrow understandings of identity was a practice of necessity - one from which we can learn . . . For Cabrera and Glissant alike, archipelagic thought is lighter and more generative than monolithic continental thought.
>
> (Marta & Rangel, 2018, pp. 25–26)

The essay stands now before the challenge of finding new versions - mobile, open, relational, and multidirectional versions - of the Latin American experience. The world's interpretative axis has shifted from time to space. From the cultural map that guaranteed and was guaranteed by the narrative of history, we have come to mapped culture, conceived as infinitely mutating combinations, and only could be organized through atlases, cartographies, mobile archives, open reencounters, and provisional orders.

In "The Muse of History" (1974/1998), Derek Walcott poses a re-reading of the American colonial experience that we can contrast with Fuentes's *El espejo enterrado*. Walcott criticizes the servitude to the muse of history that has taken place in the New World:

> In the New World servitude to the muse of history has produced a literature of recrimination and despair, a literature of revenge written by the

descendants of slaves or a literature of remorse written by the descendants of masters. Because this literature serves historical truth, it yellows into polemic or evaporates in pathos. The truly tough aesthetic of the New World neither explains nor forgives history. It refuses to recognize it as a creative or culpable force.

(Walcott, 1974/1998, p. 37)

Walcott favors memory over history: he recognizes the colonial mark in the experience - present and living - of the inhabitants of America, and he emphasizes that we are heirs to both - both the defeaters and the defeated, both the enslaved and the slaver - while also considering the need to integrate the fragments into a new unity that should not hide the marks but precisely flaunt these differentiating signs lovingly:

I accept this archipelago of the Americas. I say to the ancestor who sold me, and to the ancestor who bought me, I have no father, I want no such father, although I can understand you, black ghost, white ghost, when you both whisper "history," for if I attempt to forgive you both I am falling into your idea of history which justifies and explains and expiates, and it is not mine to forgive, my memory cannot summon any filial love, since your features are anonymous and erased and I have no wish and no power to pardon. You were when you acted your roles, your given, historical roles of slave seller and slave buyer, men acting as men, and also you, father in the filth-ridden gut of the slave ship, to you they were also men, acting as men, with the cruelty of men, your fellowman and tribesman not moved or hovering with hesitation about your common race any longer than my other bastard ancestor hovered with his whip, but to you, inwardly forgiven grandfathers, I, like the more honest of my race, give a strange thanks. I give the strange and bitter and yet ennobling thanks for the monumental groaning and sol-dering of two great worlds, like the halves of a fruit seamed by its own bitter juice, that exiled from your own Edens you have placed me in the wonder of another, and that was my inheritance and your gift.

(Walcott, 1974/1998, p. 64)

We stand at the end of a model of the essay that has been centered around a certain identitary essentialization, which is based on the strong relationship between culture, history, language, and literature. This is made evident in Glissant's (2009) "archipelagic thinking", which in his *Philosophie de la relation* he associates with "the essay's thinking, of intuitive temptation, that we could add to continental thinking, which would be, first and foremost, systematic" (p. 45). This is proposed as non-systematic thinking, a mode of thinking that is open to infinite relationships (the game of differences), although it is always localized, since, as Glissant notes, "place is unavoidable" (2009, p. 46). Glissant writes from a spatial perspective that contrasts "continent" to "archipelago" thinking. Florencia Bonfiglio (2014) states that essayists are able to generate, through writing itself, "shared places". She considers that the Caribbean essay is "that which, in relating to the Latin American interpretation essay, tries to define the boundaries of 'Caribbeanity'" (p. 20).[13] The author says that this "creates a regional culture as a product of its writers' desires for re-vinculation", turning the Caribbean into "a literary territory that assembles and interconnects insular experiences through the imaginary (re)run of a maritime geography that appears in its integration. This is how "the essay that repeats itself or the Caribbean as a *common place*" opens for us the possibility of discussing an "imaginary integration of the Caribbean" - or, in my own words, geopoetics – that promotes "a cultural integration" (p. 19).[14]

We stand at the end of a determined model of the relationship between discourses and spaces, but this does not mean we have lost the desire to find points in common and views in common. And, as Ette, Mackenbach, Müller, and Wallner (2011) put it:

> This is not about starting from a space pre-determined by its territoriality and its respective borders, but about taking the networks of forms and figures of accumulated movements as a starting point and a basis for the comprehension of an area from its relationality and dynamics.
>
> (p. 10)[15]

Essays and atlases

To illustrate a creative way of taking on the subject, and to show that imaginative solutions have led to confirm the hypothesis of "resilience" in the idea of integration, I would like to consider a fragment of a contemporary essay, Graciela Speranza's *Atlas portátil de América Latina. Arte y ficciones errantes* (*Portable Atlas of Latin America. Wandering Art and Fictions*), published in 2012. This essay proposes a new imaginary cartography of America as an alternative to the old map anchored to the mainland. She thus overcomes, through the order of aesthetics, contradictions that could not have been overcome from a traditional, or merely pragmatic or instrumental, point of view.

Speranza proposes the "atlas" as a mobile and dynamic ordering of maps and trails, and this allows her to rethink and give new solutions to the identitary presuppositions of the Latin American. The atlas allows her to move from a temporary axis to one mostly spatial, through which history becomes an operation of many paths and the task of the essayist is permanently put into a dialogue. Speranza's proposal can be understood as part of the many artistic and literary projects that, through multiple approaches, offer to trace new maps and cartographies of Latin America: festivals, book fairs, recitals, publications, blogs, websites, databases, and many other forms of exchange and productive meeting that today have seen themselves multiplied by digital culture.

Conclusion

The essay, just like the idea of cultural integration, evinces a tension between the part and the whole, the short term of the present and the longer term that considers inheritances of the past and projects of the future, based on tradition and appealing to imagination. The essay, just like proposals for integration, moves between collective spirit and imaginative freedom, between the temptation of closing and the invitation of opening. And if, on the one hand, it is imposed upon by its vocation to depict "reality" in close affinity to the chronicle, on the other, it is geared towards exploration and construction of new orders, amongst which lies imagination. This journey, which has led us through different proposals of geopoetics suggested by the essay, shows us that geopoetics consists of imaginative solutions, open to the future, that allow us to overcome the concrete contradictions of past and present.

Pedro Henríquez Ureña, in an essay titled "Discontent and Promise" ("El descontento y la promesa", in *Seis ensayos en busca de nuestra expresión*, 1928, pp. 11–35), wrote this phrase which aptly describes the encounter and articulation of resilience, integration, and imagination: "Every great work of art creates its own peculiar means of expression: it takes advantage of previous experiences but it remakes them, since it is not a sum but a synthesis, an invention".[16]

Experience and creation embrace, with a performative sense of intellectual program, in this quotation. Resilience, with its notes of resurgence, rebounding, resistance, may be well represented by artistic creation. The examples we have examined show how geopoetics can offer creative responses, propose solutions through aesthetic operations, and symbolically solve the contradictions and dispersions of real situations. In order to counter frustration, we need not only to restore but to create, to look not only to the past but also to the future and the boundless horizon with our sights set on utopia. Counterbalance discontent with the past and the present with the promise of the future.

Notes

1 Originally in Spanish: "Preguntémonos [. . .] cuáles son las razones que hacen que la unidad de origen haya llevado a una diversidad de destinos, y que hoy, la diversidad de desarrollos reclame la unidad de destinos".

2 For the way in which art history is being reconsidered and proposals about redesigning the "map" of art history and revising its geography, see the interesting volume Mattos C. Avolese & R. Conduru. (2017). *New world: Frontiers, inclusion, utopias.* São Paulo, Brasil: Comitê Brasileiro de História da Arte.

3 In a broad sense, the term 'geopolitics', conceived by the Swedish political scientist Rudolf Kjellén towards 1916, refers to the study and analysis of the complex influence of geographical factors on international politics. Centuries before this term was coined, Latin America was implicitly defined from a geopolitical dimension as it was being incorporated into the world order as a 'New World'. From this initial moment, Latin American thought has been intricately tied to 'geopolitics', incorporating a legal dimension to this concept, including judiciary notions such as sovereignty, freedom, and human rights. This is evident in a variety of texts related to the denunciation of human rights violations in the works of Bartolomé de las Casas or to the emancipation from colonial power in the writings of Francisco de Miranda, Simón Bolívar, and Bernardo de Monteagudo, among many others.

4 Federico Italiano (2008) finds a lexical relationship between geopolitics and geopoetics. He defines geopoetics as an "operative category" that "enables us to comprehend and to analyse the territorial, geographical and geo-ecological dimension of a literary text":

"The Geopoetics of an author is to be understood as his territorial intelligence, poetic and imagining ability for producing and constructing a world, his characteristic determination and presentation of the relation Man–Earth".

5 For a critical reading of Schiller's point of view, see G. C. Spivak (2012). *An aesthetic education in the era of globalization*. Cambridge, MA: Harvard University Press.

6 Following the aforementioned Fondo de Cultura Económica collection titled "Tierra Firme", in Weinberg (2017a, 2017b).

7 Originally in Spanish: "A Alfonso Reyes, gran humanista, gran escritor, en recuerdo de tantos diálogos en que su claridad definió e hizo norma y aprendizaje nuestra común esperanza en América".

8 Originally in Spanish: "Cómo se forja la cultura hispanoamericana, qué ingredientes espirituales desembocan en ella, qué formas europeas se modifican al contacto del Nuevo Mundo y cuáles brotan del espíritu mestizo, son los interrogantes que quiero responder en este ensayo de historia cultural".

9 Originally in Spanish: "Desde los tiempos en que Bolívar escribió su «Carta de Jamaica», una tarea fundamental de este Continente ha sido el diálogo entre la unidad y la diversidad. Mentiríamos si dijéramos que nuestra América es una: por todas partes surge la evidencia de su pluralidad [. . .] Y no hablo solo de la extraordinaria diversidad geográfica y biológica sino, en ella y sobre ella, de la diversidad de los pueblos y de sus culturas, o de algo más sugestivo aún, los muchos matices irrenunciables de una vasta cultura continental".

10 Originally in Spanish: ". . . una característica común de la cultura latinoamericana es que nada en ella puede reclamarse hoy como absolutamente nativo, salvo quizá esos pueblos mágicos del Amazonas que nunca han entrado en contacto con algo distinto. En otras regiones del mundo, hasta hace poco tiempo, podía hablarse de pureza, de razas puras, de lenguas incontaminadas. Aquí las mezclas comenzaron muy temprano, no para llegar a lo indiferenciado sino para producir en todos los casos cosas verdaderamente nuevas. Digamos que en nuestra cultura continental casi nada es nativo pero todo es original".

11 Originally in Spanish: "una cierta interpretación de la cultura latinoamericana como totalidad unificada alrededor de un relato de nuestra diferencia, cuyo fundamento es el realismo mágico" (p. 74).

12 Among many works on the subject of Latin American studies, see R. McKee Irwin & M. Szurmuk. (2012). *Dictionary of Latin American cultural studies*. Gainesville, FL: University Press of Florida.

13 Originally in Spanish: ". . . aquel que, emparentándose con el ensayo de interpretación latinoamericano, intenta definir los contornos de la 'caribeñidad'".

14 Originally in Spanish: "El ensayo que se repite o el Caribe como lugar común" nos abre a la posibilidad de hablar de una "integración imaginaria del Caribe" – o, en mis palabras, una geopoética – que promueve "una integración cultural" (p. 19).

15 Originally in Spanish: "No se trata, entonces, de partir desde un espacio predeterminado por su territorialidad y sus respectivas fronteras, sino de tomar las redes de formas y figuras de movimientos acumulados como puntos de partida y base para la comprensión de un área desde su relacionalidad y dinámica".

16 Originally in Spanish: "Cada grande obra de arte crea medios propios y peculiares de expresión; aprovecha las experiencias anteriores, pero las rehace, porque no es una suma, sino una síntesis, una invención".

References

Allende Serra, M. (2002–2003). Arte sin fronteras: Perspectivas de integración latinoamericana. *Pensar Iberoamérica. Revista de cultura, 2*. Retrieved from www.oei.es/historico/pen sariberoamerica/ric02a04.htm

Arciniegas, G. (1963). Nuestra América es un ensayo. *Cuadernos, 73*, 9–16.

Bello, A., & García del Río, J. (1972) [1923]. *Biblioteca Americana o Miscelánea de Literatura, Artes y Ciencias*. Caracas: Presidencia de la República. Retrieved from www.cervan tesvirtual.com/obra/biblioteca-americana-o-miscelanea-de-literatura-artes-y-ciencias-0/

Bello, A., & García del Río, J. (1973) [1826]. *El Repertorio Americano* (2 Vols.) (P. Grases, Fwd). Caracas: Presidencia de la República. Retrieved March 18, 2020, from www.cervan tesvirtual.com/obra/el-repertorio-americano-londres-18261827-volumen-1-0/

Benítez Rojo, A. (1989). *La isla que se repite: el Caribe y la perspectiva posmoderna*. Hanover, NH: Ediciones del Norte.

Bolívar, S. (1815). *Letter from Jamaica*. Retrieved February 11, 2020, from https://library. brown.edu/create/modernlatinamerica/chapters/chapter-2-the-colonial-foundations/ primary-documents-with-accompanying-discussion-questions/document-2-simon-bolivar-letter-from-jamaica-september-6–1815/

Bonfiglio, F. (2014). El ensayo que se repite o el Caribe como lugar común (Antonio Benítez Rojo, Édouard Glissant, Kamau Brathwaite). *Anclajes*, *18*(2), 19–31. Retrieved from www.redalyc.org/articulo.oa?id=22433923002

Castoriadis, C. (1989) [1975]. Spain: Tusquets.

Coronil, F. (2010). La política de la teoría: el contrapunteo cubano de la transculturación. In L. Weinberg (Ed.), *Estrategias del pensar: ensayo y prosa de ideas en América Latina Siglo XX* (t. I, pp. 357–428). México: CIALC-UNAM.

Eagleton, T. (2000). *The idea of culture*. Oxford: Blackwell.

Ette, O., Mackenbach, W., Müller, G., & Ortiz Wallner, A. (Eds.). (2011). Introducción. In W. Mackenbach, G. Müller, & A. Ortiz Wallner (Eds.), *Trans(it)Areas. Convivencias en Centroamérica y el Caribe. Un simposio transareal* (pp. 9–16). Berlin: Tranvía.

Fuentes, C. (1992). *El espejo enterrado*. México: FCE.

García Márquez, G. (1982). The solitude of Latin America. *The Nobel Prize*. Retrieved February 11, 2020, from www.nobelprize.org/prizes/literature/1982/marquez/lecture/

Glissant, É. (1990). *Poétique de la Relation*. Paris: Gallimard.

Glissant, É. (2009). *Philosophie de la Relation. Poésie en étendue*. Paris: Gallimard.

González Echevarría, R. (2001). *La voz de los maestros*. Madrid: Verbum.

Guerrero, G. (2009). La desbandada. O por qué ya no existe la literatura latinoamericana. *Letras Libres*, *93*, 24–28.

Guerrero, G. (2014). Modos, rutas y derivas del ensayo contemporáneo. De la tierra firme al mar sin orillas. *Revista de la Universidad*, *126*, 63–75.

Gutiérrez, J. M. (1846). *América poética. Colección escogida de composiciones en verso, escritas por americanos en el presente siglo. Parte lírica*. Valparaíso: Imprenta del Mercurio.

Henríquez Ureña, P. (1928). *Seis ensayos en busca de nuestra expresión*. Buenos Aires: Babel.

Italiano, F. (2008). Defining geopoetics. *TRANS- Revue de littérature générale et comparée*, *6*. Retrieved March 19, 2020, from https://journals.openedition.org/trans/299

La juventud argentina de Córdoba a los hombres libres de Sud América. Manifiesto de la Federación Universitaria de Córdoba. (1918). In G. del Mazo (Ed.), *La Reforma Universitaria (1918–1940)* (t. I. El Movimiento Argentino, pp. 1–5). La Plata, Argentina: Centro de Estudiantes de Ingeniería.

León-Portilla, M. (Ed.). (1959). *Visión de los vencidos. Relaciones indígenas de la conquista* (A. M. Garibay, Trans.). México: UNAM.

Marta, K., & G. Rangel (Eds.). (2018). *Lydia Cabrera and Édouard Glissant: Trembling thinking*. Curated by H. U. Obrist, G. Rangel, & A. Raza. [Brochure]. West Haven, CT: Americas Society.

Martí, J. (1891). *Our America*. Retrieved February 11, 2020, from www.josemarti.cu/ publicacion/nuestra-america-version-ingles/#_ednref1

Mattos Avolese, C., & Conduru, R. (Eds.). (2017). *New world: Frontiers, inclusion, utopias.* São Paulo: Comitê Brasileiro de História da Arte.

McKee, I. R., & Szurmuk, M. (Eds.). (2012). *Dictionary of Latin American cultural studies.* Gainesville, FL: University Press of Florida.

Mignolo, W. (1984). Discurso ensayístico y tipología textual. In I. J. Lévy & J. Loveluck (Eds.), *El ensayo hispánico* (pp. 45–61). Columbia, SC: University of South Carolina.

Ortiz, F. (1940). *Contrapunteo cubano del tabaco y el azúcar.* La Habana: Jesús Montero.

Ortiz, R. (2000). América Latina. De la modernidad incompleta a la modernidad-mundo. *Nueva Sociedad, 166,* 44–166.

Ospina, W. (2010). El dibujo secreto de América Latina. *Casa de las Américas, 28,* 36–46.

Paz, O. (1994) [1970]. Posdata. Crítica de la pirámide. In *Obras completas: Vol. 8. El peregrino en su patria* (pp. 267–324). México: FCE.

Picón-Salas, M. (1994) [1944]. *De la conquista a la independencia: Tres siglos de historia cultural hispanoamericana.* Caracas: Monte Ávila.

Pratt, M. L. (1991). Arts of the contact zone. In *Modern Language Association* (pp. 33–40). Retrieved March 11, 2020, from http://l-adam-mekler.com/pratt_contact_zone.pdf

Rama, Á. (1986) [1982]. *La novela en América Latina. Panoramas 1920–1980.* Montevideo, Uruguay-Xalapa, México: Fundación Ángel Rama-Universidad Veracruzana.

Speranza, G. (2012). *Atlas portátil de América Latina. Arte y ficciones errantes.* Barcelona: Anagrama.

Spivak, G. C. (2012). *An aesthetic education in the era of globalization.* Cambridge, MA: Harvard University Press.

Tylor, E. B. (2016). *Primitive culture. Researches into the development of mythology, philosophy, religion, language, art and custom* (2 Vols.). Mineola, NY: Dover Publications. [First Edition, 1871].

Vitier, M. (1945). *El ensayo americano.* México: FCE.

Walcott, D. (1998) [1974]. The muse of history. In *What the twilight says. Essays* (pp. 36–64). New York: Farrar, Straus and Giroux.

Weinberg, G. (1982). Dialéctica de la integración. *Latinoamérica. Anuario de Estudios Latino-americanos, 15,* 239–253.

Weinberg, L. (2017a). El ensayo en diálogo: de la tierra firme al archipiélago relacional. In D. Reindert & D. Vandebosch (Eds.), *Transnacionalidad e hibridez en el ensayo hispánico: Un género sin orillas* (pp. 15–35). Leiden and Boston, MA: Brill.

Weinberg, L. (2017b). El ensayo entre-espacios: hacia una geopoética del género. In C. Alba Vega et al. (Eds.), *Pensar las categorías de análisis para el estudio de la globalización* (pp. 89–104). Berlin: Tranvía – Verlag Walter Frey.

Yúdice, G. (2009). Cultural diversity and cultural rights. *Hispanic Issues On Line, 5,* 110–137.

7 The Catholic Church and the resilience of regionalism

José Ramiro Podetti

Introduction[1]

The extended presence of the Catholic Church across Spanish and Portuguese America is one of the indicia that enables thinking of otherwise extremely diverse spaces as one "region."[2] Of course, this is among many other shared indicators that enable scholars, politicians, and everyday people, to think of "Latin America" as such. It comes as no surprise that the very coinage of the expression "Latin America" and its descriptive and analytic usages are not without a history.

This chapter situates Catholic institutions and actors at the center of such an account by re-construing how agents of the Church were the first to embrace forms of regional, that is supra-national, integration in the 19th and 20th centuries. Somewhat counterintuitively, the Latin American Church has been more successful than many other secular institutions in articulating projects at a regional scale. Along these lines is that this chapter puts the Church and its institutions at the center of the resilience of Latin American "regionalism" on at least two levels. One is that of integration and coordination through specific organs and institutions; the other is the intellectual production regarding Latin America in terms of culture, identity, and challenges.

The chapter thus by showing how the process of the implantation of the Church in the Spanish and Portuguese Americas – usually referred to as the Indies – fastened together regions of the hemisphere that in every other aspect were extremely different from each other. This original Church in the Americas was, then, less Spanish or Portuguese than *Indiana* – of the Indies – and thus related to the processes of expansion through the missionization of non-European peoples and the ministration of the faithful in places where Catholicism took hold.

The Church in the Indies, however, was disrupted from within by the Iberian states. Administrators sought to wield greater control of ecclesiastical appointments through the exercise of the *Patronato Regio*[3] and measures such as the expulsion of the Society of Jesus from Spanish and Portuguese territories in the late 18th century. The "nationalization" of the Church in the Indies by the Iberian states – analogous to the process of greater temporal control over the clergy in other European countries such as France – was later transmitted to the heirs of these polities: the independent Spanish-speaking republics and the Empire of Brazil.

The study then moves on to describe this earthquake of secularization that shattered the Church of the Indies into multiple "national churches" in the 19th century. It was in this context of atomization that, as addressed here, a greater need for coordination and communication of the shared challenges of these different churches emerged. Following the works of historians and intellectuals, I then set up to explain how the very expression "Latin American" was, presumably, first applied to describe an ecclesiastical institution situated thousands of kilometers away from the region, in Rome, to train clerics and bishops in the mid-19th century.

The process to reconstitute a Church beyond the narrow scope of the national churches that started in Rome with the *Colegio Pío Latino Americano* continued through meetings of bishops in the 19th century and later became institutionalized in the mid-20th century Latin American Episcopal Council (*Consejo Episcopal Latinoamericano*, CELAM). The latter sections of this essay thus focus on the meetings (General Conferences) of Latin American bishops in the 20th century and their political, social, and intellectual relations with various "Latino Americanist" projects and processes. Arguably, it is shown in this chapter how the CELAM and its Conferences became one of the most successful spaces for Latin American integration. Even more so than its secular counterparts, the CELAM was effective in enacting changes across diverse countries and providing fuel for intellectual conversations across borders. I deliberately chose two of these intellectual foci. One was the "Preferential Option for the Poor" that took off in the 1960s and 1970s and was given greater promotion in Churchwide Councils by Latin American bishops. The other was the "theology of culture," which acquired a great salience in the 1970s and 1980s and was inextricably related to the processes of thinking of and about "Latin America." The CELAM, moreover, was also at the vanguard of advocating for greater social, political, and economic integration across countries in Latin America – a project that has still to fully flourish.

The Church in the "Indias"[4]

Between the 16th to the early 19th centuries, much of the territory in the Americas was ruled by the Spanish. It was occupied, organized, and governed through various complex political, legal, and administrative systems that had, among others, two main actors, the Crown and the Church (Podetti, 2017a, 2017b, 2019). Their importance laid on the degree of organization, unity, and control they had over their agents in the field and on their influence on the decision making, regardless of the organizational diversity and complexity of the huge regulatory normative apparatus and the infinity of the different regional realities from California to Tierra del Fuego.

The Crown and the Church were strong unifying elements in the Americas. As a matter of fact, two of the main American polities in the 15th century –

the Aztec and the Inca, which fought against the Spanish invaders in the first decades of the 16th century – had no significant contact between each other and, of course, had no shared past either. In their universal pretensions, Crown and Church endowed the Americas with common frameworks that allowed them to incorporate vastly different local social, political, and legal configurations.

On the other hand, in order to restrict this chapter to the ecclesiastic sphere – although this could also describe the secular one – it is worth mentioning that the mobility of the Church's agents, from priests (*curas*) to, especially, bishops, was quite high. This characteristic made pastors on both low and high levels of the ecclesiastic hierarchy familiar with the entire Hispanic American territory. To put just one example: in their origin, the Jesuit-Guaraní reductions in Paraguay, an especially significant social experience over the course of 150 years, played a key role at the Synod of Asuncion of 1603 given their recommendations on the matter of the pastoral care of the indigenous peoples. The bishop who organized this event, Martín Ignacio de Loyola – nephew of Ignacio de Loyola, but Franciscan – had been a missionary in the Philippines and China, and by the time he arrived in Asunción, he had already made two circumnavigations (Loyola, 1989). Therefore, it could be claimed that most of the civil and ecclesiastical leaders of the new emerging American societies between 1500 and 1800 had (apart from the same nationality, Spanish) unprecedented levels of cosmopolitanism (Polo y La Borda, 2017). The situation in Brazil was different, for Brazil kept its judicial-political unity in its territory after its separation from Portugal in 1822 and preserved the monarchy until 1889. It was because of this that in Brazil, the clergy and the episcopate did not suffer as radical changes as in Hispanic America.

The Earthquake of Secularization

The secularization processes of the 19th century displaced the Church from its virtual education monopoly (from early education through university) and took away its economic support through the various laws that amounted to confiscation. Additionally, the secularization gradually made the Church less influential and reduced its jurisdiction over basic social services like hospitals, almshouses, cemeteries, etc. After 40 or 50 years, the position of the Church in most Ibero-America had changed radically. Nevertheless, above all, it was its institutional continuity that was most radically affected. This was because if the effects of the continuous independence and civil wars were also considered, it can be stated that there was a dismantling of the priestly and episcopal structures, laicization of priests, the abandonment of state support for the priesthood, the closure of seminaries, etc. Particularly, the secularization in education had a huge impact and was accompanied by the loss of the central role of the Church in the intellectual field. Yet although this central role had already been questioned in the 18th century, there was a major Catholic Enlightenment, which was fertile in almost every intellectual field. Then, in the 19th century, the Church would drift toward a growing isolation in the intellectual field, even though several significant exceptions could be mentioned.

In the specific cases of Hispanic America and Brazil, it is important to consider that the Church was administered by the Iberian Crowns, as a consequence of the *Patronato Regio*. Even though Rome had always been the arbitrator of several issues, the clergy and the episcopate were mostly dependent on the Crown. Therefore, when independence led to the administrative separation from Spain, a peculiar situation arose. On the one hand, the republican governments considered themselves to be heirs to the *Patronato* regime; but on the other hand, they were growingly secular and anticlerical. Consequently, a singular paradox emerged, since anticlerical governments had to govern the clergy.

In conclusion, the ecclesiastical organization, which had been an important agent of integration during the occupation of the territories in the Americas and of social and political organization, was pushed away from most key decisions only a few decades after the declarations of independence. Evidently, there is simplification in the description of this process, and there were nuances across time and places. I would not argue, either, that the Church lost key sources of power. Above all, this was the result of the presence of a number of parishioners, both in urban and rural areas, who demanded religious attention. In addition, the Church devised survival strategies – and in some cases resistance – against secularization. Yet the vast, leading Hispanic-American Church became disaggregated into a group of churches of lesser influence. Its links across the whole continent disappeared, and local churches grew disconnected from both Spain (due to independence) and Rome (as the *Patronato* was now controlled by each one of the new republican governments).

Ecclesiastical reconstitution

The hypothesis presented in this chapter is that the stage of virtual "reconstitution" undergone by the Church in the 20th century, after the secularization earthquake, had a continental scope and direction in the case of Latin America. This "reconstitution" is to be understood in a partial and restricted sense, for in formal terms, the Church in the Indies and the Church of the age of secularism were one and the same. Notwithstanding this fundamental similarity, significant changes distinguished the Church of the Spanish period, the Church of the 19th century, and the Church of the 20th century from each other. The Church in the second half of the 20th century, for instance, recuperated a regional, even continental scale and dimension. Actually, the process of reconstitution out of the atomization of the national churches ended in 1955, with the founding of a permanent continental organization, the CELAM.

This process took its first steps in the second half of the 19th century. A key model was the foundation of Rome's *Seminario Americano*. As of the mid-19th century, the number of vacant parishes and priestless churches grew to an evident level in most Latin American countries. On the initiative of a Chilean priest, José Ignacio Eyzaguirre, a seminary aimed at the training of priests was founded in Rome in 1858, and it was named Pontifical Latin American College (*Pontificio Collegio Pio Latinoamericano*). As Alberto Methol Ferré has argued, this was the first institution to take the name of "Latin America" (Methol Ferré, 1987, p. 21). In any case, the college became a cradle of priests and ecclesiastical groups, who received both a "Roman" and a "Latin American" education. This detail is important since, as has just been mentioned, neither the Church of the Indies nor the Church of the secularization process had this "Roman" stamp, despite the unquestionable significance that Rome and the pontificate had to any ecclesiastical actor. Precisely, being less connected to Rome in this specific sense rendered the Church in the Americas much more reliant upon, and thus vulnerable to, the power of the state – be it the Spanish Crown or the republics of the new world. Therefore, the condition of "Roman" and "Latin American" went hand in glove with the process of the Church's reconstitution. The Pontifical Latin American College – which is still open nowadays and from which the renowned and recently canonized Archbishop Monsignor Oscar Arnulfo Romero graduated – produced a new clergy and a new episcopate who shared their training – and connections – with seminarians, priests, and bishops from every country in Latin America (Collegio Pio Latinoamericano, n.d.). Actually, the college's alumni soon acquired the nickname "*piolatinoamericanos.*"

From the councils to the general conferences

Since the early days of missionization and ecclesiastical organization in the Spanish America synods and councils met frequently.[5] Such routine assemblies was, in fact, one of the defining factors of the Church in the Indies. The tradition was interrupted completely in the 19th century, and it was not resumed until 1899, when the Pontifical Latin American College hosted a council in which 53 bishops took part. Beginning this tradition anew took an unprecedented scale. For the new meetings now encompassed the whole Hispanic/Luso-American region, "Latin America," and included among its goals the preservation of the Latin American unity as a social and cultural reality closely linked to the modern history of the Church.

The existing bibliography agrees (Pontificia Comisión para América Latina, 1999; Pazos, 1998; Piccardo, 2012) on the fact that the 1899 Conference marked the beginning of a new ecclesiastical era in Latin America, the basis upon which the Latin American Church grew in the 20th century. This led to the restoration of regular large-scale meetings of bishops, triggering a long series of ecclesiastical assemblies. These assemblies first took place on local levels – in dioceses, later in each country – to later be extended to the whole region through five Latin American councils that have taken place since 1955. These General Conferences of the Latin American Episcopate have taken place throughout the region, and the most recent was held in Brazil in 2007.

The creation of these events also fostered the enforcement of the resolutions of the Plenary Latin American Council of 1899. The Plenary became the first systematic and continental guide of the now-Latin American Church, after the communication channels between ecclesiastical units across the region had broken down in the 19th century, leading to the isolation of national churches and even local dioceses. This process led to the creation of a permanent institutional space, the CELAM, whose pastoral, coordination, training, and education activities finally rendered "Latin American" the host of Catholic churches in the region.

The new "council" cycle started in 1955 with the General Conference of the Latin American Episcopate in Rio de Janeiro, and its greatest novel contribution was the creation of the CELAM. Although its bylaws have been modified several times, its goal remains to be a coordinating body of the church in Latin America and the Caribbean. Its definition and scope of activity explain why the CELAM can be considered a resilience actor of Latin American regionalism of the second half of the 20th century. Among the most outstanding features one can mention (*Consejo Episcopal Latinoamericano*, 2009):

1   To promote episcopal collegiality, communion, and communication between the General Conferences of Latin America and the Caribbean Episcopate.
2   To study the problems shared by the Church in Latin America and the Caribbean, in order to provide criteria and guidelines for the pastoral care.
3   To strengthen the dynamic presence of the Church in the historical process of Latin America and the Caribbean, through appropriate services.
4   To promote and encourage initiatives and deeds of common interest.
5   To offer advice and other services to the General Conferences that request such aid, as per the demands of the Church in Latin America and the Caribbean and the means of the very CELAM.
6   To foster the strengthening of the hierarchical communion and to seek the proper development of bodies and movements of the Church in Latin America and the Caribbean in order to render them as efficient as possible.
7   To organize the General Conferences of Latin America and the Caribbean Episcopate whenever they are called by the Holy See, on their own initiative, or as requested by the CELAM.

(para. 4)

When the decision as to which city should be the seat of the CELAM was put to the vote among the bishops who took part in the Conference, Rome obtained 32 votes, defeating Bogotá by 2. Nevertheless, as he approved the resolutions of the Conference, Pope Pius XII suggested that CELAM'S seat should stay in Latin America and therefore in Bogotá. Chilean Bishop Manuel Larraín, in his defense of the creation of the CELAM, claimed, "Only a close-knit Latin America, whose unity lies in its action rather than in its faith and charity . . ., can provide the Church with the answer of redeeming hope people expect from it" (Botero, 1982, p. 17).

CELAM debated and found its role through a series of ordinary assemblies (11 took place between 1955 and 1968),[6] and it became more visible after the General Conferences, and especially after the Second Vatican Council (also Vatican II; 1962–1965). Vatican II, on the one hand, endowed bishops with a shared Latin American perspective through mutual understanding and coexistence in the Council's sessions in Rome. On the other, during deliberations on the implementations of Vatican II in Latin America, the CELAM had its first opportunity to play a leading regional role, and this is why the Conferences of Medellín (1968) and Puebla (1979) are so important.

Theological Latin American debates

Even though this ecclesiastical reconstitution had a "Latin Americanizing" stamp, the intersections with other "Latin Americanisms" were still incipient during the first half of the 20th century. There are important connections, and a clear example is the presence of José Vasconcelos – a committed pro "Latin America" activist since the 1920s – in the pages of the Catholic magazine *Latinoamérica*. Notwithstanding this, local episcopates were still too focused on the reorganization of dioceses, parishes, the development of the specific pastoral activities, and the challenges posed by various nation-states to the Church.

It was through the General Conferences held in Medellín (1968) and Puebla (1979) that the "Latin Americanization" of the Church became stronger and where the intersections with other "Latin Americanist" social actors developed and intensified.

The theological debates were actually a crucial part of this stage. In this context, theology in Latin America acquired a vigor and social importance that it had not had since, probably, the 16th century. Theology became a main actor in intellectual debates way beyond the secluded discussions in seminaries and the ecclesiastical institutions. Consequently, there was an unprecedented boost in the intersections between the internal process of the "post–Vatican II" Church (*Iglesia posconciliar*) and other social and political processes.

Exploring all these controversies, its many facets, and the different stances would be impossible in the space provided in this chapter. Suffice to say that the intersection of post-Vatican II theological, political, and social debates infused new life to the Church, mobilized lay and religious agents, and motivated intercommunication between the Church and society. From this point of view, it is interesting to lay out at least the topics that were disseminated to other social actors by these controversies.

In this period, the Church spread two significant topics. Under no circumstances can it be claimed that they were the only two nor the main ones. They are discussed in this chapter because their conjunction with contemporary issues of the social and political agenda – of America and the whole world – is one of the reasons that, along with the dynamism that characterized the Latin American Church of those years, explains the role played by the Church in the resilience of the continental integration during this period.

The topics are extracted from the Final Documents of the General Conferences of Medellín and Puebla. The General Conferences, being true continental "councils," are events in which the idea production and the decision making become much more intricate and impactful than those that frequently appear in the routine of ecclesiastical life. Since they have been held in almost every decade (1955, 1968, 1979, 1992, 2007), they allow for a preparation activity from the ground up. Preparations starts on the parish level through meetings that are later taken to diocesan and archdiocesan institutions, national episcopal conferences, apart from an equivalent activity to prepare the subsequent adoption of resolutions. These activities have been quite disparate in each General Conference, and, of course, each ecclesiastical jurisdiction and institution can work on them – in fact, it has happened – with different degrees of strength and commitment. Nevertheless, as a whole and, especially, from 1955 to 2007, its impact on the processes of other social actors and on the general process should be studied in detail when carrying out research on the *resilience of integration* from the perspective of the actors.

Focusing on the final documents, their definitions, and nuances should not lead to the omission of other documentation (preparatory documents, consultation documents, deliberation minutes, book and article references) that was also part, in each case, of the General Conferences. A single example will be provided: the last book published by Alberto Methol Ferré, the lengthy interview conducted by the writer and journalist Alver Metalli, *La América Latina del siglo XXI* (Latin America in the 21st Century), was written in 2006 for the preparation of the Fifth General Conference. Methol Ferré is mentioned because of his relevance as an intellectual and political advisor in Uruguay and Argentina, with a widespread repercussion on the whole Latin American region – particularly in relation to his contributions to historical and geopolitical thinking in the Church.

The chosen topics are really well known and have been thoroughly studied, which is why this analysis will not be exhaustive. Alternatively, it will be argued why they were vehicles to spread ideas that converged into actions and processes for the resilience of integration.

Preferential option for the poor

In the case of the Conference of Medellín, the topic was *preferential option for the poor*, which stemmed from the Second Vatican Council. This is due to the fact that, within the general framework of the purposes of the Ecumenical Council, the situation of the poor was declared one of the most severe issues of the time. In the first session of the Council (Planellas I Barnosell, 2014, p. 87), a group dedicated to this specific issue, called "Church of the Poor," was established. It was inspired by the French priest Paul Gauthier, by then settled in Nazareth as a pastoral worker. Even though he had published some works, his ideas had not acquired diffusion beyond the pastoral sphere. Gauthier's ideas and pastoral message did not truly transcend until he published, in 1963, the book *Les Pauvres, Jésus et l'Église* (The Poor, Jesus, and the Church). This work was widely read among several conciliar fathers, and it inspired deliberations and documents. The group Church of the Poor became more prestigious, and it contributed to Vatican II. Some of its members were the Brazilian Bishop Monsignor Hélder Câmara, who had a profound and fruitful influence in Brazil and, later, in Latin America as well (way beyond the ecclesiastical sphere), and Manuel Larraín Errázuriz, a Chilean bishop whose work at the CELAM had a significant impact on its development.

The group defined the matter as theologically important, and the Church of the Poor became a feature of the *aggiornamento* of the Church that was expected as a result of the Council. The French theologian Yves Congar was one of the key actors of the French "New Theology." He was highly influential in the deliberations and resolutions of Vatican II and participated in some meetings of the group. Congar is mentioned here because a book (Congar, 2014) also had a great impact on the Council, and it is considered a key source by the current pontiff (Pope Francis). Congar also served a pivotal role in shaping of Alberto Methol Ferré's thought, who is considered, as already explained, one of the most distinguished Latin Americanist thinkers of the second half of the 20th century.

These ideas imbued most of the Final Document of the General Conference held in Medellín (1968). Although the document remains multifaceted, its general message points to the need to move towards a "human economy," one that is at the service neither of the capital nor of the state. And that change is seen as vital to "trigger the true process of Latin American development and integration" (Second General Conference, 1968, Justice, para. 11). Later in the text, it is claimed that "without unity, Latin America will not be able to liber-ate itself from neo-colonialism, nor will it be able to realize itself in freedom, with its own cultural, socio-political, and economic characteristics" (Second General Conference of Latin America Episcopate, 1968, Justice, para. 13). The preferential option for the poor, plus several pastoral provisions – like the cre-ation of social pastoral commissions in each diocese – implied a new vision on economy, and this new economy was regarded as connected to greater regional integration, both from a social and from a political-continental perspective. Explicitly, the document (Second General Conference, 1968) states that:

> The integration process . . . presents itself as a pressing necessity for Latin America. Without intending to set norms for truly complex, technical aspects, we thus deem it opportune to highlight its multi-dimensional nature. Integration . . . is not solely an economic process; it implies other aspects . . . social, political, cultural, religious, racial.
>
> (Peace, para. 11)

Intellectual reflection on the poor brought the issue of regional integration, as a multidimensional phenomenon, to the forefront. In Chapter XIII, it is stated that "The Latin American Church must speak out and aid the continent, which faces hardships as distressful as those of integration, development, radical changes, and poverty" (Second General Conference, 1968, Education, para. 1). The preparation process and, above all, that of the implementation of the General Conference of Medellín coexisted with the most influential period of the Cuban Revolution in Latin America and with the time when youth and student activism was at its peak.

Therefore, political and ideological debates met, everywhere, with ecclesiastical debates over the meaning and scope of the conciliar reforms. Various situations, spaces, and trends for the production of theological knowledge emerged, resulting in the Theologies of Liberation.

The enormous ecclesiastical mobilization brought by Vatican II in Latin America turned the Church into a more prominent institution as it had been since before the secularization earthquake of the 19th century. This mobilization promoted a serious dialogue between the Church and different organizations of civil-society and political organizations, which had been specifically suggested at Vatican II.

The theology of culture

Regarding the General Conference of Puebla (Mexico, 1979), the chosen topic was the "theology of culture." Even though it was not as influential as the preferential option for the poor at Vatican II, it may have represented a greater theological novelty. The apostolic exhortation *Evangelii nuntiandi* (Evangelization in the Modern World, *EN*, December 8, 1975), issued by Pope Paul VI on the 10th anniversary of Vatican II and one year after the Third Ordinary General Assembly of the Synod of Bishops, took on the debates over the relationship between the Catholic Church and the different cultures in the world. This synod was the first ecumenical and ecclesiastical assembly in which the Latin American Church had a central role. Methol Ferré posited that there had been a virtuous circle of Vatican II (1962–1965), the General Conference of Medellín (1968), the General Assembly of the Synod of Bishops (1975), and the General Conference of Puebla (1979). This virtuous circle prepared, as the Brazilian theologian Henrique de Lima Vaz said, the evolution of the Latin American Church from "reflection-Church" to "source-Church" (Methol & Metalli, 2006, pp. 53–54). The "source-churches" find the sources for their own renewal within themselves, and the "reflection-churches" accompany them. This Latin American ecclesiastical leading role was the result of its new continental nature and strengthened the CELAM (*Consejo Episcopal Latinoamericano*). This position helped the Latin American Church achieve a more active role in the resilience processes of the regionalism of the final quarter of the 20th century.

Moreover, since *EN* was one of the "steps" of this virtuous circle, it was widely accepted in Latin America and, especially, at the General Conference of Puebla. Let us start by considering the emphasis on the fact that the objectives of the Council "are definitively summed up in this single one: to make the Church of the twentieth century ever better fitted for proclaiming the Gospel to the people of the twentieth century" (Pope Paul VI, 1975, p. 2). The Church was thus required to know each culture of the world (Pope Paul VI, 1975):

> The Gospel, and therefore evangelization, are certainly not identical with culture, and they are independent in regard to all cultures. Nevertheless, the kingdom which the Gospel proclaims is lived by men who are profoundly linked to a culture, and the building up of the kingdom cannot avoid borrowing the elements of human culture or cultures. Though independent of cultures, the Gospel and evangelization are not necessarily incompatible with them; rather they are capable of permeating them all without becoming subject to any one of them.
>
> (pp. 7–8)

In 1979, when the General Conference met in Puebla, Pope John Paul II (Pope John Paul II, 1979) explicitly accepted the idea that, when fulfilling the evangelizing role, the Church should be "inculturated" into all cultures and societies:

> The term "acculturation" or "inculturation" may be a neologism, but it expresses very well one factor of the great mystery of the Incarnation. We can say of catechesis, as well as of evangelization in general, that it is called to bring the power of the Gospel into the very heart of culture and cultures. For this purpose, catechesis will seek to know these cultures and their essential components; it will learn their most significant expressions; it will respect their particular values and riches. In this manner it will be able to offer these cultures the knowledge of the hidden mystery and help them to bring forth from their own living tradition original expressions of Christian life, celebration and thought.
>
> (pp. 27–28)

The Final Document of the Puebla Conference thoroughly addressed the relationship between Church and culture, mentioning, for example, that the accomplishment of the mission of the Church implies feeling "compelled to get to know the Latin American people within its historical context and with its different circumstances" (Third General Conference, 1979, para. 3). The Church adopts the role of agent of study and knowledge of the "Latin American people." The Document elaborates at length on the features of Latin American culture and its transformations in the face of external influences and the challenges of the contemporary world, also acknowledging its complexity and diversity, yet seeing it as a whole. In its first chapter, the Final Document (Third General Conference, 1979) describes a "historical vision," "the greatest moments of evangelization in Latin America" (para. 3). This approach emphasizes the importance of analyzing the Latin American present from a cultural-historical perspective: although the document mainly tackles the present and the future (three chapters), it sets out to properly assemble them with the past. That is, it arranges its assessments (of the present) and its proposals (towards the future) into a single tradition. The Church's interest in and concern about the cultural-historical perspective found roots in its own nature (Third General Conference, 1979):

> The history of the Church is, mainly, the history of the evangelization of a people that is constantly gestated: *it is born and inserted into the secular existence of nations.* The Church, when "becoming incarnate," is a crucial contributor to the birth of nationalities.
>
> (para. 3; emphasis added)

Consequently, the Document includes the work of the Church in Latin America within the particular history of its peoples, which leads the Church to the need of getting to know them and, especially, to absorb them as part of its own history. The document (Third General Conference, 1979) later characterizes culture in Latin America:

> Latin America forged, out of the sometimes painful convergence of utterly diverse cultures and races, a new *mestizaje* of ethnicities and ways of life and thinking, which allowed for the gestation of a new race, once the harsh separations that had taken place before were over.
>
> (para. 5)

It also delves into the way in which the Church took part in this process, "one of the most important chapters in the history of the Church" (Third General Conference, 1979):

> Innumerable charity, aid, and education initiatives, as well as the original syntheses of the evangelization and the human advancement promoted by the Franciscan, Augustinian, Dominican, Jesuit, Mercedarian, and other missions, are there . . . , [as well as] creativity in the pedagogy of faith, the wide range of resources that were part of all arts, from music, singing, and dance to architecture, painting, and theater. These pastoral skills are linked to a moment of significant theological thinking and intellectual dynamics that promote the creation of universities and schools and the production of dictionaries, reference grammars, and catechisms in several indigenous languages.
>
> (para. 9)

Through an explicit definition of the convergence of tradition and progress, the document (Third General Conference, 1979) defines the activity currently undertaken by the Church as the continuation of the pastoral efforts since the first evangelization:

Especially ever since Medellín, totally aware of its mission and truly open to conversation, the Church analyzes the signs of the times and is kindly willing to evangelize, in order to contribute to the creation of a new more just and humane society, which is loudly demanded by our peoples. This way, tradition and progress, which seemed opponents who were constantly inflicting harm to each other in Latin America, today come together looking for a new synthesis that joins the opportunities of the future with the energies coming from our shared roots. Therefore, in this far-reaching movement for renewal that opens a new era, amidst the recent challenges, we, the pastors, accept the secular episcopal tradition of the continent and get ready to deliver, with hope and strength, the salvation message of the Gospel to all men, preferably the poor and the forgotten.

(para. 12)

Chapter II, "Socio-cultural Vision on the Reality of Latin America," includes a series of distinctive features of this reality, the "growing interest in native values and respecting the originality of indigenous cultures and their communities" (Third General Conference, 1979, para. 19). Ever since the General Conference of Puebla, several initiatives on the role of culture – and particularly on popular cultures and traditions – in evangelization were developed. For example, a campaign for pastoral care and revaluation of popular expressions of faith was conducted, and the topic "popular religiosity" became a significant part of the theological creation. This line of thought runs deep in the works of several thinkers and trends in literary writing, academic writing, and social sciences, which construed some of the chief tenets of Latin American identity over the 20th century. From the writings in José Enrique Rodo's *Ariel* of the beginning of the century to the artistic avant-gardes of the 1920s and 1930s to the new narrative of the 1960s, the topic of cultural identity penetrated the whole sphere of cultural creation in Latin America.

In an article published in 1988, "*Los rumbos nuevos de Rodó*" (Rodó's New Directions), Alberto Methol Ferré stated that, at the Puebla Conference, the Church had resumed a process of cultural Latin American self-awareness, which had been started by the '900 Generation but cut short in the mid-20th century (Methol Ferré, 1988, pp. 49–50). Methol Ferré was trying, almost ten years after the Conference in Puebla, to connect its contributions with the already planned Fourth Conference in Santo Domingo. His intention was to discover how to preserve this cultural-historical Latin American awareness. He argued that the cultural-historical vision of the Puebla Final Document could be interpreted as a "new path" of José Enrique Rodó's ideas toward the end of the century. This hypothesis, formulated by Methol Ferré, placed the Church's theological reflection along the lines of a singular moment of Latin America's intellectual history, the '900 Generation. And he is not the only one, for historiography ascribes a big intellectual interest in Latin American regionalism to this generation as well.

As for the theology of culture, it will strengthen, in the bosom of the Church, the acknowledgment of the value of cultural identity as an evangelization tool. In the arts, literary writing, academic writing, and ecclesiastic fields, the reference is the whole continent. This does not mean that "national horizons" will vanish but that they will be naturally absorbed into Latin America. The theological debates at this stage are not specifically Mexican, Brazilian, or Argentine but Latin American instead. The new narrative of the most eminent writers of the mid-20th century is not Colombian, Cuban, Argentine, Mexican or Brazilian, but Latin American. Gabriel García Márquez, Alejo Carpentier, Jorge Luis Borges, Juan Rulfo, and Guimaraes Rosa are recognized as Latin American authors rather than as Colombians, Cubans, Mexicans, Argentines or Brazilians. Thus, the resilience of regionalism, in most part of the 20th century, is part of the significant convergence between theological production and literary and artistic production.

From Puebla to Aparecida

The General Conferences of Medellín and Puebla represented a pivotal moment for Latin America's theology. They managed to take theological debates beyond seminars and Catholic universities. These meetings belong to a very creative period, in which a "Latin American" theology emerged not as an interruption of the Catholic theological tradition but rather as though the Church in Latin America had reached maturity. This implied thinking theologically from the perspective of the Church's inculturation into the peoples of Latin America. By analogy with what was mentioned earlier, it can be argued that this was not a Mexican, Colombian, or Chilean theology but a *Latin American* one. In other words, when considering the regional context, the Catholic Church appears as the main actor of the resilience of Latin American regionalism.

Nevertheless, by the time the Conferences of Medellín and Puebla were held, the Church in Latin America was also surrounded by its own internal controversies. To some extent, these controversies were related to the approaches of the different trends that led this renewal – which would be impossible to address here. The research on the topic has led to a good summary by J. I. Saranyana (2002). These were years of dialogue between Christians and Marxists, for they were looking for things in common in spite of the contradictions between Christianity and Marxism. These were the years of debates on democracy and "armed conflict" as different paths toward profound social change. In 1967, a year before the Conference of Medellín, Methol Ferré published an article in the Catholic magazine *Víspera*, warning about inconsistencies and serious mistakes made by propagandists of the armed conflict (Methol, 1967, pp. 17–18). These controversies were lived many times with passion and generated wounds that to time to heal.

In this regard, the subsequent conferences, in Santo Domingo, Dominican Republic (1992), and Aparecida in Brazil (2007), were mainly focused on preparing a summary. These events worked on organization rather than creation, managing to express the theological Latin American thinking in a mature way.

The Fourth General Conference of Santo Domingo was summoned and developed in the context of several different commemorations of the 500th anniversary of Columbus's arrival in the Americas. Pieces of research and publications encouraged debates on the "discovery" of America, European conquests, and the history and the situation of the indigenous and Afro-American peoples. In fact, commemorations had begun even before that, as in 1984 the Catholic Church organized the preparation of the commemoration of the 500-year presence of the Church in the Americas.

The Santo Domingo Concluding Document kept and developed the theology of culture that had been built in Puebla, using the concept "culture our peoples share" (Fourth General Conference, 1992, Priority pastoral guidelines, para. 7) as framework of reference and replacing the name "Latin America" with "Latin America and the Caribbean." The Document (Fourth General Conference, 1992) described the *mestizaje* (miscegenation) question as a generic feature of Latin American society and culture and explained it within three conclusions, the broadest of which says:

> The encounter between Iberian Catholicism and the cultures of the Americas resulted in a singular *mestizaje* process which, in spite of its conflicts, emphasizes the Catholic roots as well as the Continent's particular identity. This *mestizaje* process, which can also be noticed in several forms of popular religiosity and mestizo art, is the conjunction of perennial elements of Christianity and typical elements of the Americas, and it spread over the whole Continent since the beginning.
>
> (500 years after the first evangelization, para. 4)

For the first time in the Concluding Documents of the General Conferences, "Latin American integration" got a specific mention (Fourth General Conference, 1992). The authors claimed that "experience has proven that no nation can live and develop strongly if it is isolated" and warned that "Our nations are experiencing isolation and division, while the economy of the world is getting global, and large blocs are being formed and/or redesigned. . . . These are large blocs that threaten the whole continent with isolation if it does not serve their economic interests" (Latin American Integration, para. 7–8).

As for the Church, it had to solve the "lack of communion" between local churches of the region, as this weakened the very Church's capacity for action as an integration factor (Fourth General Conference, 1992, Latin American Integration, para. 9). Among its pastoral lines, the following one can be highlighted: "To foster and accompany the efforts to achieve Latin American integration as a 'Great Homeland' [Patria Grande], from a solidarity perspective that also demands a new international order" (Fourth General Conference, 1992, Latin American Integration, para. 10).

In his opening speech, Pope John Paul II stated that "a factor that could be of great help to overcome the pressing problems that nowadays affect this continent is Latin American integration" (Pope John Paul II, 1992, p. 10). Moreover, he regarded integration as a heavy responsibility that lay with rulers. At first, the Fifth General Conference was summoned in celebration of CELAM's (*Consejo Episcopal Latinoamericano*) 50th anniversary, and thus Brazil was chosen to host it again to commemorate the first meeting. For the first time, it took place in a sanctuary,[7] the Cathedral Basilica of the National Shrine of Our Lady Aparecida, a major Catholic pilgrimage site in Latin America (it received more than 12 million visitors in 2018). Given how important popular religiosity became in Latin American theology after the Puebla Conference (Morandé, 2010; Secretariado General del CELAM, 1977), the location of the Fifth Conference was not simply fortuitous. This Concluding Document was longer than any other of the General Conferences of the Latin American Episcopate. The growing length of the Concluding Documents (Rio de Janeiro, 23 pages; Medellín, 58; Puebla, 180; Santo Domingo, 103; and Aparecida, 268) reflects how these became more significant to the Church in Latin America. The increase in theological research and publishing in the region can also account for this tendency.

The name "Latin America and the Caribbean" and the acknowledgment of a cultural common ground, "our Latin American and Caribbean culture" (Fifth General Conference, 2007, p. 12), were reasserted. In its introduction, Catholic tradition is defined as "a foundation stone of Latin American and Caribbean identity, originality, and unity" (Fifth General Conference, 2007, p. 3). The interest in and commitment to regionalism were also restated: "we aspire toward a united, reconciled, and integrated Latin America and Caribbean" (Fifth General Conference, 2007, p. 122). Several paragraphs analyzing the situation of the continent appear under the title "Socio-political dimension" (Fifth General Conference, 2007):

> In Latin America and the Caribbean there is a growing desire for regional integration through multilateral agreements, involving a growing number of countries that establish their own regulations in the fields of trade, services, and patents. Common origin combines with culture, language, and religion, and so integration involves not only of markets, but civil institutions and, above all, persons. Similarly positive is the globalization of justice in the field of human rights and of crimes against humanity, which will enable all gradually to live under equal norms, intended to protect their dignity, integrity, and life.
>
> (p. 21)

The Document (Fifth General Conference, 2007), delves into the Church's concept of Latin American unity: The dignity of recognizing ourselves as a family of Latin American and Caribbean peoples involves a singular experience of closeness, fellowship, and solidarity. We are not merely a continent, simply a geographical fact with an unintelligible mosaic of contents. Nor are we a total-ity of peoples and ethnic groups in juxtaposition (p. 123).

In addition, by repeating John Paul II's opening words from Santo Domingo, the Document (Fifth General Conference, 2007) adds: "One and plural, Latin America is the common house, the great homeland of brothers and sisters 'of peoples,' whom as His Holiness John Paul II said in Santo Domingo: 'the same geography, Christian faith, language, and culture have joined together defini-tively in the course of history'" (p. 123).

The Document also recalled that both Puebla's and Santo Domingo's Con-cluding Documents used the term "Great Homeland" or *Patria Grande* to talk about Latin America and concludes: "The Fifth Conference in Aparecida expresses its firm intention to pursue this commitment" (Fifth General Con-ference, 2007, p. 123). Nevertheless, it also notices setbacks that may prevent that ideal from coming true:

> There is certainly no other region that has so many factors of unity as Latin America . . . However, it is a unity torn apart because it is permeated by deep dominations and contradictions, still incapable of bringing together into itself "all the races" and overcoming the gap of tremendous inequality and marginalization. It is our great homeland, but it will be really "great" only when it is so for everyone, with greater justice.
>
> (p. 124)

Conclusion

The foundation of the Pontifical Latin American College in 1858 can be regarded as the first response to the secularization crisis and as a symbol of the begin-ning of the Latin American Church's reconstitution following the seculariza-tion "earthquake." Methol Ferré has claimed that perhaps the "Latin American" name of the College had been suggested by Catholic Colombian intellectual José María Torres Caicedo (Methol Ferré, 1987, p. 9). Additionally, he argued that this was the first time at institution called itself "Latin American" (Methol Ferré, 1987, p. 10) – a hypothesis also supported by other authors (Ayala Mora, 2013, p. 234). As for historiography, it mainly ascribes the origin of the name "Latin America" to Torres Caicedo as well. The Uruguayan philosopher Arturo Ardao conducted research on this and included it in several publications, calling Caicedo "Latin America's christener" (Ardao, 1990, p. 40). Still, despite Tor-res Caicedo's claim that he had first used the name "Latin America" in 1851, it was not heard until his poem "Las dos Américas" ("The Two Americas") was published in Paris in 1857 – a year before the foundation of the Pontifical Latin American College (Ardao, 1990, p. 42). José Ignacio Eyzaguirre has been also said to have named the College, for he encouraged and achieved its foundation with Pope Pius IX's support (Ayala Mora, 2013, p. 234).

The coincidence that the name "Latin America" emerged and was used to call the first seminar to train a new clergy for Latin America cleared a new path. This is the path of "Latin Americanization" described in this chapter. The recovery of the council tradition by the Plenary Latin American Council of 1899 gave greater life to this direction. The creation of the Latin American Episcopal Council (CELAM) in 1955 confirmed its institutional nature, and the five General Conferences of the Episcopate, between 1955 and 2007, developed it. Moreover, the "Latin Americanization" of the Catholic Church in the continent was responsible for the greatest international repercussion of the Latin American Church, first by creating the "Latin Americanist" theologies and, finally, thanks to the inauguration of the first Latin American pope ever, in 2013.

A proactive attitude toward Latin American regionalism is found upon analyzing the steps followed by the Catholic Church after the creation of the CELAM (*Consejo Episcopal Latinoamericano*). On the one hand, this attitude was the result of a new internal organization of a regional nature. On the other hand, it stemmed from the elaboration of a sort of theology of the "great homeland" that justified its actions.

By taking this road, the Church even preceded – as already explained – the integration processes of the 20th century. For example, the creation of the CELAM in 1955 was five years before the first treaty of economic integration in the continent: the Latin American Free Trade Association (LAFTA) was signed on February 18, 1960. The Church was aware of this early move, as indicated in the Puebla Concluding Document (p. 53).

The ecclesiastical renewal fostered by Vatican II and its implementation in Latin America helped the Catholic Church recover its leading role in the continent. What is more, some topics included in the new Latin American theology, like the Preferential Option for the Poor and the Theology of Culture, encouraged a constructive dialogue with other social actors. Considering the analysis developed in this chapter, it can be claimed that the Catholic Church plays a significant role in the resilience of regionalism. This is due to the continental system of coordination it established, which is made of institution and networks that think, deliberate, and work from a regional point of view. The several pastoral documents and instructions issued for the whole Latin American continent and the adoption of specifically Latin American theological perspectives – like the Liberation Theology and the Theology of Culture – also contributed to the fulfillment of this role.

Notes

1 I would like to express thanks for the suggestions and comments of the editors of this volume and those made by Álvaro Caso Bello.
2 This is an explicit or tacit premise of much of the literature on the region. A synopsis of the richness in studies on Christianity in Latin America can be found in Orique, Fitzpatrick-Behrens, and Garrard (2015). It should be noted, however, the abundant literature that shows how Catholicism or, more broadly, Christianity, were far from monolithic. Historians, anthropologists, and literary scholars have shown the devotional diversity that, under this umbrella, developed in Latin America since the times of the conquest, with

regional variations in the Andes and Mexico/New Spain, as well as Afro-Catholicism particularly in the Caribbean Basin and Atlantic littoral. In a recent leading handbook of Latin American history, historian José Carlos Moya (2010) notes, however, that much like Iberian languages, law, and other institutions that also had regional variations, "Roman Catholicism had a unifying and lasting effect on the entire region, both as a set of beliefs and practices and as a public institution" (p. 6).

3 Through the Patronato Real, the Holy See conferred on the kings of Spain and Portugal the authority to intervene in different aspects of the rule of the Church in the Americas.

4 "West Indies" or just "Indies" is how the Crown of Spain named the Americas. "Indian" means "belonging or relating to the Indies." For example, the "Laws of the Indies" are called "Indian Law" (Derecho Indiano). Therefore, the "Church of the Indies" was the name of the Church of the Americas between the 16th and 18th centuries.

5 The definition and scope of "councils" and "synods" are complex, given the wide range of situations of and differences between the Catholic Church and other churches. In America, during the Hispanic period, episcopal assemblies were called "councils" (gathering superiors of religious orders, theologian advisors, etc.). For example, the Third Council of Lima (Lima, 1582–1583) and the Third Mexican Council (City of Mexico, 1585) had a significant impact. Regarding the "synods," which occurred more frequently, they brought the clergy and the religious members of dioceses together. The First Synod of Asunción (Asunción, 1603) can be taken as an example (Dussel, 1979, pp. 193–194).

6 The CELAM has departments specialized in different topics and a training center that edits the *Medellín* magazine, which was first launched in 1975. It hosts general coordination meetings, biennial ordinary, and extraordinary general assemblies. Apart from the bishops, the president of the Latin American Confederation of Religious (CLAR) – which groups the religious congregations together – attends the assemblies.

7 Sanctuaries are shrines dedicated to a particular devotion – Christ, the Virgin Mary, or saints. They have mainly emerged as a consequence of the belief in some miracle in a particular place, which then receives visits from people asking for divine favors or coming back to express their gratitude. Pilgrimage and patronal holidays – which commemorate the patron saint of a city, region, or country – are traditions of Latin America's popular culture. Marian shrines, dedicated to the Virgin Mary, and Our Lady of Guadalupe in Mexico, Our Lady of Charity in Cuba, Our Lady Aparecida in Brazil, or Our Lady of Luján in Argentina are some of the most illustrative examples.

References

II Conferencia General del Episcopado Latinoamericano. (1968). *Documento conclusivo*. Retrieved from www.celam.org/documentos/Documento_Conclusivo_Medellin.pdf

III Conferencia General del Episcopado Latinoamericano. (1979). *Documento conclusivo*. Retrieved from www.celam.org/documentos/Documento_Conclusivo_Puebla.pdf

IV Conferencia General del Episcopado Latinoamericano. (1992). *Documento conclusivo*. Retrieved from www.celam.org/documentos/Documento_Conclusivo_Santo_Domingo.pdf

V Conferencia General del Episcopado Latinoamericano. (2007). *Concluding document*. Retrieved from www.celam.org/aparecida/Ingles.pdf

Ardao, A. (1990). *Nuestra América Latina*. Montevideo: Banda Oriental.

Ayala Mora, E. (2013). El origen del nombre América Latina y la tradición católica del siglo XIX. *Anuario Colombiano de Historia Social y de la Cultura, 40*, 213–241. Retrieved from www.scielo.org.co/scielo.php?script=sci_arttext&pid=S0120-24562013000100008

Botero, R. J. (1982). *El CELAM. Apuntes para una crónica de sus veinticinco años*. Medellín: CELAM.

Congar, Y. (2014). *Pour une Église servante et pauvre*. Paris: Cerf.

Consejo Episcopal Latinoamericano. (2009). *Estatutos.* Retrieved from www.celam.org/documentos/Estatutos-CELAM.pdf

de Loyola, M. I. (1989). *Viaje alrededor del mundo.* Madrid: Historia 16.

Dussel, E. (1979). Los concilios provinciales de América Latina en los siglos XVI y XVII. In *El episcopado latinoamericano y la liberación de los pobres 1504–1620.* México: Centro de Reflexión Teológica, chap. 5.

Methol Ferré, A. (1967). La revolución verde oliva, Debray y la OLAS. *Víspera, 3,* 17–39.

Methol Ferré, A. (1987). *La Iglesia en la historia de América Latina.* Buenos Aires: Cuadernos de Nexo.

Methol Ferré, A. (1988). Desde Puebla. Los rumbos nuevos de Rodó. *Nexo, 18,* 48–69.

Methol Ferré, A., & Metalli, A. (2006). *La América Latina del siglo XXI.* Buenos Aires: Edhasa.

Morandé, P. (2010). *Ritual y palabra. Aproximación a la religiosidad popular latinoamericana.* Santiago de Chile: IES.

Moya, J. C. (2010). Introduction: Latin America – The limitations and meaning of a historical category. In *The Oxford handbook of Latin American history.* New York and Oxford: Oxford University Press.

Orique, D. Th., Fitzpatrick-Behrens, S., & Garrard, V. (Eds.). (2015). *The Oxford handbook of Latin American Christianity.* New York and Oxford: Oxford University Press.

Pazos, A. (1998). El *iter* del Concilio Plenario Latino Americano de 1899 o la articulación de la Iglesia latinoamericana. *Anuario de Historia de la Iglesia, 7,* 185–206.

Piccardo, D. R. (2012). *Historia del Concilio Plenario Latinoamericano.* Tesis Doctoral, Universidad de Navarra, Pamplona, España.

Planellas i Barnosell, J. (2014). *La Iglesia de los Pobres en el Concilio Vaticano II.* Barcelona: Herder.

Podetti, J. R. (2017a). *La transformación de los señoríos en repúblicas en el origen de los estados hispanoamericanos modernos.* Montevideo: XXXI Congress of the Latin American Sociological Association.

Podetti, J. R. (2017b). Law and politics in sixteenth-century Mexico: Re-reading Alonso de Veracruz. In R. Hofmeister Pich & A. S. Culleton (Eds.), *Scholastica colonialis: Reception and development of Baroque Scholasticism in Latin America in the sixteenth to eighteenth centuries* (pp. 35–51). Rome: Fédération Internationale des Instituts d'Études Médiévales.

Podetti, J. R. (2019). Raíces cristianas del republicanismo latinoamericano. In R. Buttiglione et al. (Eds.), *Doctrina Social de la Iglesia y compromiso político en América Latina* (pp. 99–109). Santiago de Chile: Academia de Líderes Católicos y Konrad Adenauer Stiftung.

Polo y La Borda, A. (2017). *Cosmopolitanism, mobility, and royal officials in the making of the Spanish empire (1580–1700).* Ph.D. Dissertation, University of Maryland, Maryland. Retrieved from https://drum.lib.umd.edu/handle/1903/20150

Pontificia Comisión para América Latina. (1999). *Acta et Decreta Concilii Plenarii Americae Latinae.* Romae: Typographia Vaticana.

Pontificio Collegio Pio Latinoamericano. (n.d.). *Reseña histórica.* Retrieved from https://piolatino.org/el-collegio/resena-historica/

Pope John Paul II. (1979). *Apostolic Exhortation Catechesi Tradendae.* Retrieved from www.vatican.va/content/john-paul-ii/en/apost_exhortations/documents/hf_jp-ii_exh_16101979_catechesi-tradendae.html

Pope John Paul II. (1992). *Discurso inaugural de la IV Conferencia General del Episcopado Latinoamericano.* Retrieved from http://w2.vatican.va/content/john-paul-ii/es/speeches/1992/october/documents/hf_jp-ii_spe_19921012_iv-conferencia-latinoamerica.html

Pope Paul VI. (1975). *Apostolic Exhortation Evangelii nuntiandi*. Retrieved from www.vatican.va/content/paul-vi/en/apost_exhortations/documents/hf_p-vi_exh_19751208_evangelii-nuntiandi.html

Saranyana, J. I. (dir.) & Alejos Grau, C.-J. (coord.). (2002). *Teología en América Latina. Vol. III: El siglo de las teologías latinoamericanistas (1899–2001)*. Madrid and Frankfurt am Mein: Iberoamericana-Verbuert.

Secretariado General del CELAM. (1977). *Iglesia y religiosidad popular en América Latina*. Bogotá: Consejo Episcopal Latinoamericano.

8 Entrepreneurs in Latin American regional integration from 1960 to 2018

Rita Giacalone and Giovanni Molano Cruz

Introduction

Our objective is to explore entrepreneurs' interaction with different Latin American processes of regional economic integration through time. Survey studies of their positions or opinions about regional integration point to the important role they have played in the process (Salgado & Urriola, 1991; PNUD-BID-INTAL, 2001). But authors have mostly analyzed the subject from the perspective of specific agreements (Schelhase, 2008), individual nation-states (Tussie & Trucco, 2010), and the relationship between regional integration and subjects such as democracy (e.g. Haggard & Kaufman, 1995). We think that analyzing entrepreneurs' interaction with regional integration processes in Latin America, from 1960 to 2018, deepens our understanding of how regionalism has evolved since the mid-twentieth century and how entrepreneurs have contributed to its resilience.

We start from the premise that in Latin America, entrepreneurs are neither the main protagonists of regional integration nor some menacing hidden force working in the shadows but social and political actors who share with state actors the responsibility for the successes and failures of regional processes. Another premise is that, in discussions regarding entrepreneurs' involvement with regional integration, there is an underlying assumption that integration leads to economic development and produces economic benefits to firms. This assumption plays a key role in the way in which they interact with regional agreements. Accordingly, by identifying some explanatory variables of their interaction through time, we hope to improve our knowledge of both regional processes and the development models embedded in them.

In this chapter, we examine business involvement in the Latin American Free Trade Association (LAFTA, ALALC by its Spanish acronym), the Andean Community (CAN, by its Spanish acronym), the Southern Common Market (MERCOSUR by its Spanish acronym), and the Pacific Alliance (PA). First, we look at: (1) the existence of an institutional place for entrepreneurs in those agreements; (2) how did entrepreneurs organize to deal with integration? and (3) what was the entrepreneurs' position regarding the development model embedded in each agreement? Second, we discuss the elements of continuity and change in their involvement and specify some explanatory variables of the entrepreneurs' interaction with Latin American regional integration. This analysis is based on specialized literature and a review of published material emphasizing declarations and contributions by contemporary primary actors or observers.

LAFTA: entrepreneurs build economic development through integration

In 1960, LAFTA changed the national horizons of entrepreneurs' economic activities when it established the goal of developing a free trade zone. LAFTA represented the culmination of a series of studies by the Economic Commission for Latin America and the Caribbean (ECLAC)[1] regarding the need to integrate national markets into a regional framework to achieve development. The expectation was that the agreement would generate a link between entrepreneurs, integration, and development (Ferrer, 1967), but for LAFTA, the private sector was limited to industrialists.

Before LAFTA, industrialist associations had discussed the advantages offered by a regional market (Garcia, 1959), and several ECLA meetings with entrepreneurs discussed the proposed economic agreement. Some of them, such as the meeting to strengthen the railway industry in the region, were initiated by businessmen from Argentina, Brazil, and Chile (CEPAL, 1959). Also, LAFTA increased the number of industrialist associations, because new ones developed to deal with the regional process. In 1963, besides meetings of the leather, steel, automotive, and petrochemical sectors, among others, the Latin American Industrial Association (AILA) came into being (Estatutos de la Asociación de Industriales de Latinoamérica, 1963).

Simultaneously with the organizing efforts of industrialists, LAFTA convened in 1963 the First Convention of Entrepreneurs Participating in the Commercial Exchange of LAFTA Member Countries that resulted in the founding of the Association of Latin American LAFTA Businessmen. Subsequently, LAFTA also institutionalized periodical meetings with different sectors. In 1966, LAFTA established the Business Affairs Advisory Committee (CCAE, by its Spanish acronym), made up of officially accredited representatives of the top national industrial associations. Their function, like that of sector meetings, was to make recommendations and proposals to the LAFTA Permanent Executive Committee.

Between 1963 and 1972, there were 176 sector meetings with the participation of 7,367 entrepreneurs. According to the first LAFTA Executive Secretary, Romulo Almeida, 19 sector organizations participated in those meetings in 1965. With their participation, entrepreneurs showed their interest in shaping economic integration mechanisms (Informe Mensual de Integración Latinoamericana, 1970). The LAFTA annual rounds of negotiations were relatively successful insofar as they included commodities and recommendations made by the entrepreneurs during the sectorial meetings (Baldinelli, 1967, p. 45).

LAFTA recognized the role of entrepreneurs in the practical designing stage of the agreement (i.e. when the formal agreement became implemented). Its authorities claimed that it was essential to obtain more support from governments and entrepreneurs to fortify the agreement (Se va a tratar plan de financiamiento, 1963, p. 143). Participating entrepreneurs accepted their role in LAFTA, and AILA statutes included the objective of coordinating national private-sector associations around trade questions and problems (Estatutos de la Asociación de Industriales de Latinoamérica, 1963, p. 745). Besides, they shared the "spirit" of LAFTA's integration. In the first meeting between the private sector and LAFTA, Mexican entrepreneur Guillermo Nasser Quiñones considered the LAFTA agreement "historic, unavoidable and necessary" and claimed that businessmen had the responsibility to translate it into cooperative actions overcoming national interests and to partake "of a plurinational or Latin Americanist feeling" (Nasser Quiñones, 1963, p. 736). For Jose Zabala, general manager of the Chilean company *Manufacturas de Cobre*, Latin American integration was urgently needed (Zabala, 1967, p. 63). The Uruguayan Chamber of Industry, initially skeptical about LAFTA, argued in 1966 that the regional process was fundamental to Uruguay and that the country needed a long-term integration policy (Rivarola, 2003, p. 173).

Nonetheless, disagreements between governments and entrepreneurs developed during LAFTA implementation. The most important one was that even though the latter insisted on including state financing of regional trade, coordination of trade policies, harmonization of exchange rates, simplification of formalities, etc., to facilitate industrial complementarity, LAFTA maintained automatic tariff reduction as its main instrument. Disagreement was clear during the process to compile national lists of goods to be subjected to tariff elimination, as well as in the compilation of the common list.

LAFTA members could establish bilateral sector agreements, whose tariff reductions were incorporated onto national lists, but this mechanism was implemented rather slowly, because its inclusion of the most favored nation clause permitted non-signatories to obtain the same benefits without making concessions. Until 1964, only two agreements of this type had been signed, but between 1965 and 1969, there were 25 after it was decided that only signatories would benefit from those agreements (Baldinelli, 1967, p. 48). By 1970, the industrial complementarity stipulated by LAFTA had not involved any industrial programming (Prebisch, 1972), and the Caracas Protocol postponed until 1980 the establishment of a free trade zone, effectively ending the tariff-reduction process (Conclusión de la IX Conferencia, 1970, p. 14). Although Elvio Baldinelli, director of industrial affairs, considered that LAFTA's receptivity to entrepreneurs' recommendations was little (Baldinelli, 1967, pp. 46–47), Gustavo Magariños, LAFTA secretary, declared that negotiations with entrepreneurs had produced 249 tariff reductions (Dos opiniones divergentes sobre la IX Conferencia, 1970, p. 18). In Chile and Uruguay, entrepreneurs' associations were driving forces behind LAFTA (Rivarola, 2003).

However, one factor that reduced entrepreneurs' influence on LAFTA was the diverging interests of the largest countries (Mexico, Brazil, Argentina), middle-sized countries (Chile, Colombia, Peru, Venezuela), and the smallest ones (Bolivia, Ecuador, Paraguay, Uruguay). For the small economies, LAFTA was not positive, because the biggest countries dominated intra-regional trade of manufactured goods (Tironi, 1976, p. 65). Most nations needed to expand their productive systems to obtain benefits from regional preferences, while Brazilian, Argentinian, and Mexican entrepreneurs did not question LAFTA's trade opening because their exports increased (Almeida, 1980; CEPAL, 1979). Before LAFTA, public and private sectors followed their national development plans' guidelines (Herrera, 1983) based on the principles of industrial substitution with state support. The entrepreneurs' positions in the conflict between large and small economies show that, in the late 1970s, their economic interests still adjusted to the development models of their own nations.

In 1980, when in Latin America the dismantling of state-led industrialization policies was beginning in Chile and Mexico, and in the world open markets were becoming the norm (Bertola & Ocampo, 2016), the Latin American Integration Association (LAIA, ALADI in Spanish) substituted LAFTA with a regional system of preferences and differential treatment. LAIA strengthened monetary cooperation (Ocampo, 1990) and produced a relative increase in intra-regional trade and services (Baldinelli, 2010; CEPAL-ALADI, 2012) besides incorporating Cuba (1998) and Panamá (2009). Regarding their relationship to entrepreneurs, there was little change between LAFTA and LAIA. In 1988, the CCAE became the Business Advisory Board (CASE, by its Spanish acronym), under the umbrella of the State Representatives Committee and with more limited functions. Nevertheless, LAIA continued organizing annual business meetings that, in 2019, brought together 600 entrepreneurs from its member countries (Expo Aladi will summon more than 600 companies, 2019).

CAN: entrepreneurs move towards an open economy

The founding agreement of CAN, signed in Cartagena (Colombia) in 1969, included three mechanisms: trade liberalization, a common external tariff, and a common regime for foreign direct investment. With the creation of Andean regionalism, member countries committed to promoting industrial substitution. As usual, the responsibility for generating and increasing trade among members fell on entrepreneurs, but governments retained the role of planners and negotiators that allowed them to settle the agreement's economic and political orientation. Unlike LAFTA, where industrial-sector meetings of entrepreneurs formed the basis for economic negotiations among governments, the Andean agreement resulted from negotiations among governments, and entrepreneurs channeled their demands through them. Despite some opposition (Guerrero, 1979, pp. 397–398), entrepreneurs and workers obtained representation in the Economic and Social Advisory Committee (CAES, by its Spanish acronym) established in the Cartagena Agreement. CAES representatives came from the most important business associations of member countries, like ANDI (National Association of Industrialists) in Colombia and Sofofa (Industrial Development Society) in Chile. Before 1969, there were already subregional business associations in cattle raising, agriculture and transport, and joint ventures, such as the *Flota Mercante Grancolombiana*.

Simultaneously with the dynamics of regional integration, contacts among entrepreneurs took place outside CAES, in the Andean Council of Industrialists, the Andean Chamber of Manufacturers of Auto-parts, the Andean Exporters' Council, and the Permanent Colombian-Venezuelan Business Committee – the latter after Venezuela's entrepreneurs changed their negative perception of Andean integration and their government joined the agreement in 1973. A year later, when intra-regional exports grew (Hojman, 1981) the Association of State Communication Enterprises of the Andean Agreement was born.

CAES made few proposals during its lifetime because delegates prioritized their sector or national interests rather than those of the region (Ramírez, 2000). This suited the interests of Andean bureaucrats who attached little importance to CAES (Guerrero, 1979, p. 150). However, entrepreneurs asked for more participation instead of being informed of decisions after they had been taken. In 1983, those demands led to changing CAES into two separate councils, one for entrepreneurs (the Entrepreneurial Advisory Council, CCEA by its Spanish acronym) and another one for workers. The CCEA is formed by representatives of national business associations and has an autonomous organization, the possibility of initiating discussions, participating in the Andean Council of Foreign Ministers, the Andean Commission, and the Andean General Secretary, and attending working groups' and experts' meetings.

Entrepreneurs had a proactive participation on Andean regulation of foreign direct investment (FDI) and institutional reforms of the Cartagena Agreement. After December 1970, when the Andean integration process approved Decision 24, a common code for the regulation of foreign companies and their investment within member countries, entrepreneurs adopted different positions (Ardila, 1991). In Colombia and Venezuela, where entrepreneurs were closely linked to their governments, business supported the decision. In Bolivia and Ecuador, both governments and private sectors considered that the measure affected their interests (Tironi, 1976, p. 71). In each case, entrepreneurs from sensitive sectors to a common policy regarding FDI (petrochemical, manufacture, automotive, etc.) concerted their positions with governments, including Chile, which in 1976 used Decision 24 as an argument to leave CAN. In the 1970s, most FDI went to Colombia and Venezuela (Hojman, 1981, p. 156) and Andean disagreements about the benefits of Decision 24 were exploited by American companies (Tironi, 1977).

In the 1980s, Andean integration stagnated because it had been unable to implement a common external tariff, all its members were suffering the negative effects of the external debt crisis, and governments had incurred multiple postponements of decisions (Salgado, 1984). In addition, in 1981, a border conflict between Ecuador and Peru had produced armed clashes between their armies. Notwithstanding, in 1982, the 'common regime for the development of Andean multinational companies' (EMA, by its Spanish acronym) obtained the enthusiastic support of business (Cherol & Nuñez, 1983, p. 426). Out of the 51 companies EMA founded through the years, in 2017, 43 were still in operation (CAN, 2017, p. 94). During CCEA meetings in 1983 and 1984 (in Guayaquil, Lima, Caracas, and Barranquilla), entrepreneurs prepared a document titled "Andean Business Alternative" addressed to Andean regional institutions. In 1987, the Quito Protocol included the most significant business recommendation – the modification of Decision 24 and actualization of the EMA (Garland, 1989, p. 50).

CAN has never been characterized by the political homogeneity of its governments. After its creation in 1969, member countries mutated towards political paths opposed to the governments that had promoted the creation of Andean regional integration (Molano Cruz, 2011, pp. 39–40). Thus, in a first moment, political and ideological factors framed the evaluations of the mechanisms of economic integration and the positions of their private sectors (Tironi, 1976; Véliz, 1969). Later on, entrepreneurs' position vis-à-vis integration became more pragmatic. Their interests in terms of economic advantages or disadvantages determined their support or alienation from their respective governments and the regional integration process (Giacalone, 1997, pp. 6–8). But in the 1990s, the private sector and governments agreed on the opening of markets as a means of economic and social development.

In 1989, in Galapagos (Ecuador), CAN decided to accelerate integration with the objective of reaching a free trade zone among members and general trade liberalization. A year later, a survey of more than 200 Andean industrialists found that entrepreneurs considered indispensable for establishing a free trade zone to surmount obstacles posed by transport deficiency and complex national administrative measures (Salgado & Urriola, 1991, p. 9). During the 1990s, Latin American entrepreneurs favored expanding regional markets without state planning or control (De Lombaerde & Garay, 2008), and in CAN, this produced the usual tensions that any exercise of this type generates. Anyway, the free trade goal offered regional businesses a certain stability in relationship to national economic adjustment programs (Echavarría, 1998). Moreover, United States (US) and European FDI grew in CAN countries (Dunning, 2002).

In this context, entrepreneurs attempted to establish dialogues with their governments to defend their interests and assume a common position regarding the Andean free trade zone. After long negotiations with private-sector associations, Colombia and Venezuela (Desempantanado el Pacto Andino, 1991) freed their mutual trade in 1992, while other CAN members postponed the implementation of the free trade zone (Escobar, 1991). The successful outcome of trade liberalization between Colombia and Venezuela led their governments to establish a common external tariff and to negotiate trade opening with Mexico. The result was the signing of the Group of Three free trade agreement in 1993, after the adoption of an Andean norm by which any CAN member can sign bilateral trade agreements with other Latin American and Caribbean countries.

In the 1990s, CAN adopted the export-led development model associated with open regionalism, and Andean governments assumed a common position regarding preferential trade access in the US and Europe, on behalf of the war on drugs (Molano Cruz, 2011). The opening of their economies favored the expansion of big economic groups with a high degree of internationalization (exports, joint ventures, etc.) and diversified production (Giacalone, 1997).

By the middle of the 2000s, political divergences produced changes in development models. In Colombia and Peru, entrepreneurs' influence over executives and congresses grew (Serna & Bottinelli, 2018, p. 54), liberalization became deeper, and their governments signed trade agreements with the US and the European Union (EU). In 2012, they joined with Chile and Mexico to establish the PA. Meanwhile, Bolivia, Ecuador, and Venezuela rejected free trade treaties and associated in the Bolivarian Alliance for the Peoples of Our America created in 2004. In these three countries, entrepreneurs became part of a belligerent opposition. For example, in 2002 in Venezuela, the president of the main business association (Fedecamaras) and former president of the Andean Cartagena Agreement Board led a *coup d'état* with trade union, political and ecclesiastic support.

In the twenty-first century, CAN institutions work to preserve and reproduce a collective identity among member states (Prieto, 2016), while entrepreneurs have maintained their support for CAN and economic integration. CCEA organizes business rounds and finances Andean entrepreneurs' participation in forums in the United States, Europe, and non-Andean Latin American nations.[2] In 2006, CCEA regretted Venezuela's withdrawal from CAN to enter MERCOSUR (Martínez, 2006). To confront the 2008 crisis, entrepreneurs exalted CAN as the most favorable scenario for economic growth and asked their governments to resolve their divergences in order to pursue common regional goals (CAN, 2009, p. 38). In 2018, CAN General Secretary Walker San Miguel relaunched the CCEA and called its members to propose measures and present initiatives on economic and financial matters that would contribute to further Andean integration (CAN relanza Consejo Consultivo Empresarial Andino, 2018).

MERCOSUR: entrepreneurs emphasize economic benefits over integration

In the formative stage of MERCOSUR (1986–1991), governments did not incorporate entrepreneurs in its design or institutional makeup. However, in 1994 when MERCOSUR established a Consultative Economic and Social Forum (CESF) with trade union and business representatives, business sectors became interested because governments were discussing its conversion from a free trade zone to a customs union. CESF aimed at granting legitimacy to the bloc, but its members exercised more influence at the national level than in

MERCOSUR (Genna, 2017, p. 174). In 2002, after measures to fight inflation and facilitate macroeconomic stability collapsed in Brazil and Argentina, a newly created MERCOSUR Technical Assistant Sector (SAT, Spanish acronym) recommended more interaction with social and economic actors, but the outcome was the MERCOSUR Parliament (Dri & Paiva, 2016).

Other two institutional initiatives aimed at increasing entrepreneurs' participation were: first, in 2002, the Production Chains Competitivity Forums that seek the entrepreneurs' advice on how to develop sub-regional complementarity in value chains. Their peak years were 2006 to 2008, when the Inter-American Development Bank provided funds to create a management unit for the wood and furniture chain. Later, the private sector retreated from the initiative, claiming lack of proper financing for projects and public agencies' extreme intervention in decision making (Botto, 2015, pp. 96–97).[3] Second, the MERCOSUR Productive Integration Program was approved in 2008, the most important project of which was to develop a network of MERCOSUR suppliers to substitute foreign suppliers of the Brazilian oil company Petrobras. However, until 2015, MERCOSUR had not invited business to participate (Botto, 2015, pp. 101–102).

Schaposnik (1986) conducted a survey of Argentinian entrepreneurs when Argentina and Brazil signed the Program for Integration and Economic Integration (PICAB, by its Spanish acronym). He found that most entrepreneurs were against the agreement due to practical aspects, had negative perceptions of integration agreements, or did not know enough about them. In 1993, another survey that included entrepreneurs of Argentina, Brazil, Paraguay, and Uruguay (Achard, Flores, & Gonzalez, 1993, 1994) found a growing positive attitude and better knowledge (Mellado & Ali, 1995), but businessmen were reticent to sacrifice sectors' interests. The first bilateral automotive agreement between Brazil and Argentina was an exception because it involved large foreign companies willing to restructure production to benefit from regional-scale economies (Botto, 2015, p. 95).

Business did not participate in the negotiation process, but domestic interests shaped MERCOSUR's structure through the ratification process. National legislators defended the economic interests of their subnational jurisdictions, granting political representation to industries with important roles in them. Industries with low values of production relative to Argentinian and Brazilian GNP (gross national product) but located in the smallest subnational economies became protected sectors because their eventual disappearance due to trade opening would have had a strong negative impact on those economies (Pezzola, 2018).

The year 1993 looked like a watershed in business involvement, highlighted by the creation of the MERCOSUR Industrial Council (CIM) by the UIA (Argentine Union of Industrialists) and the National Industrial Confederation of Brazil (CNI). CNI and UIA began discussing CIM in 1991 and later incorporated the top industrial associations of Paraguay and Uruguay.[4] But this was an isolated instance, and in 1994 Argentinian industrialists from the iron and steel, textiles, sugar, and paper sectors still presented position papers to the Ministry of Economics and were mostly unable to influence the outcome of their demands in MERCOSUR. The petrochemical association was able to obtain better results because, since its participation in LAFTA/LAIA negotiations, it had hired professional technical staff (Botto & Quiliconi, 2010).

The US proposal of a Free Trade Area of the Americas (FTAA; 1994) accelerated business interest in organizing and led governments to incorporate business in trade negotiations. As a result, by 2002 the UIA, the Argentine Chamber of Commerce, and the Argentine Rural Society developed specialized agencies to deal with regional integration, though hampered by lack of resources and technical staff (Bouzas & Avogadro, 2002). As business associations in Argentina and Brazil acquired technical expertise, they became involved in transnational associations (Schelhase, 2008). It is uncertain, however, if this was due to interest in MERCOSUR or if it resulted from the FTAA negotiation. Anyway, when the CNI organized the Business Forum of the Americas in 1997, claiming lack of coordination to conduct trade negotiations (Schelhase, 2008, pp. 58, 91), the forum created a Brazilian defensive coalition not a MERCOSUR one.

Entrepreneurs' links with MERCOSUR followed the characteristics of their national political and economic contexts. For Maxfield (2004, p. 72), in Argentina and Brazil, entrepreneurs' interaction with their governments in the 1990s was "dysfunctional," a fact that reflected a tradition of *"poor government accessibility and business organization"* linked to those countries' low dependence on trade and lack of internationally competitive companies. The Brazilian state's corporatist structure produced more business involvement, but in MERCOSUR's formative stage, entrepreneurs did not believe that it would be signed or that it was necessary to promote industrial exports (Schelhase, 2008) because Brazilian trade flows were positive. Moreover, during MERCOSUR original negotiation, the Brazilian administration was in confrontation with the private sector (Veiga, 2002), and during the customs union negotiation, the government had to pressure entrepreneurs to accept tariff levels. CNI and the Industrial Federation of São Paulo (FIESP) attempted to represent industry, but by making the consultation sectoral, the government weakened its bargaining position (Botto & Quiliconi, 2010, n/p).

Starting in 2003, MERCOSUR witnessed a change in its governments' political orientation and an economic boom due to high international demand for commodities. This worked against integration, because governments that want to stress their autonomy and power are unlikely to deepen integration when their economies are prosperous (Lomeu Campos, 2016). When Brazilian foreign policy focused on transforming Brazil into a global player and a South American leader, Brazil lost partial interest in MERCOSUR in favor of larger global and regional arenas. FIESP and other business associations considered the possibility of returning MERCOSUR to a free trade zone to facilitate Brazil's foreign economic dealings (Vigevani, De Mauro Favaron, Ramanzini Junior, & Alves Correia, 2008, p. 20).

In Argentina, President Néstor Kirchner established links with large companies, which, thanks to the resulting access to government contacts, benefitted from exporting to the booming Venezuelan market. In the Fernández de Kirchner administration, after the global crisis of 2008, confrontation between the government and the agricultural sector over state retention of firms' benefits was prevalent. If the first Kirchner administration generated a political clientele of entrepreneurs, the following ones adopted a confrontational position toward the private sector (Gras, 2008). Entrepreneurs failed to act as a unified front because the volatile economic and political national context led them to concentrate on short-time objectives in MERCOSUR (Escuder & Iglesias, 2009, pp. 81, 83). The 2008 financial crisis did not generate a collective reaction, but it weakened institutions like SAT (Dri & Paiva, 2016) and diminished Brazilian interest in MERCOSUR.

Regarding the relationship between entrepreneurs and development models, in 1991, like in CAN, MERCOSUR members were transiting from industrial substitution to trade opening, and governments assumed that economic development was the duty of the state. Consequently, governments privileged national over regional interests and granted a central role to state actors (Botto, 2015, p. 107). According to Phillips (2004, pp. 86, 92), national development models reverberated in MERCOSUR's design, but their differences led governments to formulate economic policy independently from their partners, as well as to grant entrepreneurs different degrees of participation. Brazil in the 1990s saw MERCOSUR as a safe market for its industrial goods and an investment area (industrial development model), which meant a high degree of coincidence between the state, industrialists, and business interests. Argentina was more inclined towards trade and macroeconomic coordination (orthodox development model) than industry, and it negotiated MERCOSUR without consultation with economic actors, even though government–business relations were cooperative. As entrepreneurs acted through their governments, their inputs to MERCOSUR were incorporated into government positions, together with their support for development models (Phillips, 2004, pp. 100, 103, 108).

During the exporting boom, MERCOSUR governments looked for ways to increase the volume of state revenue derived from exports of natural resources (new agrarian extractivism). In Argentina this meant increasing taxes on agriculture export revenues and exacerbating conflict with the private sector, especially after the 2008 crisis (Grugel & Riggirozzi, 2012). In Brazil, the exporting boom sustained the expansion of Brazilian business abroad without the need to resort to taxes. State support for a wide diversification of exports and markets through the National Development Bank (BNDES; Boschi & Gaitan, 2009) acted as a bond between business and the government. Only after the crisis dragged on, the business–government coalition broke up, leading to the impeachment of President Dilma Rousseff (2011–2016).

At the same time, entrepreneurs discussed the possibility of organizing a transversal business lobby in MERCOSUR (*Comercio y Justicia*, 2019, March

29). In Brazil, the CNI promoted convergence between MERCOSUR and PA to recover Brazilian market losses in Chile, Colombia, and Peru due to these countries' free trade treaties with the US and the EU (EFE-Gestión Perú, 2018). These actions demonstrate increased entrepreneurs' willingness to participate in MERCOSUR or use the agreement to strengthen their economic position.

Since 2016 Argentina and Brazil have been moving toward new forms of international insertion linked to a different development model in which trans-regional trade relations and investments acquire added value together with business participation in global and regional value chains (Molano Cruz, 2016). The MERCOSUR-EU agreement (2019) and negotiations with the PA (Chile, Colombia, Mexico, Peru) are examples of the influence of this model on regional integration.

Summarizing, in each change of development model in member nations, entrepreneurs' support for MERCOSUR seems linked to perceived economic benefits rather than to conceptual or development notions. In January 2016, FIESP instigated Brazilian participation in US mega-agreements, such as the Transpacific Partnership (TPP), because if these went through without Brazil, their products would lose additional market share in their member countries. Entrepreneurs who were ideologically committed economic liberals – and closer to open regionalism – "*begged for protection the minute imports threatened their profitability*" (Maxfield, 2004, p. 77).

Pacific Alliance: entrepreneurs align with regional integration

In 2012, representatives of the most important business associations of Chile, Colombia, Mexico, and Peru formed the Pacific Alliance Business Council (CEAP, Spanish acronym) with the stated goals of developing links with markets in the Asia Pacific region, promoting PA, and giving advice to other entrepreneurs. CEAP is the only spokesperson for the private sector, and its demands go to the High-Level Group (Declaración del CEAP, 2014).[5] Nevertheless, it is not formally part of PA institutional structure.

PA assigns a central role to entrepreneurs without granting them institutional participation. Regarding how official representatives see the entrepreneurs' role in PA, Colombian Ambassador to Mexico Patricia Cárdenas considers that they "*are the blood that runs through the Alliance veins, i.e. . . . without you the Alliance would not have much reason to exist*" (cited in Salinas, 2016). The Mexican Secretary of Trade declared that commerce within the PA would improve based on the relationships built between private sectors (Mexico. Secretaría de Comercio, 2012).

Entrepreneurs have not objected to the lack of an institutionalized role because they consider themselves partners of their governments. According to Bernardo Larrain, CEAP-Chile president, PA resulted from both government and business initiatives, so entrepreneurs have the right to ask governments to maintain a pragmatic approach, regardless of changes in their political orientation, and the strength of entrepreneurs' participation is "its capillarity" with their respective states' trade apparatus (cited in Nuñez, 2018, n/p). For the Mexican Council of Foreign Trade (COMCE), the PA represents a new model of private–public partnership in regional integration, because entrepreneurs directly say what they want, so they do not consider themselves advisors to negotiators but regional negotiators (Sergio Contreras in Gandara, 2018a, p. 62).

CEAP declarations at parallel business meetings during PA summits show that the measures they have proposed have been incorporated into PA's decisions, and CEAP's agenda has incorporated subjects proposed by governments. The language of the declarations is technical, so they do not intend to persuade governments but to provide them with information about needs, opportunities, and technicalities. These declarations highlight the business know-how that governments need to make decisions. However, the discourse of CEAP's national chapters has a political objective as well: to persuade other entrepreneurs and domestic public opinion of the benefits of PA and the development model it envisions (Giacalone, 2019a).

As in the cases of the CCAE (LAFTA) and the CCEA (CAN), in the Pacific Alliance, CEAP is headed by representatives of the most important business associations, such as the Production and Trade Confederation (CPC) and Sofofa in Chile, ANDI in Colombia, COMCE in Mexico, and the National Confederation of Business Associations (CONFIEP) in Peru. These associations are key actors in the national development programs of Chile and Mexico since the second half of the 1980s and of Colombia and Peru since the 1990s.

In PA, entrepreneurs' involvement in regional integration seems to be embedded in a strong relationship with their own states and the export-led development model. This alignment can be explored through entrepreneurs' historical ties to the state in each member nation, especially because there is also a strong similarity among their development models and a relative consensus regarding them.

Starting in the 1940s and 1950s, Chilean business associations became strong to face organized trade unionism and an interventionist state (Bull, 2004, p. 206). But when invited to participate in trade negotiations by the military government in the 1970s, they could not take advantage of the invitation because they lacked the necessary technical expertise. After associations got professional personnel, the government came to depend on Sofofa's technical knowledge for trade negotiations in the 2000s (Bull, 2004, pp. 2007–208, 219). During the democratic transition, entrepreneurs cultivated personal relations with politicians (Flores, 2006), and this made possible the continuity of their participation in regional integration under all administrations.

In Colombia, the creation of the Non-Governmental Group to Coordinate International Relations (CORI; 2008) allowed entrepreneurs to exert influence on economic foreign policy and interact with entrepreneurs from other nations (Cepeda Ladino, 2014). If their technical knowledge and experience is a key consideration, equally important is a similar outlook on matters of economic development between state actors and the biggest economic groups. This common outlook pushed government and entrepreneurs to look for enlarging and diversifying external markets after Venezuela shut trade with Colombia (2010). Closeness between big business and government is exemplified by their proactive participation in peace negotiations between the guerrilla and the Colombian government (Rettberg, 2013) and the fact that Juan Manuel Santos's Defense Minister had previously been ANDI's president.

In Mexico, entrepreneurs gained a positive image by participating in the movement to promote democratic elections in the 1980s and 1990s, and since then, they have taken up lobbying at the Executive and Legislative levels (Alba, 2006). When the 1982 debt crisis led Mexico to replace its development model and apply macroeconomic reforms, the North American Free Trade Agreement signed in 1992 represented a major change in trade policy. Entrepreneurs played a crucial role during NAFTA negotiations, so it made sense to incorporate them into PA.

In Peru, in the 1990s, the state diminished its presence in the economy while the government isolated itself from business, so firms left sector associations to strengthen their lobbying capacities (Vasquez, 2005, pp. 472–473) and avoided politics due to the loss of prestige of politicians and political parties. In the 2000s, entrepreneurs went back to political activity to counteract economic losses due to protectionist policies in Argentina and Venezuela. The Pedro Pablo Kuczynski administration (2016–2018) showed a change of attitude demonstrated by the number of entrepreneurs in his cabinet (Durand, 2017). CEAP-Perú is formed by Asociación de Exportadores (ADEX), Cámara de Comercio de Lima (CCL), and Sociedad de Comercio Exterior (Comex), Confederación Nacional de Instituciones Empresariales Privadas (CONFIEP), and Sociedad Nacional de Industrias (SNI), and their cooperation with the state is helped by the fact that the Peruvian economy has grown since 2012, and its exports in 2019 represent a large share of Peru's GDP.

Chilean foreign economic policy promotes free trade agreements with developed nations and links with neighboring nations. Chile's rejection of MERCO-SUR's invitation to become a full member in the 2000s was linked to the fact that both subscribed to different forms of international insertion – MERCOSUR promoted trade between Brazil and Argentina but did not have a joint international insertion strategy, and Chile wanted to maintain its independent insertion. The status of associated membership, achieved in 1996, was a better option for business because it did not exclude Chile from trade with MERCOSUR and let it maintain autonomy in trade policy. Becoming a member of a weakly institutionalized MERCOSUR under Brazilian dominance did not find government's or entrepreneurs' support (Fernandois & Henriquez, 2005, p. 71) except by Sofofa (Rivarola, 2003). But Chile became an associated member of CAN (2007) after Venezuela left the agreement in 2006, showing the importance of a common outlook regarding integration and development.

In Colombia, CEAP proactively broadcasts an image of Asia Pacific that goes beyond considering it a region for conducting business – it represents an export-development model that entrepreneurs and governments want to reach through PA (Giacalone, 2019b). Big businesses support that model because they can make strategic alliances within and outside Colombia, update technologies, switch production, reorganize operations, etc., and whatever benefit they reap, this becomes specific to their firms and not to the sector (Chase, 2005, pp. 33–34). The CEAP-Colombia president summarized the entrepreneurs' position by stating that *"we are the force that moves the Alliance"* – and for him, the PA represents the largest Latin American public–private association (EFE, 2017, n/p).

In Mexico, support for PA comes from dynamic and modernized economic regions, sectors, and firms, but also from companies founded during the industrial substitution period. PA interpretation as a US–led effort supported by Latin American right-leaning governments is not accurate because, for Mexican business, PA diversifies exports and investments outside North America. Juan Pablo Castañón, president of the Coordinating Business Council (CCE), claims that PA is key to get the US to re-evaluate Mexico as a trade partner (in Lopez & Muñoz, 2012, p. 21). By striving to establish a direct partnership with Asia Pacific, the agreement helps economic diversification and undermines US companies in Latin America.

In Peru, however, there is no consensual support for the development model. Recognizing that situation, Juan Francisco Raffo (Business Consultative Council of the Asia Pacific Economic Cooperation Forum, APEC), considers that business should do more than support that model – entrepreneurs need to convince public opinion that open markets have taken millions of people out of poverty (EFE, 2016, November 18). Thus, the CEAP role is to provide technical expertise and links with other entrepreneurs in PA and to propagandize the benefits of export-led development internally.

PA governments and entrepreneurs promote a development model of open regionalism that is different from the open regionalism model of the 1990s (Kuwayama, 2019). Presently, economic liberalization needs cooperation efforts on value chains, productivity, competitiveness, and social inclusion to reduce or eliminate transaction costs by substituting intraregional trade of finished goods for trade of parts and components. This model is based on Baldwin's (2011) twenty-first–century regionalism, involving trade links with investments and services, or the so-called World Trade Organization (WTO) plus subjects. For this model, business *"active engagement"* is fundamental to achieve its aim and justifies PA's close interaction with entrepreneurs.

Conclusion

Since the mid twentieth century, Latin America has explored different forms of economic regionalism and kept alive the idea of a regional horizon for integration. For more than three-quarters of a century, the private sector has been involved in Latin American regionalism. And, if agency matters in regional integration, entrepreneurs' perceptions and actions are key elements

Table 8.1 Entrepreneur's organization, participation, and position towards development model in LAFTA/LAIA, CAN, MERCOSUR and PA (1960–2018)

Agreements	Entrepreneurs' Organization	Participation	Development model
LAFTA/LAIA	Industrial sector organizations	Institutionalized (CCAE) (CASE in LAIA)	Support for Industrial import substitution
CAN	Sub-regional, national, and sector associations	Institutionalized (CAES, CCEA)	Industrial substitution in transition to open integration
MERCOSUR	Multiple non-strong business associations	Institutionalized (CESF)	Open integration with state-centric mechanisms
PA	Unitary business transversal association (CEAP)	Non-institutionalized	Support for Open integration + WTO plus measures

to understand the process of establishing intra-regional economic links in Latin America. The following table summarizes our findings regarding entrepreneurs' institutional participation, their organization, and their support for the development model incorporated in regional economic integration agreements between 1960 and 2018.

The table shows that the existence of institutionalized forms of private-sector participation in an agreement says little about their capacity to exert influence upon it. In fact, the PA case suggests the opposite, i.e. that entrepreneurs with non-institutionalized participation may have influence on a regional agreement. In MERCOSUR, it was mostly nil, and in PA, it does not exist. However, the importance of the link between entrepreneurs and regional integration has grown since LAFTA.

The way in which entrepreneurs organize to channel their demands to agreements seems to be more important. Regional processes led to founding new entrepreneurs' associations and helped establish links among them (joint ventures, annual business forums, etc.). From LAFTA to PA, their organizations have moved from industrial sectors to national and sub-regional associations, and the latter became stronger in PA. In both LAFTA and CAN, institutionalized participation by industrialists seems to have had weight in the practical redesign of the agreements and their implementation. So, in different ways, entrepreneurs have been key social actors behind the promotion and maintenance of regional integration in Latin America (Tussie & Trucco, 2010).

Our long-term historical perspective analysis (1960–2018) shows that entrepreneurs have contributed to the resilience of Latin American integration through two courses of action:

1   By helping to generate, consolidate, and give dynamism to dialogue between the private sector, the state and the integration authorities in CCAE/CASE

(ALALC/ALADI), CCEA (CAN), CESF (MERCOSUR), and CEAP (AP), they originated and supported cooperation initiatives that led to the maintenance or reformation of regional institutions and objectives; and

2   By promoting the incorporation of the expectations and demands of entrepreneurial associations in regional agreements, entrepreneurs have upheld the idea of regional integration, even when their rhetoric did not openly include it as a political objective.

In conclusion, though technical personnel (experts) and politicians have played a central role in the origin and evolution of Latin American regional integration, we claim that entrepreneurs have also been actors in that process, albeit little studied. Their contribution to the resilience of regional integration is not small but merits further research.

Notes

1   The Economic Commission for Latin America (ECLA) was established in 1948. In 1984 its name changed to Economic Commission for Latin America and the Caribbean (ECLAC), but its Spanish acronym (CEPAL) has remained unchanged.
2   According to CAN (2017, pp. 109–112), between 1998 and 2002, there were five business forums in which entrepreneurs participated in 20,861 business appointments and made deals in the amount of 273 032 781 dollars. Between 2012 and 2016, 748 Andean companies participated in trade promotion fairs, and 2,844 entrepreneurs attended business meetings organized by CAN.
3   By 2014, except for the automotive and a few other sectoral agreements, the movement to develop sub-regional value chains had not advanced. The major problems chains faced were: (1) lack of synchronism in Argentinian and Brazilian macroeconomic policies and (2) uncertainty about market access (Rozemberg & Svarzman, 2014, pp. 7, 10–11, 16).
4   CIM organized working groups on sector issues, but these groups had little influence in MERCOSUR (Birle, 1997). In 2009 CIM opposed Venezuela's entry to MERCOSUR to no avail.
5   All CEAP declarations in https://alianzapacifico.net/download-category/ceap/.

References

Achard, D., Flores, M., & González, L. E. (1993). *Estudio de la variable política en el proceso de integración regional de los países pequeños del MERCOSUR y de las opiniones de sus elites sobre dicho acuerdo.* Buenos Aires: BID-INTAL.
Achard, D., Flores, M., & González, L. E. (1994). *Las elites argentinas y brasileñas frente al MERCOSUR.* Buenos: BID-INTAL.
Alba Vega, C. (2006). Los empresarios y la democracia en México. *Foro Internacional, 46*(1), 122–149.
Almeida, R. (1965). Stade actuel de l'intégration latino-américaine. *Tiers Monde, 23,* 609–642.
Almeida, R. (1980). Reflexiones sobre la integración. *Estudios Internacionales, 13*(52), 417–459.
Ardila, H. (1991, March 24). Pacto Andino: libertad a inversión extranjera. *El Tiempo.* Retrieved May 23, 2019, from https://eltiempo.com/archivo/documento/MAM-49639
Baldinelli, E. (1967). Experiencias y perspectivas de las reuniones sectoriales y de los acuerdos de complementación (ALALC). In Banco Interamericano de Desarrollo

(Ed.), *Los empresarios y la integración de América Latina* (pp. 39–50). Buenos Aires: BID-INTAL.

Baldinelli, E. (2010). Intervención en el. *Coloquio 50 años del proceso de integración latinoamericana 1960–2010* (pp. 41–43). Montevideo: ALADI-SGI.

Baldwin, R. (2011, May 23). *21st century regionalism: Filling the gap between 21st century trade and 20th century trade rules* (WTO Staff Working Paper ERSD-2011-08). Geneva, Switzerland. Retrieved August 22, 2015, from https://wto.org/english/res_e/reser_e/ersd201108_e.pdf

Bértola, L., & Ocampo, J. A. (2016). *El desarrollo económico de América Latina desde la independencia.* México: Fondo de Cultura Económica.

Birle, P. (1997). *Los empresarios y la democracia en Argentina. Conflictos y coincidencias.* Buenos Aires: Universidad de Belgrano.

Boschi, R., & Gaitan, F. (2009). Politics and development: Lessons from Latin America. *Brazilian Political Science Review* (Online), 4 (no.se). Retrieved July 11, 2019, from http://socialsciences.scielo.org/scielo.php?script=sci_arttext&pid=S1981-38212009000100006

Botto, M. (2015). América del Sur y la integración regional: ¿Quo vadis? Los alcances de la cooperación regional en el MERCOSUR. *CONfines de Relaciones Internacionales y Ciencia Política, 11*(21), 9–38.

Botto, M., & Quliconi, C. (2010). The influence of Academia on MERCOSUR's tariff policy. In *Research and international trade negotiations* (pp. 143–175). London: Routledge. http://doi.org/10.4324/9780203870747

Bouzas, R., & Avogardo, E. (2002). La elaboración de políticas comerciales y el sector privado: Memorando sobre Argentina. In *El proceso de formulación de la política comercial. Nivel I de un juego de dos niveles* (pp. 1–11). Buenos Aires: BID-INTAL.

Bull, B. (2004). *Business regionalization and the complex transnationalization of the Latin American states* (Working Paper No. 2004/02). Norway: Center for Development and the Environment, University of Oslo. Retrieved January 21, 2019, from https://duo.uio.no/bitstream/handle/10852/32647/1/wp2004_02_bull.pdf

Cepeda Ladino, J. C. (2014, February 27). *La política exterior transpacífica de Colombia a comienzos del siglo XXI: actualidad y perspectivas.* Tunja: Universidad Pedagógica y Tecnológica de Colombia. http://doi.org/10.2139/ssrn.3157366

Chase, K. A. (2005). *Trading blocs: States, firms, and regions in the world economy.* Ann Arbor, MI: University of Michigan Press. http://doi.org/10.3998/mpub.133506

Cherol, R., & Nuñez del Arco, J. (1983). Andean multinational enterprises: A new approach to multinational investment in the Andean Group. *Journal of Common Market Studies, 21*(4), 409–428.

Comercio y Justicia (2019, March 28). *Empresarios de Brasil y Argentina buscan reactivar el MERCOSUR.* Retrieved May 14, 2019, from https://comercioyjusticia.info/blog/comercio-exterior/empresarios-de-brasil-y-argentina-buscan-reactivar-el-mercosur/

Comisión Económica para América Latina (CEPAL). (1959). *La industria de material ferroviario rodante en América Latina.* Octavo período de sesiones, Panamá, May. Consejo Económico y Social, E/CN.12/508.

Comisión Económica para América Latina (CEPAL). (1979). *ALALC: el programa de liberación comercial y su relación con la estructura y las tendencias del comercio zonal,* Consejo Económico y Social-CEPAL, E/CEPAL/L.195, May 14.

Comisión Económica para América Latina–Asociación Latinoamericana de Integración (ALADI). (2012). *30 años de la integración comercial en la ALADI.* Montevideo: ALADI.

Comunidad Andina (CAN). (2009). *La Comunidad Andina en el 2009. Principales noticias sobre el proceso andino de integración.* Retrieved from http://comunidadandina.org/StaticFiles/20 1161192622Comunida_Andina_2009.pdf

Comunidad Andina. Secretaría General. (2017). *Rumbo a los 50 años. El arduo camino de la integración*. Arequipa: Comunidad Andina.

Conclusión de la IX Conferencia: el Protocolo de Caracas y el Plan de Acción 1970–1980. (1970). *Comercio Exterior*, enero, 14–17.

Declaración del Consejo Empresarial de la Alianza del Pacifico (CEAP). (2014). Punta Pita, México, June 19.

De Lombaerde, P., & Garay, L. J. (2008). El nuevo regionalismo latinoamericano. In P. De Lombaerde, J. Briceño Ruiz, & K. Shigeru (Eds.), *Del Regionalismo latinoamericano a la integración interregional* (pp. 3–35). Madrid: Siglo XXI.

Dos opiniones divergentes sobre la IX Conferencia. (1970). *Comercio Exterior* (Mexico), enero 18.

Dri, C. F., & Paiva, M. E. (2016). Parlasul, um novo ator no processo decisório do Mercosul? *Revista de Sociologia e Política*, *24*(57), 31–48. http://doi.org/10.1590/1678-987316245703

Dunning, J. (2002). L'Amérique latine comme tremplin pour l'internationalisation des firmes européennes. *Problèmes d'Amérique latine*, *46–47*, 41–79.

Durand, F. (2017). *Juegos de poder. Política tributaria y lobby en Perú, 2011–2017*. Lima, Perú: Oxfam.

Echavarria, J. J. (1998). Flujos comerciales en los países andinos: ¿liberalización o preferencias regionales? *Coyuntura Económica*, *28*(3), 87–118.

EFE. (2016, November 17). Los empresarios de APEC alertan de aumento del proteccionismo en Asia Pacifico. *América Economía*. Retrieved (2019, August 12) from https://www.efe.com/efe/america/economia/los-empresarios-de-apec-alertan-aumento-del-proteccionismo-en-el-asia-pacifico/20000011-3099107

EFE. (2017, June 29). Empresarios de Alianza Pacífico, con la mira puesta en Asia-Pacífico. *El Mundo*. Retrieved August 12, 2019, from http://elmundo.com/noticia/Empresarios-de-Alianza-Pacificocon-la-mira-puesta-en-Asia-Pacifico/354854

EFE-Gestión. Perú. (2018, July 23). *Empresarios de Brasil piden acuerdo con Alianza Pacífico ante pérdida de mercados*. Retrieved August 11, 2019, from https://gestion.pe/mundo/internacional/empresarios-brasil-piden-acuerdo-alianza-pacifico-perdida-mercado-239319-noticia/

El Tiempo. (1991, March 16). *Desempantanado el Pacto Andino*. Retrieved June 21, 2019, from https://eltiempo.com/archivo/documento/MAM-43557

Escobar, M. (1991, December 4). Empantanado acuerdo en el Pacto Andino. *El Tiempo*. Retrieved June 21, 2019, from https://eltiempo.com/archivo/documento/MAM-202596

Escuder, M. L., & Iglesias, G. (2009). *Los determinantes domésticos del regionalismo en Argentina: actores, instituciones y proceso de formulación de políticas* (LATN Working Paper 108). Buenos Aires, Argentina. Retrieved from http://latn.org.ar/wp-content/uploads/2015/01/wp-108.pdf

Estatutos de la Asociación de Industriales de Latinoamérica (AILA). (1963). *Comercio Exterior* (Mexico), October, pp. 745–747.

Expo ALADI will summon more than 600 companies from Latin America in Bucaramanga. Retrieved August 11, 2019, from http://expoaladi.org/en/

Fernandois, J., & Henriquez, M. J. (2005). ¿Contradicción o díada? Política exterior de Chile ante el MERCOSUR *Estudios Internacionales*, *38*(148), 55–77. Retrieved from http://jstor.org/stable/41391806.

Ferrer, A. (1967). Empresarios, integración y desarrollo. In BID (Ed.), *Los empresarios y la integración de América Latina* (pp. 15–38). Buenos Aires: BID-INTAL.

Flores Andrade, A. (2006). Una inevitable (y exitosa) convivencia política: empresarios y gobiernos socialistas de Chile y España. *Foro Internacional*, *186*, 720–740. Retrieved from https://dialnet.unirioja.es/servlet/autor?codigo=1044697.

Gándara, G. (2018a). Los empresarios en la Alianza del Pacifico. Entrevista a Sergio Contreras. *Comercio Exterior, 16*, 60–62. Retrieved from https://revistacomercioexterior.com/revistas/16/1542357212835.pdf

García, R. (1959). Problemas de la integración industrial latinoamericana. *Revista de Economía y Estadística, 3*(1–3), 99–117.

Garland Iturralde, G. (1989). El Consejo Consultivo Empresarial Andino y la concertación en el Grupo Andino. *Themis. Revista de Derecho, 1989*, 49–51.

Genna, G. M. (2017). Measuring integration achievement in the Americas. In P. De Lombaerde, & E. J. Saucedo-Acosta (Eds.), *Indicator-based monitoring of regional economic integration* (Vol. 13, pp. 159–182). Bruges: UNSR. https://doi.org/10.1007/978-3-319-50860-3.

Giacalone, R. (1997). Asociaciones empresariales, integración y estado. Colombia y Venezuela, *Nueva Sociedad, 151*, 155–167.

Giacalone, R. (2019a). La inserción internacional en Asia Pacifico de la AP en la visión de sus empresarios. In G. Palamara (Ed.), *Nuevas estrategias de inserción internacional para América Latina* (pp. 57–93). Bogotá: Universidad Externado de Colombia.

Giacalone, R. (2019b). Relación, reputación y riqueza. Claves del discurso empresarial colombiano sobre Asia-Pacífico. In R. Giacalone (Ed.), *El Pensamiento Empresarial Latinoamericano en el siglo XXI* (pp. 245–274). Bogotá: Universidad Cooperativa de Colombia.

Gras, C. (2008). Empresarios rurales y acción política en Argentina. *Estudios Sociológicos* (Mexico), *XXX*(89), 459–487. Retrieved from http://jstor.org/stable/41938092

Grugel, J., & Riggirozzi, P. (2012). Post-neoliberalism in Latin America: Rebuilding and reclaiming the state after crisis. *Development and Change, 43*(1), 1–20. Retrieved from https://onlinelibrary.wiley.com/doi/full/10.1111/j.1467-7660.2011.01746.x

Guerrero Cordero, M. (1979). *Diez años del Grupo Andino. Memorias de un protagonista.* Bogotá, Colombia: CIID.

Haggard, S., & Kaufman, R. (1995). *The political economy of democratic transition.* Princeton, NJ: Princeton University Press.

Herrera, F. (1983). La Banca de Fomento Latinoamericana y la empresa privada. *Estudios Internacionales, 61*, 3–13.

Hojman, D. (1981). The Andean Pact: Failure of a model of economic integration? *Journal of Common Market Studies, 20*(2), 143–147.

Hoy Bolivia. (2018, mayo 17). *CAN relanza Consejo Consultivo Empresarial Andino y confía en su aporte a la integración.* Retrieved from https://hoybolivia.com/Noticia.php?IdNoticia=265205&tit=can_relanza_consejo_consultivo_empresarial_andino_y_confia_en_su_aporte_a_la_integracion

Informe Mensual de la Integración Latinoamericana. (1970). *Comercio Exterior*, febrero, pp. 893–896.

Kuwayama, M. (2019, March 2). *Pacific Alliance: A Latin American version of "Open Regionalism" in practice* (Discussion Paper Series DP2019-02). Kobe, Japan: RIEB, Kobe University.

Lomeu Campos, G. (2016). From success to failure: Under what conditions did MERCOSUR integrate? *Journal of Economic Integration, 31*(4), 855–897. Retrieved from https://econpapers.repec.org/article/risintegr/0701.htm

López, D., & Muñoz, F. (2012). El inicio formal de la Alianza del Pacífico. *Puentes: Análisis y Noticias sobre Comercio y Desarrollo Sostenible, 13*(4), 1–36.

Martínez, M. T. (2006, May 1). Empresarios en contra de la disolución de la CAN. *El Universo.* Retrieved from https://eluniverso.com/2006/05/01/0001/9/ACF93E5828064BAE9102110FF96B4BA8.html

Maxfield, S. (2004). The dynamics of state-business relations in the formulation of Latin American trade. In V. Aggarwal, R. Espach, & J. Tulchin (Eds.), *The strategic dynamics of Latin American trade* (pp. 59–82). Stanford, CA: Stanford University Press.

Mellado, N., & Ali, M. L. (1995). *Opinión de los sectores sociales sobre el MERCOSUR y sus alternativas*. La Plata: Universidad Nacional de La Plata.

Mexico. Secretaria de Comercio. (2012) *Aprobado el acuerdo marco, instrumento constitutivo de la Alianza del Pacífico*. Comunicado de Prensa No. 277/12. Retrieved June 30, 2019, from http://sice.oas.org/whatsnew_pending/Mexican_Senate_approval_Pacific_Alliance_s.pdf

Molano Cruz, G. (2011). The Andean integration process: Origins, transformation and structures. *Integration and Trade Journal, 15*(33), 35–45.

Molano Cruz, G. (2016). *The Latin American-EU interregionalism vis-à-vis the Trans-Pacific and Trans-Atlantic Trade and Investment Partnership Agreements* (UNU-CRIS Working Papers). Retrieved August 24, 2019, from http://cris.unu.edu/latin-american-eu-inter-regionalisms-vis-%C3%A0-vis-trans-pacific-and-trans-atlantic-trade-and-investment

The Moment for MERCOSUR's Trade Agenda is Now. (2018, July 25). *Stratfor Worldview*.

Nasser Quiñones, G. (1963). La responsabilidad del sector privado en el desarrollo del intercambio en los países de la ALALC. *Comercio Exterior*, October, 736–737.

Nuñez, L. (2018, June 5). ¿Qué le piden los empresarios a la Alianza del Pacífico? *Al Navío Noticias de Ida y Vuelta*. Madrid. Retrieved from http://alnavio.com

Ocampo, J. A. (1990). New economic thinking in Latin America. *Journal of Latin American Studies, 22*(1), 169–181.

Pezzola, A. A. (2018). The deep roots of protectionism in the Southern Cone: Constituent interests and MERCOSUR's Common External Tariff. *Latin American Politics and Society, 60*(4), 69–92. Retrieved from https://researchgate.net/publication/307970084_The_Deep_Roots_of_Protectionism_in_the_Southern_Cone_Constituent_Interests_and_MERCOSUR's_Common_External_Tariff

Phillips, N. (2004). *The Southern Cone model: The political economy of regional capitalist development in Latin America*. London: Routledge.

Prebisch, R. (1972). La integración económica en América Latina. In E. Wyndham-White (Ed.), *La integración latinoamericana en una etapa de decisiones* (pp. 29–45). Buenos Aires: INTAL.

Prieto, G. (2016). *Identidad colectiva e instituciones regionales en la Comunidad Andina. Un análisis constructivista*. Bogotá: Pontificia Universidad Javeriana.

Programa de Naciones Unidas para el Desarrollo (PNUD)-Banco Interamericano de Desarrollo (BID)-Instituto para la Integración de América Latina y el Caribe (INTAL). (2001). *América Latina a principios del Siglo XXI: Integración, identidad y globalización. Actitudes y expectativas de las élites latinoamericanas*. Buenos Aires: PNUD-BID-INTAL.

Ramírez, S. (2000). El aspecto social y la participación en la Comunidad Andina. In A. Serbin, et al. (Eds.), *Ciudadanía y mundialización: la sociedad civil ante la integración regional* (pp. 211–236). Madrid: CIDEAL-INVESP-Nueva Sociedad.

Rettberg, A. (2013, November). *Peace is better business, and business makes better peace: The role of the private sector in Colombian peace process* (GIGA Working Papers 240). Hamburg Retrieved from https://giga-hamburg.de/en/system/files/publications/wp240_rettberg.pdf

Rivarola, A. (2003). Mirrors of change: Industrialist in Chile and Uruguay. *Revista de la Cepal, 91*, 169–183.

Rozemberg, R., & Svarzman, G. (2014). *Integración productiva y cadenas de valor en el MERCOSUR* (LATN Working Paper 157). Retrieved from https://academia.edu/35860623/WP_157_Cadenas-de-valor_Rozemberg.pdf

Salgado, G. (1984). El Grupo Andino: problemas y perspectivas. *Estudios Internacionales*, *17*(68), 459–492.

Salgado, G., & Urriola, R. (1991). Introducción. In *El fin de las barreras. Los empresarios y el Pacto Andino en la década de los 90* (pp. 7–13). Bogotá: FESCOL-Nueva Sociedad.

Salinas, S. (2016, April 5). *Los empresarios son la sangre que corre por las venas de la Alianza.* Cámara de Comercio México-Colombia. Retrieved from http://ccmexcol.com/los-empresarios-la-sangre-que-corre-las venas-la-alianza.html

Schaposnik, E. (1986). *Los sectores dirigentes argentinos y la integración en América Latina.* La Plata: Universidad Nacional de La Plata.

Schelhase, M. (2008). *Globalization, regionalization, and business: Conflict, convergence, and influence.* London: Palgrave Macmillan.

Serna, M., & Bottinelli, E. (2018). *El poder fáctico de las élites empresariales en la política latino-americana.* Buenos Aires: CLACSO-OXFAM.

Tironi, E. (1976). Las estrategias nacionales de desarrollo y la integración de los países andinos. *Estudios Internacionales*, *34*, 58–102.

Tironi, E. (1977). La Decisión 24 sobre capitales extranjeros en el Grupo Andino. *Estudios Internacionales*, *10*(38), 12–26.

Tussie, D., & Trucco P. (2010). *Nación y Región en América del Sur. Los actores nacionales y la economía política de la integración sudamericana.* Buenos Aires, Argentina: Teseo-LATN-Flacso.

Vásquez Huanan, E. (2005). *Estrategias del poder. Grupos económicos en Perú.* Lima: Universidad del Pacífico.

Veiga, P.da, M. (2002). O 'policy making" da política comercial no Brasil: Os caminhos da transição. In *El proceso de formulación de la política comercial. Nivel I de un juego de dos niveles* (pp. 13–21). Buenos Aires: BID-INTAL.

Véliz, C. (1969). Centralismo, nacionalismo e integración. *Estudios Internacionales*, *3*(1), 3–22.

Vigevani, T., De Mauro Favaron, G., Ramanzini Junior, H., & Alves Correia, R. (2008). O papel da integração regional para o Brasil: universalismo, soberania e percepção das elites. *Revista Brasileña de Política Internacional*, *51*(1), 5–27.

Zabala, J. (1967). El aporte extranjero a la integración latinoamericana. In *Los empresarios y la integración de América Latina* (pp. 63–79). Buenos Aires: BID-INTAL.

Conclusions

José Briceño-Ruiz and Andrés Rivarola Puntigliano

The aim of this book has been to deepen in the understanding about regionalism in Latin America. Our task is focused in the inquiry on why, despite crises and setbacks, the idea and action of 'regional integration and cooperation' have been so resilient. This 'resilience' has been analysed in other publications (e.g. Rivarola Puntigliano & Briceño-Ruiz, 2013). In this book we have explored further the driving forces behind the processes of regional integration and cooperation in Latin America. This has implied a deeper analysis of the concept of 'resilience'. As Pia Riggirozzi (2015, p. 3), accurately pointed out, our former publication lacked a more consistent explanation of this concept, which is central to the analysis. We fully agree with Riggirozzi on the need of exploring further on 'resilience' as the preservation of an 'idea', as well as on resilience as a kind of 'resistance' that contributes to the recovery of regional projects from disturbances and setbacks. This book has tried to consider questions asked by Riggirozzi, such as "what factors govern how resilient a given project is likely to be under changing political and economic conditions? How does a resilient idea change and manifest in a changing context?" (Riggirozzi, 2015, p. 3).

The overall issue related to 'resilience' is analysed in the introduction and in Chapter 1. Inspired by the use of the concept of 'resilience' in different disciplines and areas of research, we have become particularly interested in how it is used in research on ecosystems and psychology. This allows us to go beyond the general use of the concept as synonymous with 'resistance'. There is of course also much 'resistance', but in ecosystem theory, 'resilience' is also linked to a broader analysis of systems. One can here go beyond single units or particular 'events' in a certain period of time, searching for cultural, social, geopolitical and economic systems. These are created and act within a particular territorial setting, which is the framework of existence and interaction. As an example, a cultural system might be composed by units belonging to a national territory, or 'space', but this might be connected and sometimes takes its own form within a regional space. The same happens with other dimensions of society, economy or geopolitics. Regional systems are generally connected to and often originated in national or sub-national systems. They might sometimes also be connected to broader international and global ones.

These connections might sometimes be in the form of 'integration', but there are also many conflicts.

Since colonisation, Latin America has been part of the formation of a global system. This has an important economic side, but there are also cultural, security and geopolitical dimensions. Sometimes acting as separated systems, other times as interwoven parts, a web of systems is identified with different names. A more recent one could be 'globalisation'. Yet there has never been a one-dimensional 'global' or even 'hegemonic' system that confront local ones, such as those from Latin America. As with everything in life, there is a constant change in dominating features of the 'global' framework, pushing for changes at local levels. Global systemic changes are often caused by the emergence of new local systems, pushing for processes of transformation. Systems react to external shifts or challenges – by broader systems or other units within a system – through rejection, adaptation or transformation. In all cases, resilience is a strong component of this, for example, through systemic 'adaptation'. This reflects the capacity of a system to adjust its responses to change in external drivers and internal processes, although it does not necessarily need to alter any of the structures that surround it. Adaptation might take the form of an 'isomorphism', in which organisations revise their goals and structure to conform to the ideals and myths perceived as successful. When these mimicked forms clash with established ways of doing things, organisations solve the problem by what is called 'decoupling'. This takes place when organisations maintain standardised and legitimating formal structures while their activities vary in response to practical considerations (for examples of 'decoupling' in Latin American organisations, see Rivarola Puntigliano, 2003, p. 8).

Processes of adaptation and change might differ in time and space. That is, some parts of the regional system might, during some periods or places act, as drivers of continuities (perhaps even draw-backs) while others become bearers of transformations. This shows the need of transcending time and space to grasp the complexity of this process. As described in Chapter 1, a central element to understand systems and resilience is history. As for the case of Latin America, many of these systems, have existed for a long time or might be composed of units with long histories. Thus, the systems and/or their units contain memories of past exposures to disturbances that transform them into 'memory carriers'. Hence, resilience is, in our view, linked with a *longue durée* perspective in which systems accumulated 'memory', sustaining continuity in new forms of integration initiatives. This 'memory' contains different kinds of experiences, successful or not, that are accumulated and developed by 'carriers' and 'vectors'.

However, even if the systemic analysis is important to explain and understand the resilience of regionalism, it is not enough. Actors play a central role in our study. The actors (individuals, social organisations, states and their institutions) are not just passive recipients of the influence of the systemic forces. They also shape the constitution of society. Their action is certainly related to the structure of society, and there is a mutual interaction with structural and systemic forces, a process Giddens described in his structuration theory. In this framework, actors (or agents) are critical actors in the resilience of regionalism. The chapters of this book deepen in the analysis on how actors such as political and business organisations or leaders, diplomats, the Catholic Church and intellectuals have been part (sometimes even with unintended actions) of the resilience of Latin American regionalism. This is a central methodological aspect of this book. For us, actors are not just objects in a relationship of power (Dahl, 1957, p. 203); they are also agents through which we can understand local reaction to structural (systemic) changes.

In our view, the interaction between system and units is critical to understand resilience. As described in Briceño-Ruiz and Rivarola's chapter concerning the systemic influences on Latin American regionalism, systemic factors have been decisive from the early years of political independence, in the emergence of proposals of regional integration and cooperation. Hence, the Congress of Panamá in 1826 was a response to Simon Bolivar's fears of an attempt by the Holy Alliance to reconquest the former Spanish territories. Moreover, the Hispanic Americanism led by José Enrique Rodó and Manuel Ugarte was the result of the increasing US hegemony in the continent. In these two cases, a pervasive systemic factor was the uneven distribution of power in the international system that led Latin American countries to promote regionalism as a mechanism to strengthen their relative power in that system. When Raúl Prebisch and the Economic Commission for Latin America promoted a Latin American Common Market in the 1950s, the core idea was to use economic regionalism to modify the pattern of insertion of the region into an international economic system that had been shaped by the center/periphery dichotomy. Latin America was part of the periphery, and the economic regionalism was conceived as an instrument to advance regional industrialization, and it was a mechanism to overcome that 'peripheral' status of the region. Along this line, we see regionalism as a response to a systemic constraint: the asymmetric configuration of the international economic system.

As shown by the cases presented in this book, these systemic variables are crucial in countries' decision to promote regionalism. Eduardo Vidigal's chapter analyses the Brazilian case, a country in which a sector of the political and economic elites was reluctant to further a rapprochement with its Latin American neighbours. However, as Vidigal explains, that view was superseded since the 1960s due to factors such as the Cold War and the need to confront US hegemony in the Americas. Moreover, the promoters of national developmentalism in Brazilian governments aimed to improve the Brazilian position in the world economic system through the creation of a regional market in which the industrial production sold was a component of the Brazilian strategy. Parthernay's study on Central America also evidences the extent to which external factors has contributed to the configuration of regional initiatives in that part of the world. Like Vidigal, Parthenay describes the old tradition of regionalism in the isthmus and how, despite its failures, it never disappears, but it has been re-created and relaunched. These two chapters show how the Braudelian long term historical analysis is crucial to understand the resilience of regionalism in Brazil and Central America.

However, as argued previously, the action of the units within a system is fundamental to understand the resilience of Latin American regionalism. Along this line, different chapters of the book have analysed the extent to which relevant actors have shaped Latin American regionalism. Andrés Rivarola Puntigliano demonstrates that regionalism has been an issue for Latin American militaries. The armed forces are at the inner core of national state systems, something that does not exclude broader integration-oriented and in some cases even supranational agendas. Rivarola's study shows that the militaries have been part of the creation of regional systems, contributing their own 'memories' and views of society and the future. The idea of 'autonomy' and the concept of 'development' are two elements through which the military found regional synergies with other militaries across the region, but also with other groups. In this way, they, in several times, joined forces to create regional platforms related to security, economy and even culture.

One of the organisations that was part of these synergies was the Catholic Church, as is examined by Ramiro Podetti's chapter in the book. Like the military, the Catholic Church has deep roots in Latin American history dating back to colonial times, from where a 'continental' identity took form. That is particularly the case of the Church, which has been a leading actor in the emergence of 'Latin America' as concept and institution, as is the case of the Latin American Episcopal Council. As Podetti holds, during the 20th century, the Church has even recreated itself and its role in the region through a process of "Latin Americanisation".

In the forging of regional systems, we also find another group that stems from the inner core of national states, in some cases, like Brazil, also with roots in the colonial period: the diplomats. José Briceño-Ruiz, María Antonia Correa and Enrique Catalán have shown the important role diplomats have played in the promotion of regional initiatives. The diplomats have been bearers of institutional memories. This contains early initiatives, related to security or economic issues, to integrate Latin American countries in order to confront external challenges, like those promoted by Lucas Alamán in the 1830s (the so-called Family Pact) or by the Barão of Rio Branco in the early 1900s (the ABC Treaty). Thus, when the region again, has been confronted by external (systemic or not) challenges, the diplomats have played a key role in promoting and leading the creation of regional systems, as is more recently evidenced by the action of diplomats such as Dante Caputo in the rapprochement between Argentina and Brazil in the 1980s and Celso Amorim in the formation of UNASUR in the 2000s. Briceño-Ruiz, Correa and Catalán go beyond diplomats, and they also analyse the role of technocrats, in particular those working in international institutions such as the UN's Economic Commission for Latin

America (CEPAL) and the Inter-American Economic Bank, that also fostered regionalism in Latin America. Without doubt, Raúl Prebisch was the leading figure, but other international public servants such as Felipe Herrera, Víctor Urquidi, Felix Peña, Juan Mario Vacchino, Enrique Iglesias and Gert Rosenthal also were committed in furthering regionalism in Latin America. They were important drivers that, with concrete actions, helped in the construction of the resilience of regionalism in that part of the world.

Economics is crucial to understand the resilience of regionalism, and the analysis of action of the economic actors is critical. Rita Giacalone and Giovanni Molano, in their chapter on business, states and geopolitics in Latin American regional integration, explore the role of private-sector entrepreneurs. This is more closely related to economic systems but, in the case of Latin American regional structures, also related to other dimensions. As the authors hold, economic agents have been central actors of regional integration. It is important to note that this group, like the others mentioned earlier, has had components that at sometimes have rejected regionalism or sometimes simply been indifferent. In this study, the focus has been on their role in the 'resilience' of regional integration. This part clearly shows how agents from the private sector has been involved in different processes of regional integration, often in close relationship with the national state apparatus.

The cultural dimension is crucial to understanding the resilience of regionalism in Latin America. Liliana Weinberg made an important contribution to understanding this dimension of regional unity by highlighting the way literature, particularly the essay, has somehow help to construct the idea of Latin America. For her, many thinkers and writers in this region have gone beyond the geographic or even telluric influences on international politics and policies and tried to offer a more creative and imaginative conception and re-creation of the territorial and geographical dimensions through literary texts. She calls this geopoetics, an original way of conceptualising historical periods and broader cartographies that have contributed to the formation of the idea of Latin America as a region united by strong cultural links.

Altogether, the different actors analysed in this book represent part of the web of systems that compose Latin American integration platforms and initiatives. It is in their history, interests and identities that we find the driving forces of regional integration processes and their resilience. History, politics, economy, faith and literature all are factors that, promoted by myriad actors, have contributed to the resilience of regionalism in Latin America. These actors behaved in the framework of limitations and opportunities given by the structure of the international system, but at the same time, they challenged aspects of that structure and made efforts to transform it.

There is still much more to analyse and research on this issue. Our hope is that this book is a step forward in the understanding of the complex of the persistent resilience of Latin American regional integration. The academic agenda remains open in order to deepen even more the analyses of the resilience of Latin American regionalism.

References

Dahl, R. A. (1957). The concept of power. *Behavioral Science, 2*(3), 201–216.

Riggirozzi, P. (2015). Resilience of regionalism in Latin America and the Caribbean: Development and autonomy. *Canadian Journal of Latin American and Caribbean Studies/Revue canadienne des études latino-américaines et caraïbes, 39*(3), 463–466. https://doi.org/10.1080/08263663.2014.1022032

Rivarola Puntigliano, A. (2003). *Mirrors of change: A study of business associations in Chile and Uruguay*. Stockholm: Institute of Latin American Studies, Stockholm University.

Rivarola Puntigliano, A., & Briceño-Ruiz, J. (2013). Resilience of regionalism in Latin America and the Caribbean. *Development and Autonomy*. London: Palgrave Macmillan.

Index

Printed in the United States
By Bookmasters